Transgender Resistance:

Socialism and the Fight for Trans Liberation

Transgender Resistance:
Socialism and the Fight for Trans Liberation

Laura Miles

Transgender Resistance:
Socialism and the Fight for Trans Liberation
by Laura Miles

First published by Bookmarks in 2020

c/o 1 Bloomsbury Street,
London WC1B 3QE
www.bookmarksbookshop.co.uk

ISBN
978-1-910885-83-3 (pbk)
978-1-910885-84-0 (Kindle)
978-1-910885-85-7 (ePub)
978-1-910885-86-4 (PDF)

Typeset by Bookmarks Publications
Cover design by Simon Guy

Printed by Halstan & Co Ltd, Amersham, England

Contents

Acknowledgements

Many of the ideas and arguments in the book have been the result of countless discussions at trade union meetings, conferences and political events, my involvement in LGBT+ awareness and training programmes for various organisations and institutions, and innumerable personal discussions over the years both face-to-face and online.

However I want to warmly thank and acknowledge the help of a number of friends and comrades who have offered unfailingly valuable advice and constructive criticism as this project has progressed and have been indispensable to the production of *Transgender Resistance*.

Huge thanks to Nicola Field, Noel Halifax, Sue Caldwell, John Parrington and Sheila McGregor who took the time to read and comment on early drafts of the book and to offer guidance and correction of errors in various places. Any remaining errors are down to me!

Sally Campbell and Colm Bryce at Bookmarks trimmed, edited and offered advice on what had been an unwieldy original draft and tweaked it into something that was much sharper and more focused, as well as managing the actual production of the book. I'm also very grateful to Simon Guy for the eye-catching cover design.

Above all, thanks are due to my partner Sheila Hemingway for her unfailing support and solidarity and her constant encouragement to write this book as well as her tolerance of the countless hours spent researching, drafting and re-drafting the material.

Preface

When I was about seven or eight years old and beginning to become aware that I seemed "different" to other kids there was virtually no information available about sex, sexuality or gender that might have been useful to me. Even into my teens and beyond there were no transgender role models or publicity that were not tainted and diminished by sensational press story lines or social disapproval, ignorance and disgust. While I eagerly but surreptitiously read what information I could find about April Ashley or Christine Jorgensen, their treatment in the public realm only served to reinforce my fears.

It was certainly enough to convince me that the very worst thing in the world would be for my burgeoning sense of gender confusion to cease to be a deep, dark secret. And so, like so many others who struggled with their sexuality or gender identity during those years, I sought to repress it and didn't share my feelings with anyone for almost two decades, so great was the fear of being unmasked.

Coming out for me was a long, slow and fairly painful process. Most of the time dealing with — repressing — my "issue" had felt like trying to keep afloat without a life jacket in a choppy sea.

The first and most difficult part was coming out to my partner and admitting that I cross-dressed. From then on I was involved for a few years with a cross-dressing group, the Beaumont Society, in the 1980s and then began coming out to friends and comrades. Sometime later, I was referred via my GP for assessment to the gender identity clinic at St James's Hospital, Leeds.

In 2002 I found myself publicly declaring my trans status

during an equality debate at an annual conference of my trade union, the National Association of Teachers in Further and Higher Education (NATFHE). Until then I had been a socialist militant and a rank and file union activist, a health and safety representative, departmental representative and delegate to the union's Yorkshire and Humberside Regional Council.

However, my 2002 revelation radically expanded the breadth of my union activism. I grew in confidence and became involved with trade union LGBT equality groups, being part of the union's delegation to the annual Trade Union Congress LGBT conference, and then being elected for a number of years until 2015 as an LGBT representative on the national executive of the University and College Union (UCU). I also at various times played leading roles in the union's Equality structures and committees.

I was part of the increasing visibility of trans trade unionists who have played leading roles in various unions such as Unison, the Rail Martime and Transport union and the Nattional Union of Teachers (now the National Education Union, NEU), but I believe I was the first open trans person to be elected to the national executive of a British trade union.

In 2008, after much agonising, I decided to push ahead with my gender transition while continuing to work full-time as a senior lecturer at Bradford College. As is the experience with most transgender people, this was a difficult and traumatic time for my family and my partner. We got through it, if not unscathed then, perhaps, emotionally bruised but wiser from the experience. I was very fortunate to have a partner prepared to back me despite the upheaval to her life, a supportive family, and employers thankfully keen to demonstrate their inclusivity. Backed by union colleagues and socialist comrades, my transition at work was relatively painless. My colleagues were consistently and brilliantly supportive and my students, almost without exception, were interested but unfazed.

Thus my general approach to transgender politics and activism, and to writing this book, has not only been informed by my political activities as a revolutionary socialist and trans person but also by much of my working life spent as a social science teacher in further education colleges in Yorkshire.

Introduction
LGBT+ politics today

It used to be the case than when people discussed questions of gender they were referring exclusively to women's oppression, feminism and sexism. It also used to be the case that when people referred to what we label today as LGBT or LGBT+ rights[1] they mainly meant the situation for gay men and lesbians.

Today, women's oppression and homophobia remain very real matters of concern but in addition gender identity, transphobia and trans-misogyny have emerged as widely recognised issues of oppression. Trans people's lives and their struggle for equal rights and liberation have gained a much higher profile in recent times and become lively, often heated and acrimonious, topics of discussion and debate, much of it poorly informed and malignly intentioned. Many younger trans and non-binary people have become energetic and effective advocates of new ways of thinking about gender, sexuality and human relationships in the face of societal disapproval, institutional transphobia and gender orthodoxy.

When we look around at trans people's lives even in "liberal" parts of the world we can appreciate the insecurity that seems to be growing again for many trans people and LGBT+ people more generally. Indeed, a report by human rights group ILGA-Europe in May 2018[2] showed that the UK had dropped from first place to fourth in European LGBT+ rankings, largely as a result of a transphobic media surge from 2016 on.

From around the middle of 2016 a significant assault has been mounted on trans people's rights and aspirations. In Britain this has focused on the provisions of the 2004 Gender

Recognition Act (GRA). Hostile commentators have been lining up to oppose some fairly limited proposals to amend the Act, which is the key piece of legislation, along with the 2010 Equality Act, that enshrines various legal rights for trans people.

I will examine in more detail in a later chapter the government proposals to update the GRA that were met with such vocal opposition from the anti-diversity right wing, particularly some right wing newspapers, but also from some radical feminists and others normally considered to be on the left.

However, we can note here that very unfortunately some coverage of trans issues became increasingly strident and negative over the past few years. Newspapers and media outlets have routinely carried scaremongering half-truths, distortions and outright transphobic smear pieces seeking to paint trans people and their organisations as gender zealots out to corrupt the minds and bodies of vulnerable and impressionable young people. Apparently, it is claimed, we are trying to undermine "our" family values and generally bring civilisation as we know it to an untimely and sticky end. It is no exaggeration to say that such media coverage has often amounted to a moral panic, or more prosaically, a shit storm.

The right response to all this, it seems to me, must be robust resistance to the false claims and rhetoric being retailed, supported by sound arguments to expose damaging fallacies and bad faith assertions.

A central aim of *Transgender Resistance* has been the hope that it might contribute to genuine and respectful debate about how the struggle for trans rights and trans liberation can best be achieved. I've set out to discuss how socialist ideas and principles can point the way to an understanding of different gender and sexuality expressions in the past, the roots of the transphobia we experience today, and how we can organise ourselves to fight for a trans-liberated future.

Combatting such oppression is the stuff of transgender politics and is consequently also the stuff of socialist politics.

Transgender Resistance is a contribution towards filling a gap in the socialist literature on oppression and an argument for locating trans politics and the struggle for trans liberation within a Marxist framework. Building on previous relevant material I'll strongly suggest that Marxism has the analytical tools to address oppression in capitalist society, including the oppression of trans and non-binary people.[3]

I will argue that the fight for liberation from oppression and the task of transforming the capitalist system are in reality the same fight. The capitalist system has now created conditions that threaten human civilisation and the very existence of humanity and millions of other species on Earth. The system's imperative for continued growth at all costs that results in resource wars, deforestation, global warming, rising seas and melting ice, as well as intensified attacks on workers' rights and conditions, human rights and democracy, simply digs humanity's hole ever deeper.

As a consequence of austerity and anger at establishment politicians many countries have experienced an erosion of the political centre — the sometimes-precipitous decline of support for mainstream centrist political parties. Political polarisation of historic proportions has seen fascist, racist, homophobic and transphobic organisations gain support on the one hand and left wing, socially progressive organisations (like the Jeremy Corbyn-led Labour Party in Britain) develop on the other.

Political instability is growing in country after country. The world's ruling classes are jittery. We are living in a period of great economic, social and political volatility. This impacts on LGB and transgender people as it does on the working class in general and on other oppressed groups like women or BAME (black, Asian and minority ethnic) people.

As the dangers and the pressures grow populists and demagogues of the far right poison and polarise the political landscape and seek to scapegoat the vulnerable and oppressed to lever themselves into power and keep themselves there. Donald Trump's unexpected election victory in 2016 hugely boosted the right and far right across the world.

Figures such as Trump and his friends around the world are the rotten fruit of an economic and political system in crisis, plagued by long term stagnation or low growth, and low profitability.

But there is also resistance. The defeat of the fascist, racist

Golden Dawn in Greece during 2019 shows that mass resistance and solidarity can turn the tide on racist bigotry.[4] The rise of figures such as Jeremy Corbyn in Britain and Alexandria Ocasio-Cortez and Bernie Sanders in the US shows there is hope for a radical socialist alternative. The inspiring worldwide movement against climate change, especially the active involvement of so many young people, gives us hope that massive social movements from below can challenge the super-rich minority who are ruining the world. The uprisings and protest movements from Hong Kong to Chile to Sudan show that, no matter how harsh the repression, people will still fight back.

This is the context in which the struggle for trans rights and ultimately trans liberation is taking place. I will argue that those rights that we have won so far are increasingly under threat in a world where far right and fascist ideologies are becoming increasingly mainstreamed. This means that trans people in our resistance have to engage in the broader struggles against the system generating these horrors as well as the defence of our current rights and lives.

Transgender Resistance is written for all those trans people who have faced the hard choice of either hiding who they really are and continuing to live within the restrictions of the binary gender closet, or of having to battle incomprehension, hostility, ridicule, discrimination, marginalisation and often the loss of family as well as personal violence in their struggle to lead an authentic life.

It is for the past, present and future trans pioneers and rebels who, sometimes at the cost of their own lives and well-being, have put their heads above the gender conformist/gender binary parapets to fight for trans rights and trans-liberation.

Sometimes they have done this as individuals but often they have stood alongside others to form mutual support and self-help groups or to campaign in community-based organisations, trade unions and socialist parties to struggle against violence and injustice and for equal rights for LGBT+ people and others.

It is also written for those many non-trans supporters of trans people who want to be part of a more informed solidarity, and for those who may find they have gender variant members of their family, or trans people who they study and work with or perhaps strike and march alongside.

The struggle for trans rights and trans liberation is an end in itself but also, if it is to be successful, must be part of a universal vision of the working class to unite all the oppressed in a fight to overthrow the oppressive and exploitative capitalist system that fabulously enriches a tiny minority while smothering the lives and the potential of the vast majority of the rest of us, whether we are trans or cisgender.

Fundamentally, I will argue that rather than believing we should change ourselves to fit the world and all its inequalities, oppressions and exploitation, we need to engage in a fight to radically change the world. We need socialism.

Chapter 1
Transgender visibility and backlash

> It is a paradox of the transsexual bid for emancipation that the more visible trans people become, the more they seem to excite, as well as acceptance, a peculiarly murderous hatred.[5]

Trans people constitute perhaps one percent of the population, using a relatively narrow definition of transgender to mean "people who go through or would like to go through gender transition", but a somewhat larger percentage using a broader definition to include those who cross dress or identify as non-binary in some way.[6] Either way, trans people and their lives have become markedly more visible and more openly discussed today than even a couple of decades ago.

Through the hard work and efforts of countless activists there are now many support organisations for trans and non-binary people, something that could only have been dreamed of forty or fifty years ago. One factor that has helped make this possible has been the almost universal access to the internet where information can be accessed at the click of a button — information that was previously either very difficult to get hold of or simply non-existent.

So it is certainly the case today that there are many more trans role models available, and social attitudes generally have undoubtedly shifted in Britain and in many other countries towards more liberal views on LGBT+ matters just as they have on other diversity issues.

This has coincided with the passage of significantly more liberal social equality legislation in many countries. Who would have thought even a mere decade ago that a formerly socially conservative Catholic society like Ireland would become a beacon of progress through adopting same-sex marriage, a progressive gender recognition act that includes self-declaration, and deliver a referendum outcome of almost a two-thirds majority in favour of removing the repressive anti-abortion 8th Amendment of the Irish Constitution, clearing the way for legal abortions? The situation in the Republic of Ireland now puts to shame the continued repression and lack of progress on matters like abortion rights in Northern Ireland, part of the United Kingdom.

Such changes are testaments to the effects of women's and LGBT+ campaigning in Ireland together with the declining reputation of the Catholic Church and the old establishment and the growth in confidence of ordinary people energised by mass working class activism in recent years such as the fight against water charges and austerity.

Another factor has undoubtedly been the growing number of trans role models. In Britain and elsewhere we have seen more trans characters on our screens. One high profile example was the 2015 feature film *The Danish Girl* about the pre-Second World War transsexual Lily Elbe, played by non-trans (cisgender) actor Eddie Redmayne. While generally well received as a biopic of a key historical trans figure, the film was criticised by some trans people who suggested it failed to convey the complexity of being transgender.

For 16 years *Coronation Street* had a transgender character, Hayley Cropper, played by cisgender actor Julie Hesmondhalgh. Other soaps followed suit. In 2015 *Hollyoaks* cast transgender actor Annie Wallace as a trans teacher, while EastEnders briefly featured Riley Carter Millington, another trans actor, as a trans character called Kyle. The US Emmy award winning TV series *Transparent* centred on a character who comes out as trans to her family late in life, again played by a cisgender actor, Jeffrey Tambor.[7]

While the airing of more positive trans stories and

characters in films and soaps is something to be welcomed some trans people have suggested that the fact that such roles are still mostly being played by cisgender actors perpetuates the dangerous myth that being trans is inherently inauthentic and is just about role playing.

The media exposure has been far from universally positive. *Little Britain*, *The League of Gentlemen* or even adverts such as those for Bounty kitchen roll, have too often presented trans lives and behaviour as sources of (un)easy laughs.

Another grievance has been that too often trans people are stereotyped as sex workers. The film *The Dallas Buyers Club*, with Jared Leto, another cisgender actor in a trans role, is a recent example, while *The Crying Game*, one of the few high-profile portrayals of a trans character in the 1990s, also played into this narrative. Even highly-praised, sensitive portrayals, such as Sean Baker's 2015 film *Tangerine*, about two black trans women sex workers in Los Angeles, can have the effect of limiting the public perception of trans people.

Sebastian Lelio's Oscar-winning *A Fantastic Woman* (2017) shows how this works, with central character Marina, played by trans actor Daniela Vega, having to fend off insults, prejudices and attempted assault by people who assume she is a prostitute.

Girl, by Belgian film maker Lukas Dhont, won the 2018 Camera D'Or prize at the Cannes Film Festival. Dhont's first feature film is an intense and sympathetic study of a trans girl's struggle to succeed at ballet school and live an authentic life in line with her gender identity. It is based on the life story of ballet dancer Nora Mansecour, played by cisgender actor Victor Poltser. It did however receive criticism from some trans people[8] who suggested it seriously misrepresented trans lives, especially in respect of young trans people, by playing into cisgender and misogynist obsessions with trans people's bodies and especially genitalia and failing to address subtler psychological aspects of gender diverse expression.

Emmy-nominated US actor Laverne Cox from *Orange is the New Black*, a trans woman, made the cover of *Cosmopolitan South Africa* in January 2018. Cox has also had an effigy in Madame Tussaud's San Francisco since 2015.

Non-binary actor and model Indya Moore became the first non-binary person on the cover of *Elle US* in 2019, although trans models Valentina Sampoia and Lea T had been featured earlier in international editions of the magazine. Many trans and non-binary people will welcome such exposure, while others may feel that objectifying women's bodies like this should not constitute the pinnacle of trans achievement.

In 2013 Paris Lees, a trans journalist and blogger who founded *Meta*, the first mainstream trans magazine in Britain, became the first out trans person to appear on the BBC's flagship political debating forum, *Question Time*. In 2018 she also became the first trans woman to appear on the cover of *Vogue*.

There have been a number of trans-themed British documentaries in recent years, such as the BBC's *Being Transgender* and Channel 4's *My Trans American Road Trip* about the US "bathroom wars" over trans people's rights. The media have also carried high profile interviews with transgender individuals like Janet Mock and Caitlin Jenner, one of the Kardashian clan.

ITV's three part drama *Butterfly* by Tony Marchant aired in October 2018 to mostly sympathetic and supportive reviews. The drama follows 11 year old Max's unhappiness as a boy and his growing desire to transition which exposes the family's disorientation and conflicting emotions.

In politics it has taken decades of campaigning before trans could be said to have crept some way closer to the mainstream. There have been only a handful of (unsuccessful) trans parliamentary candidates for various parties. In 2013 Nikki Sinclaire of the UK Independence Party (UKIP) became the first successful British transgender MEP although she was only outed after she left the role.

There have also been just a few successful trans candidates in local politics. The Militant Tendency's Rachael Webb, a councillor in Lambeth, south London, was probably the first in the early 1980s, followed by Liberal Democrat Mark Rees in Kent in 1994. There were at least four trans candidates in the 2015 general election for the Greens, Labour and Liberal democrats, and nine in the 2017 general election. If nothing else these examples demonstrate the diversity of political views among trans people.

Backlash

The flipside of greater trans visibility has been the development of a disturbing backlash.

In 2016 the BBC's children's channel, CBBC, came under attack from sections of the media and some Conservative politicians and "family campaigners" for showing *Just a Girl*, a fictional audio diary that followed gender variant 11 year old Amy as she joined a new school. The *Daily Mail's* front page screamed, "Fury at BBC Sex Change Show for 6-Year-Olds".

A BBC film broadcast in January 2017, *Transgender Kids: Who Knows Best?*, was poorly received by trans people who saw it as an attack on hard-won gains and on the demand for self-declaration, as well as promoting a sub-text that somehow trans people can and should be "cured".

The programme amounted to an implicit attack on gender identity clinics (GICs) that support a child-centred affirmative approach towards young people who may be questioning their gender identity or who present as transgender or non-binary. It sought to sow seeds of doubt about perceiving trans as anything other than a form of mental illness.

Mermaids,[9] a charity that offers advice and support to transgender children and their families, has also been subject to attacks in *The Times*[10] and elsewhere.

CJ Atkinson, author of a children's book, *Can I tell you about Gender Diversity?* reported that their book had sparked a media furore in the right wing press even before it was published in January 2017.[11] The press presented poorly-informed transphobic criticisms rather than recognising a real need indicated by the fact that in December 2016 Childline reported it was receiving a record eight calls a day from children and adolescents suffering bullying over gender dysphoria and transgender issues.[12]

In November 2017 Natasha Devon, the Conservative government's sacked former "children's mental health tsar", was widely misreported and subsequently harassed and abused online after she gave a speech during which she praised some schools that had adopted gender-neutral terms to address pupils. In a *Times Educational Supplement* column she explained:

In making sweeping assumptions about gender, sexuality and identity we can create a culture in which anyone who deviates from the established archetypes feels excluded from the community and therefore doesn't have this need fulfilled. One way we as educators could help to avoid this is by using gender-neutral language when addressing groups of pupils... Several schools already do this. City of London girls' school, for example, asks speakers to refer to year groups as "students" rather than "girls" to be as inclusive as possible... Meanwhile, I received death and rape threats, messages questioning my sanity, calling me a "f**king idiot", trying to insult me through the prism of questioning my own gender, calling me fat and ugly, suggesting I should be burned as a witch and, perhaps most offensively, claiming that I am single-handedly responsible for the current poor mental health of British children.[13]

The case of British trans teacher Lucy Meadows was a prominent example of negative media exposure that ended tragically. In 2012 she committed suicide after being ridiculed in the *Daily Mail* by right-wing columnist Richard Littlejohn.[14] Littlejohn called for her sacking after she began her gender transition at school, despite the school taking a positive and supportive line.

An article by Lucy's former partner in *The Independent* detailed some of the press harassment she had faced.[15] At her inquest the coroner singled out the adverse media attention as being "sensational and salacious" and a contributory factor to the intolerable pressures she had been experiencing. "To you the press, I say shame, shame on all of you" were his closing words.

Thousands signed a petition calling for Littlejohn's sacking (he was not sacked). Motions supporting Lucy were passed at trade union conferences and socialist members of her union, the National Union of Teachers (NUT), organised a solidarity demonstration in her home town.

The potential to organise rapid collective responses over

outrageous issues like this has been a new factor compared to 30 or 40 years ago. This is thanks primarily to many years of LGBT+ campaigning that has generated significant networks of activists and supporters, but also to the rise of the internet and social media — there is no doubt that the ability to react quickly to examples of transphobia has at times helped to deliver important publicity and campaigning victories.

For example, in March 2018 the editor of the British Association of Counselling and Psychotherapy's house magazine, *Therapy Today*, felt forced to make a full apology after publishing a letter from the transphobic organisation, Transgender Trend. The letter, which accused the BACP of promoting "political ideology" by advocating a supportive approach to trans children, provoked a huge outcry among counsellors and practitioners.

An open letter exposing the blatant falsehood of many of the claims in the Transgender Trend letter was organised and quickly attracted hundreds of signatures. It pointed out that:

Transgender Trend are not a therapeutic organisation, they are a group set up by parents who refuse to accept their children's gender identity which campaigns against supporting gender diverse young people. As therapists we are acutely aware of the damage done to LGBTQ+ young people by family rejection and all research bears this out.[16]

The truth is that there remain significant risks to coming out as, or being perceived as, transgender. In some parts of the world attitudes and legislative changes have actually become more negative and regressive not just for trans people but for LGBT+ people as a whole.

Thus the UN report on hate crime[17] in 2015 showed continuing high levels of homophobia and transphobia. One summary of the report noted:

Violence motivated by homophobia and transphobia is often particularly brutal, and in some instances characterized by levels of cruelty exceeding that of other hate crimes. In every region in the world, the UN continues to receive reports of physical and psychological abuse perpetrated against individuals perceived to be LGBT. In addition, LGBT people are targets for religious extremists, paramilitary groups, and extreme nationalists, and also risk being ostracised by their families and communities.[18]

Remembering our dead: transphobic violence

Transgender Day of Remembrance (TDoR) has been observed on 20 November every year since its inception in 1999, following the murder of US African-American trans woman Rita Hester the previous year. It exists to raise awareness about the high level of violence experienced by trans people around the world and to improve recording of transphobic murders.

The 2018 TDoR report revealed a total of 369 reported killings of trans and gender-diverse people between 1 October 2017 and 30 September 2018, an increase on the 2017 figure of 325 and the 2016 figure of 295. Most of the murders occurred in Brazil (167), Mexico (71), the United States (28), and Colombia (21).[19]

It is possible that the increase in numbers is partly a result of better monitoring and recording — but the figures are undoubtedly still significantly underestimated because many deaths go un-notified, or the victim's gender is misidentified, or the jurisdictions in which their deaths have occurred simply do not recognise transphobic hate crimes. The figures do not include those who took their own lives.

There are several glaring factors which can be unpacked from the data for trans murders. Thus the figures from the Transgender Day of Remembrance and the National Coalition of Anti-Violence Program's annual *Hate Violence Report*[20] show that black and Hispanic trans women in the US and elsewhere are more at risk than white trans people. In 2013, for example, similarly to other years, over 58 percent of trans homicide victims were black or Hispanic. In the US during 2019 all the trans women murdered up to September (15) were black or Hispanic. Both trans women and trans men experience a disproportionate degree of sexual and domestic violence.[21]

There are many murders of transgender people around the world annually but there are many more deaths through suicide. The figures for what has been termed suicidality of transgender people are truly staggering.

Since 2001 surveys in the US and elsewhere have found

that between 25 and 43 percent of trans people have attempted suicide at some point. In Australia surveys of LGBTI people found suicide rates between 3.5 and 14 times higher than their heterosexual, cisgender counterparts.[22]

However, as a means to counter the limiting notion that trans people are victims, many activists have felt it is important to *celebrate* trans lives as well. In 2009 Rachel Crandall of Michigan, US, initiated the International Transgender Day of Visibility that now, each 31 March, celebrates the lives, creativity, resilience and energy of trans people and helps to raise awareness of the fightback against transphobia.

Trans acceptance and transphobia

In general bigots and transphobes have been operating, at least until quite recently, in social conditions less favourable to their views than in the past. The removal of repressive laws, as was the case with the 1967 Sexual Offences Act, or the implementation of some limited legal rights in many jurisdictions, has generally been accompanied or even preceded by increasingly liberal public attitudes towards sexual orientation and trans identity.

Social attitudes in Britain, particularly among young people, as indicated by a range of surveys such as the British Social Attitudes survey,[23] have become more favourable towards gay and bisexual people and to trans and non-binary people and transgender issues — although noticeably less so for attitudes to trans people than towards LGB people. This was similar to previous US findings.[24]

However, the results of a more recent large-scale survey of attitudes to LGBT+ people in the US carried out for GLAAD by The Harris Poll and published in mid-2019 were alarming. They indicated that attitudes to LGBTQ people were growing *less* favourable among one group which has traditionally been the most sympathetic — the young. The number of Americans aged 18 to 34 who were "comfortable" interacting with LGBTQ people had slipped from 53 percent in 2017 to 45 percent in 2018 — the only age group to show a decline. That was down from 63 percent in 2016. Driving the dilution of acceptance were young women whose overall comfort levels plunged from 64 percent in 2017 to 52 percent in 2018.[25] This may well be a consequence of both the toxic discourse around LGBT+ rights in the US and elsewhere and growing political polarisation as a consequence of the system's ongoing crisis.

Thus while social attitudes towards LGBT+ people have clearly shifted towards greater levels of acceptance over the long term, prejudice and discrimination remain widespread, particularly regarding trans and non-binary people in public life. The 2016 British Social Attitudes survey mentioned above found, for example, that while:

> The vast majority of people (82 percent) describe themselves as "not prejudiced at all" to transgender people...less than half of people say suitably qualified transgender people should definitely be employed as police officers or primary school teachers (43 percent and 41 percent respectively).[26]

The evidence is clear. Gender transgressive people, as I will show in the following chapters, are still widely subject to marginalisation, hostility, violence and hate crime even in societies where such discrimination is legislated against, and there is now some evidence that persistent anti-trans agitation in the mainsteam and social media can have a negative impact on social attitudes and government's willingness to promote or defend trans rights.

It seems that Jacqueline Rose's comment at the top of this chapter was well founded; that by their very presence trans people stimulate a fundamental angst about the almost universal assumptions people often continue to hold dear — their "common sense" — about gender and sex binaries, about what it is to be male or female, about "normality" and its desirability, and about what we mean by being a man or a woman — or neither.

Chapter 2
Has oppression always existed?

One of the most common objections to socialism and, for that matter, to trans people's right to exist and be respected, is that it isn't "natural", that it doesn't fit with human nature. Karl Marx argued that ideas about society, including those about sex, sexuality and gender, emerge, ultimately, from how we organise the production of what we need for life, and how we organise the reproduction of the next generation of labour itself.

As the material conditions for this production and reproduction change and develop so do the prevailing ideas, the "common sense" notions of what's normal or right, in any society. That doesn't mean, however, that ideas are determined in a crudely mechanical way by the economic base of a society, nor that the dominant ideas in a society are the *only* ideas. The point is that ideas are not immaculately conceived out of thin air. They have sources and purposes and are linked to the interests of particular social classes.

We are continually exposed to a hotch-potch of ideas in society at any given time but some are more widely shared and accepted than others and form elements of dominant ideologies. All sorts of pressure groups exist aiming to promote what might sometimes be unpopular causes in the face of public disinterest or disapproval and these can often directly challenge dominant ideologies. One example is trans support groups in the many countries that have repressive laws and policies oppressing trans people.

Ideas about how we organise ourselves and produce goods and services are never class-neutral. Those that promote support for the royal family, hostility towards trade unions, propose more immigration controls and promote the defence of family values and the notion of a stable, ordered society generally don't want to admit the class bias inherent in them. By digging below the surface, however, people can find out in whose class interests this or that idea is being promoted. Doing so allows us to recognise that essentialist ideas[27] about gender and sexuality don't reflect truths at all but rather ideological *claims* that serve the interests of the dominant class.

Once we are able to draw back the curtain of ruling class distortion and flim-flam that constantly seeks to influence our thinking we can appreciate that it is the material circumstances in which we are forced to live in capitalism that distort and limit everyone's gender expression and sexuality, not just those of LGBT+ people, by seeking to constrain us within sometimes explicit, sometimes implicit, binary gender expectations.

Regarding sexuality and gender, this means that the social, cultural and political attitudes we encounter today are not matters of immutable human nature but are derived from the particular social relations in capitalist class society that arise from how we organise ourselves to perform labour on nature.

Pre-class societies

What evidence we have from archaeology and anthropology strongly suggests that gender variant and non-binary gender identities, as well as various forms of sexual orientation, have existed in most if not all human cultures and probably throughout human history as recognised aspects of sexuality and gender expression, despite some more recent societies regarding them as being abnormal and beyond the pale.[28]

It is also widely accepted by anthropologists now that, while there were usually gendered divisions of labour in pre-class hunter-gatherer or foraging societies, this didn't mean that men necessarily dominated women or that women were confined to the home.

Foraging by both men and women provided the bulk of the group's nutrition; hunting by mainly men, perhaps with women, children and dogs as adjuncts, provided important but intermittent calories. In such societies, male and female roles might differ due to differentiated biological reproductive capabilities but this would not necessarily mean significant differences in social status or power between the genders.

Women's ability to gestate and lactate would have had implications for who did the hunting and the gathering at any given time. A heavily pregnant or nursing woman might be less likely to take part in hunting, but this would not hamper her involvement in gathering and foraging for much of the time or performing other vital tasks for the group.

Chris Harman, writing about what we can surmise about ancient hunter-gatherer societies, suggests:

> There was almost always a division of labour between the sexes, with the men doing most of the hunting and the women most of the gathering. This was because a woman who was pregnant or breastfeeding a child could only take part in the hunt by exposing it to dangers, and thus threatening the reproduction of the band. But this division did not amount to male dominance as we know it. Both women and men would take part in making key decisions, such as when to move camp, or whether to leave one band and join another. The conjugal unit itself was loosely structured. Spouses could separate without suddenly jeopardising their own livelihood or that of their children. Missing was the male supremacism which is too often assumed to be part of "human nature".[29]

The marginalisation of sexual and gender non-conformists

The existence of transgender people is not peculiar to modern societies. Trans is not explicable as an expression of modern societal angst or a particular response to capitalist alienation.

In hir[30] book *Transgender Warriors*, which examines transgender behaviour from pre-history to the present, Leslie Feinberg showed how evidence of trans people's existence can be traced back into antiquity, despite attempts to erase it — and them — as class societies emerged.

Feinberg also assembled evidence that convincingly

demonstrated that homophobia and transphobia have not always existed:

> The more I studied, the more I believed that the assumption that every society, in every corner of the world, in every period of human history, recognized only men and women as two immutable social categories is a modern Western conclusion. It's time to take another look at what we've long believed was an ancient division of labor between only two sexes.[31]

Feinberg described evidence that there has been a minority of people from earliest recorded times, both male-identified and female-identified, who have sought to live outside of what class societies have later designated as the normal expectations of behaviour associated with their biological sex. This evidence suggests that such gender variance has been tolerated or even encouraged for certain roles seen as vital in those societies.

Feinberg points to priestess religions that worshipped goddesses like the Great Mother in a range of pre-Christian, pre-Islamic societies across the Middle East, North Africa, Europe and Western Asia. Some of these priestesses were male to female transsexuals, as were some of the shamans among nomadic hunter-gatherers and other clan societies as far afield as Africa, North and South America and Asia.

We should be careful not to over-generalise about or romanticise gender variant or homosexual behaviour in pre-class societies as it is difficult in most cases to confidently speculate about how people lived in pre-literate times where no writing and relatively few monuments and artefacts have survived. Nevertheless, the existence of transsexual priestesses is well documented from ancient times. Modern interpretations of this phenomenon, however, vary widely according to the political perspective of the person doing the interpreting.

Feinberg refers to David Greenburg who argued in *The Construction of Homosexuality* that the role of trans shamans probably dates back to the late Palaeolithic period (roughly 10,000 to 50,000 years ago) if not earlier.[32] On the other hand, feminist researcher Merlin Stone thought that it was only as class societies, or what we know as "civilisation", emerged and men began to gain power over women that men chose to be castrated and adopt the priestess roles in order to displace women.[33]

Feinberg, however, suggests two reasons why Stone's view may be the less likely interpretation.[3]. First, the threat to the goddess religions came from the new, male-dominated, male deity religions such as Judaism and Christianity, which were arising within the early class societies in these regions at the time. It is known that the priestesses struggled to protect and continue their religions in opposition to the new gods.

Second, it seems counter-intuitive to suggest that these males who rid themselves of their "maleness" to become priestesses would be able to curry much favour or influence with male rulers, as Stone suggests.

It seems that a strong case can be made that pre-class or early class societies often had conceptions of gender roles and gender variance which were more subtle and accommodating of transgender people than trans people experience within the bounds of a modern capitalist gender binary conception.

A case for this might also be made based on analogy from examples of hunter-gatherer societies that survived into recent times. Some of these have been subject to intensive anthropological studies. Evidence from shamanistic traditions in various native American societies and in some Asian societies, as well as the history of trans communities such as the hijra in the Indian sub-continent (who worship the Mother Goddess Bahuchara Mata or the half male, half female incarnation of the Hindu god Shiva, Ardhanarisvara) also suggests that in former times gender variant people were more accepted than today.[35]

Gender and sexuality in North American First Nation societies

Some writers on the lives of First Nations in North America have referred to the existence of "berdaches", a term sometimes applied to apparently transgender people. The term berdache has been used to denote genetic males among First Nation Americans who dressed as women, did women's work and often had sex with non-berdache men.

The term, however, is regarded by many as derogatory. As Pat Califia has pointed out it does not derive from any Native American languages.[36] It may well be originally Persian, moving via Arabic and Spanish to French. It was used to refer to the passive partner in gay male intercourse and Califia suggests it is a misapplied term, an example of native gender variant people being viewed through Western homophobic lenses.

In fact, the original Native American terms used, such as the Lakota "winkte", the Cheyenne "he man he", and the Crow "badé" all have meanings like "not man/not woman" or "half man/half woman". In other words, they focus on gender rather than sexuality.[37]

How widespread were transgender people in these societies? Will Roscoe's book *Changing Ones: Third and Fourth Genders in Native North America* suggests that rather than being ostracised or forced into obscurity, gender-variant people were embraced by some 150 tribes, serving as artists, medicine people, religious experts, and tribal leaders.[38]

Others have documented how many societies considered that there were not two but three, four, or more genders.[39] Some seemed to tolerate both gender-variant and homosexual relationships. The experience of being a Two-Spirit person — one whose gender status was different from both men and women — was thought to confer a capacity for wisdom and greater understanding of the human condition.

Early Jesuits in the Americas, such as Joseph-Francois Lafitau, often encountered transgender people. In 1711, having spent six years among the Iroquois in the northeast of North America, he reported seeing (but clearly not appreciating) "women with manly courage who prided themselves upon the profession of warrior" as well as "men cowardly enough to live as women".[40]

Having a Two-Spirit wife was often seen as increasing the resources for the family group or the tribe. This seems to make sense, particularly in hunter-gatherer and nomadic societies, where resources and the necessities of life may be scarce or seasonal and birth rates had to be kept low, while all members of the group would be expected to contribute to the successful raising of the young.

Where the division of labour is along the lines of a person's reproductive role, and carries little or no social superiority for either sex and where everybody contributes to production in the social unit, the choices people make about their gender and sexuality are unlikely to be perceived as a threat to the group. It is only once control by an emergent ruling class has been achieved over women's reproductive capability that this gender assignment becomes closely aligned to sex and reproductive capacity.

Despite the erosion and discouragement of gender variant traditions in some First Nations people by the subsequent spread of Christianity and Judeo-Christian moral values, they persist in some places to this day. Some modern First Nation LGBT+ activists have in recent times sought to reclaim their history and values, including their trans history.[41]

It would, again, be mistaken to assume an unduly romantic or uncritical view of gender variance in First Nation societies. Pat Califia argues that some Western gay and transgender historians have been naïve about the extent to which such gender variant or same-sex behaviour was accepted.[42] He suggests that social attitudes varied quite a lot from region to region and tribe to tribe.

Califia also points to a serious problem for transgender history in general — the way that it has frequently been subsumed within the history of varieties of sexual orientation. He argues that some gay writers have misappropriated, misunderstood or misrepresented gender variant roles and behaviour as being only about sexual orientation. He accuses Johnathan Katz of doing this in his *Gay American History* of 1976.[43]

Similarly, Susan Stryker has argued that the history of trans people and of trans rebels has been largely either hidden altogether or buried within lesbian and gay history.[44]

The subjugation of women

Leslie Feinberg argued that the historical subordination and oppression of women as class societies emerged resulted in greater rigidity of gender roles and stricter policing of gender boundaries.[45] Referring to Friedrich Engels's groundbreaking 1884 work *The Origin of the Family, Private Property and the*

State[46], Feinberg shows how he drew on the then recent work of the American anthropologist Lewis Henry Morgan who had studied indigenous American and other societies.[47]

Engels's classic work identified the emergence of the patriarchal family and class societies as the key to understanding women's historical subordination and oppression.[48]

It was the development from matrilineal (descent traced through the female line) hunter-gatherer clan societies to patrilineal (descent traced through the male line) class societies, that led to the downgrading of status and the specific gendered and sexual oppression of women.

The reason that this dispossession was possible was because men increasingly came to control the forces of production as agriculture developed and more children were needed to work the land. Women's reproductive and infant nurturing roles largely or at least frequently precluded the possibility of continuous heavy labour in the fields where ploughs, oxen and cattle farming came to predominate. As some in the society were able to accumulate greater wealth, the "some" who controlled and traded the growing surpluses were the men who primarily used, or got others to use, these key forces of production.

Engels put it this way:

> With the herds and the other new riches, a revolution came over the family... The herds were the new means of acquiring these necessities; the taming of the animals in the first instance and later their tending were the man's work. To him, therefore, belonged the cattle and to him the commodities and the slaves received in exchange for cattle. All the surplus which the acquisition of the necessities of life now yielded fell to the man; the woman shared in its enjoyment, but had no part in its ownership... The division of labour within the family had regulated the division of property between the man and the woman. That division of labour had remained the same; and yet it now turned the previous domestic relation upside down, simply because the division of labour outside the family had

changed... The domestic labour of the woman no longer counted beside the acquisition of the necessities of life by the man; the latter was everything, the former an unimportant extra.[49]

Engels did not directly address sexual orientation or gender variant behaviour in his book, but considering another century or more of evidence since the publication of *The Origin* we can extend Engels's insights on women's oppression to help us understand the oppression of non-heterosexual and gender variant people as well.

The policing of gender and sexuality

The patriarchal family structure that increasingly replaced matrilineal and matrifocal clan societies imposed female monogamy within ruling class families so that the inheritance and accumulation of wealth, property and titles could be more easily assured. The men had to know who their children were, at the cost of women's sexual autonomy. In addition to demanding greater control over women's sexuality, prohibitions and strictures against cross dressing and other cross-gender behaviours in this period of social and economic transition seem to have been increasingly enforced.

Evidence of this process can be found in the Bible. Those fond of quoting biblical strictures on sinful behaviour will often refer to Leviticus 18.22 and 20.13, verses which prohibit homosexuality (at least male homosexuality), and Deuteronomy 22.5 (also the fifth and final book of the Jewish Torah) which prohibits cross dressing as an abomination: "A woman shall not wear that which pertaineth unto a man, neither shall a man put on a woman's garment; for whosoever doeth these things is an abomination unto Jehovah thy God."

The Bible-citers tend to be quite selective, however, since these prohibitions are actually included as part of a long list of things the chosen people at the time were not supposed to eat, touch, have sex with or wear and which carried some pretty robust and disturbing penalties, frequently death related.

The term "sodomy" itself derives from the alleged sinful goings-on in the ancient city of Sodom which required its destruction, along with Gomorrah, for its refusal to reject these abominable ways of the flesh. More likely, perhaps, the destruction was due to the cities' refusal to accept the authority of new laws and their subjugation to rival authorities — the accusations were a very convenient justification. It remains the case, though, as Mario Mieli has pointed out, that: "The ancient Hebrews were the first people in history to condemn homosexuality".[50] Since then the proscriptions in the Old Testament, enthusiastically promoted by priests and priests' assistants (Levites) have passed through Judaism into Christianity in particular.

What these Biblical strictures actually give us are examples of law-setting by ruling groups of that period seeking to consolidate their class control in order to further accumulate their wealth and power in a part of the world that was rapidly growing more prosperous and interconnected.

The imposition of these sorts of behavioural proscriptions and prohibitions happened over quite long periods of time in parts of the ancient world between the 11th and 7th century BCE as significant surpluses began to be accumulated through trade and conquest.

Feinberg presents a range of evidence that this was so.[51] Zie writes, "Hostility to transgender, sex-change, intersexuality, women, and same-sex love became a pattern wherever class antagonisms deepened".[52]

The fact that gender-variant behaviour had to be so forcefully prohibited, Feinberg argues, suggests that this behaviour had been fairly common practice — and tolerated at least to some extent — in earlier societies.

Some of the sharpest clashes between the old ways of what Engels in *The Origin of the Family* calls "primitive communist societies" or Morgan called "barbarism" and the emergence of expansionist Christian class societies and empires can be found in the chronicles of European conquest and colonisation of the Americas from the Middle Ages onwards.[53]

The Catholic Church and the Spanish and Portuguese states' approach to native cultures was based on the elitist and racist notion that these societies needed to be subjugated and sometimes enslaved for their own good (not merely, of course,

for Spanish and Portuguese primitive accumulation of capital).
The ideological justification for this brutal process often came
from a very willing Christian Church, which shared in the booty.

In 1530 the Spanish conquistador Nuño Beltrán de Guzmán
reported that the last person he captured in a battle, who
"fought most courageously, was a man in the habit of a woman,
for which I caused him to be burned".[54]

There was often systematic persecution and eradication of
transgender or non-binary people. One of Feinberg's illustrations in *Transgender Warriors* is a 1594 engraving by Theo-
dore de Bry of Balboa's Panama expedition which shows him
using dogs to murder two-spirit people in the Americas.[55] To
Balboa these trans people, often highly respected as healers,
teachers and sometimes female-born hunters and warriors in
their own societies, were examples of diabolical and primitive
debauchery. When the Spanish invaded the Antilles and Loui-
siana, "they found men dressed as women who were respected
by their societies. Thinking they were hermaphrodites or
homosexuals, they slew them".[56]

The impact of colonialism was genocidal in the Americas.
But it was not just the Portuguese or Spanish empires that
tried to stamp out any acceptance and respect for variant sexualities and cross-gender expression. The history of the British
Empire's relationship with less industrially advanced societies
is also instructive in this respect. The imposition of Christian
legal codes on colonial possessions such as India and various
African countries by Britain and other imperialist countries
clearly included the intent to criminalise and eradicate both
sexually "perverse" and gender transgressive behaviour.[57]

The family in capitalism

Writers on sexuality and the family such as Jeffrey Weeks and
John D'Emilio have pointed out a major contradiction in the
nature of the modern family.[58] [59] While the developing capitalist
mode of production in the 18th and 19th centuries was in practice creating the conditions for the emergence of freer sexual
relationships and gender roles among working class people,
it was simultaneously undermining the family as a social unit
which could provide relatively cheaply for the reproduction of

the working class.

This was a scary prospect for sections of the capitalist class, along with the growing capacity for workers to organise themselves into unions and challenge the dreadful conditions they were expected to endure in the new factories and city slums.

It may be difficult today to grasp just how appalling conditions were for working people at the time. In his 1845 book *The Condition of the Working Class in England*, Engels showed how industrial capitalism consumed working class lives.[60] The average lifespan for working men in Manchester was 17. It was 16 in Bethnal Green and only 15 in Liverpool. This was at a time when the middle class male lifespan averaged 52 years. A few years later, in *Capital*, Karl Marx described the appalling social and working conditions faced by both agricultural workers in the countryside and industrial workers in the burgeoning towns and cities.[61]

The long hours of work in the developing factories, mills and mines were physically and emotionally draining, insecure, dangerous and badly paid. Workers' leisure time to spend with each other or their children was at an absolute minimum. Often children from the age of four or five worked in the mills and mines alongside their parents, risking death and severe injury with little or no time for schooling. These are the kind of conditions that fuelled the growth of the great working class Chartist movement of the 1830s and 1840s that demanded political representation and changes to working conditions among other things.

The family, for working class people, had all but disappeared as the population shifted from peasant life to industrial urban life. Workers of all ages and genders were living in shared accommodation, often provided by the companies they worked for. Bed-sharing and sleeping in shifts was common. Fast food took the place of the farmhouse kitchen and there was little time for leisure or community-building.

Some in the bourgeoisie were genuinely horrified by the poverty and degradation that they saw around them and that was exposed in investigations like the Mines Commission of 1842. These led bourgeois reformers to look for means to ensure the working class family's survival, not only in the interests of workers but much more importantly, for them, in the longer term interests of capitalism.

Rapidly expanding capitalist enterprises not only needed workers in the here and now but also required the working class to provide the necessary reproduction of the next generation of workers as cheaply as possible.

In response, a series of Factory Acts (1833, 1844, 1847) were passed which restricted hours of work. Aimed initially at child labour, they later included women's labour, and men's working hours subsequently benefitted indirectly. The 1844 Act prevented children and women from working nights or for shifts longer than twelve hours, and this was further reduced to ten hours by the 1847 Act. In 1842 legislation preventing women from working underground in mines was passed, though some women continued to work in mining on the surface.

Measures like these were double-edged. On the one hand the legislation was intended to exclude women from industrial occupations such as working underground in mines (not least because of the potential for "immorality" when men and women were working together half-naked) and might be seen as reducing women's work opportunities and pushing down family incomes. On the other hand, such legislation was often campaigned for and welcomed by working class people as a measure of workplace protection and a recognition of the need to reduce the high levels of mortality among working class people.

The ideological assertion of the role of the nuclear family — father as breadwinner, mother focused on the home and caring for children — was not something simply imposed on the working class. Much of the legislation was also about attempting to mould the working class family in the image of the bourgeois family to enable the capitalist class to exert greater control of the working class through encouraging identification with middle class values of morality — "family values", the Church, temperance and the discouragement of sex outside marriage.

The legislative changes had also to be underpinned by an ideological drive towards notions of fidelity (at least for women) and the strict regulation of sexual behaviour. This had implications for attitudes and prohibitions towards homosexuality and cross-gender behaviour.

This is the background to D'Emilio's claim that homophobia is built into the ideology of the nuclear family and capitalism itself. He writes:

> On the one hand, capitalism continually weakens the material foundation of family life, making it possible for individuals to live outside the family, and for a lesbian and gay male identity to develop. On the other, it needs to push men and women into families, at least long enough to reproduce the next generation of workers. The elevation of the family to ideological pre-eminence guarantees that a capitalist society will reproduce not just children, but heterosexism and homophobia. In the most profound sense, capitalism is the problem.[62]

Weeks has pointed out that the bourgeois family was "both the privileged location of emotionality and love…and simultaneously an effective policeman of sexual behaviour".[63]

We can certainly extend this analysis to the experience of trans people, who do not easily fit within the strict delineation of gender roles in the nuclear family — and so suffer the psychological and social effects of being made to feel they are "outsiders".

The material expansion in much of the world in the decades after the Second World War once again opened opportunities (at least in principle) for different living arrangements, different sorts of relationships and the expression of different sexualities and gender identities. Sexuality and sexual activity, largely due to the development of efficient methods of contraception, perhaps most notably the contraceptive pill since this was under the direct control of the woman herself, has increasingly become separated from procreation and the care of the next generation of labour, the cost of which is still borne by individuals not societies. Nevertheless, political battlegrounds have developed over contraception, abortion rights, same-sex marriage, gay rights such as gay adoption and so on.[64]

Despite many more people now living in single parent families or alone this does not alter the basic fact that the nuclear family and the ideology promoting it remain the ideal in modern capitalist societies. Transphobia is part of the oppressive ideological justifications that serve to maintain the heterosexual social order, "family values" and norms of appropriate sexual and gender expressive behaviour.

The nuclear family is a site of conflict between people's need for emotional and physical support and sustenance and a potential hell of domestic violence, bullying, poverty and unfulfilled potential. It remains crucial to the inculcation and perpetuation of the oppression suffered by women, non-heterosexual and gender variant people and a site where both the dispossession of labour power and the denial of dreams are prepared for.

Chapter 3
Biology, gender and gender identity

> Every newborn human inherits gender constructions as an obligatory part of their developmental system: gender stereotypes, ideologies, roles, norms, and hierarchy are passed on via parents, peers, teachers, clothing, language, media, role models, organisations, schools, institutions, social inequalities…and, of course, toys.[65]

> The strict division between "nature" and "culture" evinced in many "essentialist" versus "constructionist" debates thus does not make sense insofar as it artificially separates two aspects of what ultimately produces behaviour.[66]

In late March 2017 a big orange bus began a tour of the East Coast of the United States. Organised by a trio of right wing groups — the National Organization for Marriage, the International Organization for the Family, and CitizenGo — it was dubbed the Free Speech Bus by its organisers. It was intended to carry its message of transphobia to towns and cities to galvanise the silent majority who, its organisers believed, would welcome the opportunity to reject notions of gender variance and gender fluidity.

In keeping with Donald Trump's penchant for appointing the-last-person-anyone-rational-would-appoint-to-that-role, in the same week that the Free Speech Bus began its trundle through East Coast cities he appointed Donald Severino as head of the Department of Health's Office of Civil Rights (OCR).

This body is supposed to ensure that no-one in the United States is blocked from getting healthcare through the prejudices of providers. Yet Severino had campaigned *against* the legislation that protects trans people in this regard and had previously accused the OCR of abuse of power in "trying to coerce everyone...into pledging allegiance to a radical new gender ideology".[67] He had made his transphobic views clear in a report for the far-right Heritage Foundation in 2016 in which he said: "On the basis of religious teachings, moral reasoning, scientific evidence, and medical experience, many have strong grounds to hold that one's sex is an immutable characteristic."

No doubt the orange bus organisers will have felt they were winning new friends in high places with Severino's appointment.

On the sides of this bus packed with gender-orthodoxy evangelists were stencilled stylised stereotypical figures of girls and boys, emblazoned with XX or XY, and the words:

It's Biology: Boys are boys...and always will be.
Girls are girls...and always will be.
You can't change sex. Respect all.
Sign now to defend freedom of speech.

The "Respect all" in a campaign message intended to whip up disrespect towards and invalidation of trans people seemed a little clunky. Similarly the call to sign up for free speech, while typical of the topsy-turvy illogic with which bigots justify their campaigns to *restrict* free speech and close down genuine democratic discussion, might seem hypocritical for a bus tour clearly intended to get some people to stop going on about transgender rights.

Campaign organiser Joseph Grabowski of the National Organization for Marriage was reported saying that being transgender is a disorder and trans people should "live that out privately" and not in public.[68] Public, of course, includes using public toilets (or bathrooms in American English). Grabowski believes that if people come across trans people using their gender appropriate bathroom they should "speak up if they feel uncomfortable and let the business owner know. This can't be considered transphobic or bigoted".[69] No doubt in the bad old segregationist days in the US if someone had seen a black person using a white restroom they should have "spoken up if they felt uncomfortable and let the business owner know" because, in Grabowski-world, that couldn't have been considered racist.

The Free Speech bus in reality was promoting views about sex and gender that, while popular in some people's versions of common sense, are fundamentally out of step not only with any humane or liberating policies or politics, but also with what we know about the science and evolution of sex, sexuality and gender.

Is it true for instance that at the genetic, gonadal, biological levels "boys are boys and girls are girls"? Well, modern scientific evidence suggests a rather more complex and nuanced take on sex and gender.

Certainly science, albeit sometimes quite bad science, from neuroscience through anthropology to evolutionary sociology and psychology, has often been keen to hunt down "fundamental" genetic or brain structure differences between males and females that would bolster binary and essentialist notions of gendered behaviour. In 1991, for example, Simon LeVay claimed to have found evidence that the cause of homosexuality was to be found in brain differences between gay and straight people — claims which were subsequently discredited on methodological and other grounds.[70]

In terms of such supposed or assumed fundamental differences between men and women, populist books like John Gray's 1992 best seller *Men are from Mars, Women are from Venus* have sought to popularise this "never the twain shall meet" ideology.[71]

In Gray's view, shared by many others, men and women are so different psychologically that they need "his and hers" approaches to relationship issues and problem solving. His book touched a nerve in popular culture in the 1990s and subsequently tapped into a lucrative spin-off market, a treasure trove of book sequels, faddy counselling approaches and speaking tours, even fragrance lines and travel guides (his and hers, obviously).

These ideas have been effectively challenged by writers such as Deborah Cameron. In her book *The Myth of Mars and Venus* she writes:

> The idea that men and women differ fundamentally in the way they use language to communicate is a myth in the everyday sense: a widespread but false belief. But it is also a myth in the sense of being a story people tell in order to explain who they are, where they come from, and why they live as they do. Whether or not they are "true" in any historical or scientific sense, such stories have consequences in the real world. They shape our beliefs, and so influence our actions. The myth of Mars and Venus is no exception to that rule.[72]

Those attracted to this myth of an apparently neat, essentialist binary gulf between men and women might be disappointed to discover that life really isn't that simple, even at basic biological levels, let alone when it comes to sexuality, gender and gender identity. And if things are so much more complex and interesting in terms of human biology and the structure and development of our gonads, genitalia and brains, how much more informative and exciting ought it to be to consider how sexuality and gender emerge and interrelate with the hugely variable material, economic, social, psychological and political circumstances that each of us encounters from birth.

As Cordelia Fine has put it, "while the male and female reproductive systems have stayed the same across human history[73], as the developmental system has changed — whether through the introduction of contraception, equal opportunity legislation, paternity leave, or gender quotas — brains, hormones, behaviour, and roles have changed".[74]

Intersex

Undeniably, sex binary and gender binary ideologies remain very influential, even hegemonic, in the modern capitalist world as they have done in class societies for hundreds of years at least.

Consider the birth of a child somewhere, anywhere, in the world. When the child is born doctors, nurses, midwives or those otherwise attending the woman will ascribe it as a boy or a girl on the basis of a fairly perfunctory look at its genitals, assuming this has not been done already via a pre-natal ultrasound scan. Does it have an "inny" or an "outy", is the outy of an acceptable size, are there any obvious physical anomalies present in the genitalia? Medical staff are very unlikely to check the child's chromosomes to see whether it has XX (female chromosomes), XY (male chromosomes) or some other combination or arrangement.

Nevertheless, a small minority of people are born outside the assumed sex binary who may possess a variety of intersex conditions. The Intersex Society of North America estimates that roughly one in 1,500 to 2,000 babies are born visibly intersexed each year.[75] In Britain the charity DSD Families reports that around 130 children are born each year with differences of sex development (DSD)[76]and worldwide, according to the Office of the UN High Commissioner for Human Rights, up to 1.7 percent of people have intersex traits, about the same proportion of the world's population as people with red hair.[77]

There are at least thirty conditions which can lead to the development of atypical physical sexual characteristics. Many such intersex conditions would not be detected at birth or possibly at all under most circumstances, unless the person were to have a chromosome test. When there are detectable biological anomalies some of those affected have in the past been described by the inaccurate, offensive and outmoded term "hermaphrodite".

Such medical conditions may arise from a variety of causes. These include insensitivity to the male hormone androgen, or chromosomal or genetic inconsistencies with one's apparent physical sex, or several other biological conditions.

Even when it comes to what are considered to be the most fundamental elements of biological sex, our chromosomes, there is variability and diversity, as Myra Hird describes:

Although discussions of chromosomes tend to focus

on the genes inherited from the father (because it is these genes that define the sex of the child) all people must have at least one X chromosome because so many essential genes are contained on the X chromosome. All foetuses spend their first six weeks in an XX womb and her amniotic fluid, undergoing the same development until the release of testosterone for the majority of XY foetuses. The only thing that does not exist is a pure (Y or YY) male. There has been a case of a boy born with an XX configuration, however. This boy's ovum split several times before being fertilized by sperm, providing further evidence that parthenogenic reproduction extends to humans. All cells usually contain a conglomeration of our biological parents' chromosomes. This means that our bodies live in a permanently fertilized state, with only our egg and sperm cells qualifying as sexed (haploid): the vast majority of our cells are intersex (diploid).78

However the medical profession, in reflecting the dominant gender binary ideology in capitalist society, has generally been unwilling to simply accept such variation. In the claimed interests of the child, medical practitioners traditionally have offered concerned parents the technological sophistication available to them to surgically and/or hormonally shoehorn such people into one of two genders. This has usually been carried out without allowing the person most concerned the right to exercise any choice in the matter, generally because they were too young to know what was going on.

In practice this has meant carrying out surgical procedures (sometimes many such procedures) on infants and young children that are either very difficult or impossible to reverse. Many intersex people and their organisations rightly regard this as oppressive, unwarranted and intrusive at best, and as a form of genital mutilation at worst.79 Depending on a particular child's physical development such procedures may include operations to reposition the urethral opening (for urination), phalloplasty (the creation or augmentation of penile material), vaginoplasty (the creation of a vaginal opening), as well as hysterectomy or orchidectomy (the removal of ovaries or testes).

Thus the UK Intersex Association urges medical practitioners and family members of an infant with an apparent intersex condition to be cautious and consider the long term interests of the child. Most conditions do not require urgent medical intervention for the health of the child.

It is for these reasons that, politically, intersex people are generally considered to be in the same boat as others subject to oppression based on their sexuality or gender identity. In many cases, and for the past two decades or so, acronyms in this field have often reflected this sense of inclusion, such as LGBT+, LGBTI, LGBTQI, or LGBTQI+ ("I" for intersex, "Q" for questioning or queer) and so on.

However, many people, including some poorly informed or malignly intentioned transphobes, continue to confuse intersex and transgender. Being transgender relates to a person's gender identity and is not the same as having an intersex condition. Intersex relates to a physical condition whereas being transgender relates to the lack of "fit" between a person's birth-assigned gender and their sense of gender identity. According to the current state of knowledge a trans person is no more likely to have morphological or other biological intersex manifestations such as chromosomal, endocrinal or physical inconsistencies than the average person.

A number of news sources fell into this confusion when reporting on South African athlete Caster Semenya's unsuccessful appeal in April 2019 against a ruling by the International Amateur Athletics Association that would require her to medicate with hormone blockers to reduce her natural testosterone levels if she wished to continue competing.[80] While Semenya does not discuss her situation publicly she does not claim to be transgender and almost certainly has an intersex condition that means her body naturally generates testosterone at relatively high levels for a genetic woman (she has a form of hyperandrogeny).[81] Many intersex people certainly see themselves as falling under the transgender umbrella due to such inconsistencies, which includes how intersex people may have been inappropriately assigned at birth and subsequently treated socially and medically.

Brains and brain sex

Some researchers in recent years have claimed that structural brain differences can be found between the brains of cisgender males and females and those of trans women.[82] Such studies have generally taken two forms: either examination under the microscope of brain slices from certain tiny areas of the brain, usually the hypothalamus; or brain imaging of such areas by magnetic resonance imaging (MRI) or positron emission tomography (PET) scans.

The brain-slicing studies have used post-mortem brain samples of transsexuals and compared these to similar post-mortem samples of apparently "normal" or non-trans men's and women's brains. In the first such study originally published in the 1990s it was claimed that in tiny areas of the hypothalamus, "the bed nucleus of the stria terminalis (BSTc), a brain area that is essential for sexual behaviour, is larger in men than in women. A female-sized BSTc was found in male-to-female transsexuals".[83]

The researchers hypothesised that "gender identity develops as a result of an interaction between the developing brain and sex hormones", since it appeared that differentiation in size was not the result of the hormonal regime in adulthood, based on the fact that several of the transsexuals had ceased hormone treatment some months before death. The fact that they had ceased the hormone regime before their deaths, however, would not necessarily reverse any morphological effects.

A significant advantage of brain imaging over peering at slices of brain under a microscope is that you don't need to be dead to be a subject. Despite this, sample sizes in published studies are still quite small. The experimental technique generally used has been to look for sexually dichotomous responses (particularly in the hypothalamus and the "olfactory brain" — the part of the brain dealing with smell) to particular stimulations, for example certain smells and pheromones.

If researchers can find systematic differences between men and women they could then compare these to transsexual women and very occasionally a transsexual man. Several studies over the last ten years claimed to have found that transsexual women's brains showed results closest to cisgender women or somewhere between typical male and typical female brains.[84] Once again, however, it is not clear that any brain differences could not have been due to the effects of taking hormones.

One such study was reported by Julie Bakker of the University of Liege and colleagues at the Centre of Expertise on Gender Dysphoria at the VU University Medical Centre, The Netherlands, presented to the European Society of Endocrinology's annual meeting in May 2018.[85]

The researchers examined brain activation scans (by MRI) of 160 participants reacting to a pheromone stimulus. The participants were trans-identified adolescents compared to a control group of cisgender adolescents.

The research suggested that the brain activation patterns and thus the sexual differentiation of the trans young people's brains were closer to those of their desired gender exhibited by the relevant cisgender controls than those of their natal gender. They also suggested that some brain structural differences were detected along similar lines. The researchers were suggesting, reflecting their implicit acceptance of the medical model in explaining trans, that their results might form the basis for early diagnosis and thus better access to therapy for gender dysphoria. Their focus was on causation rather than addressing transphobia.

It's worth noting however, once again, that the results obtained don't rule out the possibility that differences in task performance or brain structure might be due to the puberty blocker hormones the trans subjects were taking, or indeed to the gender identity and gender role of the trans person rather than the other way round — ie what was cause and what was effect.

Notwithstanding the way in which the media have frequently picked up study results like this and simplistically claimed "gender is in the brain" or that "brain differences cause trans", it certainly is the case that some scientists have concluded that results such as these are "suggestive" of brain differences in transsexual people compared to cisgender people, or at least that transsexual women's brains show some similarities in structure and activity with cisgender women's brains.

There are other problems with this sort of research, however. The researchers in the original brain slicing study admitted that there was no evidence in humans that the larger size of the BSTc is related to masculinity. They based their assumption that there might be such a link on research data from rat brains because in some cases rats can effectively model human physiology

Second, the research samples are almost always small — the sample size reported in the original Luders et al paper referred to above was only six transsexuals' brains. In subsequent years the research team was able to increase the sample size, but it was still very small to claim any robust statistical validity.

Third, in the case of a number of the brain imaging studies, the researchers did not control for sexual orientation and this could have been another variable that might have confounded results (including, it seems, the recently reported Bakker study).

Nevertheless, many transgender people seem to welcome, indeed they find very attractive, the possible validity of such research outcomes. For them, identifying a biomedical explanation for being trans strengthens the case both for refuting those who argue that being transgender is a lifestyle choice, and for promoting arguments for more funding and better access to medical intervention. This is no test of the scientific validity of such claims, however. Some gay people welcomed the claimed identification of a "gay gene" by LeVay decades ago for similar social and political reasons, but the scientific evidence for this was subsequently shown to be flawed.

How robust is the evidence? Critics of neuroscience such as Cordelia Fine suggest that the evidence presented by such "neuro-pundits" for male/female differences is weak and contested and hence the comparison with transgender people's brain structure or brain activity is conceptually very weak as well.

Other researchers (Rebecca Jordan-Young at Barnard College in New York, Analis Kaiser at the University of Freiburg, Daphne Joel at Tel Aviv University, and Gina Rippon at Aston University) have promoted evidence challenging the psychology of male/female dichotomy in the human brain, linked in particular to foetal testosterone levels.[86]

In direct contrast to the claims being made in some quarters, these researchers point to the empirical weaknesses that support this view of the sexually dimorphic brain. Instead they promote interpretations of research strongly indicating the brain's plasticity or malleability over time and through interactions with our social and physical environments. While this view doesn't exclude the possibility of male/female brain differences, these have not been proven. They criticise the evidence used to promote notions of hardwired inflexibility inherent in some sociobiological approaches to the explanation of human behaviour patterns.

Not the least of the criticisms of these brain-fishing expeditions is that our behaviour, personality and desires cannot just be read off from physical or functional differences in localised areas of the brain, even if these exist. In addition, and fundamentally, a *correlation* between various stimulants and perceived activity in areas of the brain is not the same as *causation.*

Our knowledge and understanding of the brain are still quite limited, but what we do know is that it is a highly complex and integrated organ and has the potential for continuous adaptation and change throughout life.[87] When it comes to the sex of the brain it is becoming ever more clear with more detailed analyses of brain cells that to speak of the "male" brain or "female" brain is a misconception. Some scientists have been developing the notion of a "mosaic" brain, the idea that our brains have unique patterns or mosaics of regions with variable "maleness" or "femaleness" in each.[88]

The empirical evidence for "brain sex", and thus for brain sex being the determinant of gender identity, is weak and unconvincing. A Marxist view of sex starts by recognising that it is neither simple nor one-dimensional. It is true that human reproduction depends upon the existence of two sexes. However the division of labour in reproduction and production predates capitalist society and is rooted in the family and the emergent division between material and mental labour. Once these devolve onto different individuals the stage is set for the unequal distribution of what is produced and "the latent slavery in the family, [of wife and children — LM] though still very crude, is the first property..."[89]

In *The German Ideology*, written in the mid-1840s, Marx talks about the first division of labour being the sex act.[90] But as pointed out above, in pre-capitalist and pre-class societies there were degrees of fluidity in terms of adoption of gender roles which did not assign more or less importance to male and female roles. So being a particular sex could lead to a variety of gender roles and choices of gender roles as ascribed by particular societies.

Marx and Engels continued: "The production of life, both of one's own in labour and of fresh life in procreation, now appears as a double relationship: on the one hand as a natural, on the other as a social relationship".[91]

Marx and Engels talk about the "natural" division of labour between the sexes but they mean here "that which seems natural to a given society" rather than "something fixed or essential in nature". Thus "natural" should not be taken to mean they saw gender as biologically determined. What is "natural" for them constitutes a dialectical concept influenced by both objective and subjective factors. Human reproduction through the sex act (and other forms of insemination as well today) produces children but how they are nurtured and raised is flexible and depends on the social order into which they are born.

How brains do gender

Most people continue to see the matter of someone's gender as not merely important but fundamental to understanding the essential underpinnings and determinants of a person's life.

I've referred to Cordelia Fine's work above and in her fascinating and very funny books she has shown how assumptions of male/female differentiation, for example in the supposed fundamental differences in language use or other mental abilities and aptitudes such as "emotionality" or spatial ability, are just that — assumptions.

The terms in which such supposed differences are explained or justified may have changed over the decades but recent science seems to be employed just as badly and uncritically as ever, Fine claims, by many working in this field or by those carving out lucrative careers popularising the notion of fundamental and essential gender differences.

Fine argues that the discovery (or re-discovery) of so-called fundamental differences between male and female abilities and aptitudes and concomitant differences between the brains of males and females is actually nothing new. Such supposed differences have served to justify women's oppression and their second class status in society for centuries.

The discoveries of biological differences between men and women (rather than the pre-Enlightenment view that women were just an "inversion" of men) helped to underpin the ideology of superiority/inferiority applied to gender — women are emotional and weak and made for child bearing and nurturing, and men are strong and competitive, less nurturing and emotional, and designed for reading maps, fixing taps and doing mental arithmetic. If this was not due to women's head size (smaller than men's, of course) it was to do with having erratic hormones or the misfortune to think with the wrong side of the brain.

Without claiming that there can be no possible differences between the brain structures or functions of men and women (not least because we just don't know for sure yet), even if clear gender differences were to be found — and that is a very big if, for reasons which I have summarised above — then we should still not, as many researchers and commentators insist on doing, assume that brain = mind. We cannot read the person from their brain structure, nor does the evidence suggest we can read off the gender identity of the person. For human brains hormones are certainly important factors but social context is a major determinant. Thus any male/female differences that might exist become especially significant when the social and political context, as in class societies, is one of women's oppression and subjugation.

Brain structure has inherent plasticity and adaptability. Changes to connectivity between neurones can result throughout our lives from interactions with our physical and social environments. On the one hand an under-stimulating environment can stunt the brain's growth and development. For example, there is empirical evidence from MRI scans and EEG (electroencephalogram) evidence that the inhumanely restricted environments of the appalling Romanian orphanages discovered after the fall and execution of Nicolae and Elena Ceausescu[92] in 1989 caused parts of the incarcerated children's hippocampuses to fail to develop normally. It seemed that this was almost irreversible unless addressed early enough in infancy.[93]

On the other hand, there is evidence that greater environmental exposure, stimulus and practice can physically enhance parts of the brain. London black cab drivers learning the traditional "knowledge" have shown increases in the size of their grey matter — the brain cell bodies — in a part of the hippocampus as measured in MRI scans.[94]

Such examples point to the possibility of radically different conclusions that might be drawn from the evidence discussed earlier. The apparent differences in the brains of trans women, their greater similarity to cisgender women rather than men, might be due to the aspirations, roles, behavioural patterns and habits developed over sometimes many years living in female roles by these trans women. In other words, even among adolescents, could the way trans people think of themselves and how they live their lives be influencing their brain morphology rather than their brain morphology "causing" them to be trans?

The attraction of trans essentialism

When it comes to explanations of the development of a person's gender identity, common sense and much of the literature invites us to take an either/or approach. Either gender identity is a result of the chromosomes we inherit from our parents which determine (usually) binary development of mostly unspecified gender specific aspects of the brain; or it is perceived as strongly socially malleable and thus socially determined.

Undeniably and perhaps understandably, particularly in the past, many trans people have taken an essentialist and binary view of the relationship between biological sex and gender. Such a view treats gender as somehow natural and given — "a man's mind in a woman's body", "a woman's mind in a man's body". A glance at a selection of trans people's autobiographical writing, particularly those from an older generation, will tend to confirm this.[95] Being transgender is still often presented in the media in this oversimplified way.

This attraction to essentialism is analogous to the attraction the approach has for some gay people. It bolsters a notion that sexual orientation is not a matter of choice or socialisation — it is hardwired. Thus it is not a gay person's "fault" they are gay and homophobia is therefore unjust and unfair.

There are some obvious problems with the direction this logic leads in. If a state has extreme homophobic or transphobic views and wants to eradicate such behaviour among its citizens, and if one's gender orientation really is hardwired and cannot be eradicated by education, therapy, medical intervention and so on, then for some people in power, especially those infected with eugenicist ideas, the solution that presents itself is the removal or eradication of gays or trans people.[96] This is essentially what the Nazis attempted in Germany.

There is a less bestial version of this essentialist view, though. If transgender people's problem is that somehow the wrong switch got thrown at some point early in life, then what they now need is to find ways to get back to the gender they were really supposed to have been.

What follows from this is the notion that since this could have happened to anyone and is beyond the individual's control it should follow that the trans person should not be penalised and should be enabled to live their life in the gender of their choosing. This has been a common view among transgender people and it broadly dovetails with the dominant, pathologising, gate-keeping medical approach to gender identity.

"Gender dysphoria", the medical diagnosis which superseded "gender identity disorder" in the most recent edition of the psychiatrists' bible, the *Diagnostic and Statistical Manual* (DSM-V[97]), denotes discomfort or distress due to the mismatch between a person's inner sense of gender identity and their biological sex.

Many trans people, such as Julia Serano[98] believe that while the diagnosis of gender dysphoria may be less prescriptive, pernicious and pathologising than the previous "gender identity disorder" it does not describe a real condition and should be dropped altogether from the DSM. Increasing numbers of trans people resent the requirement for any medical diagnosis to access treatment and feel there are serious problems with such an essentialist approach to gender identity.

Sex, gender and gender identity

Some transgender people have traditionally drawn distinctions between those who are "transsexual" and wish to physically transition by undertaking gender affirmation genital surgery (for many, with the aim of "passing" as their desired gender), and those who are "merely cross-dressers" or "fetishists". The "true" transsexuals are contrasted with those who don't intend to or cannot transition for health, financial or political reasons, or who don't perceive themselves as on one side or the other of a gender binary.

However, others such as Juno Roche in her 2018 autobiography,[99] have rejected the whole notion of "passing" and feel that their trans status, and being perceived as trans rather than one or the other "safe" pole of binary gender, is authentic, legitimate and desirable, not least in that it avoids, in her view, inadvertently reinforcing oppressive gender stereotypes.

In an article about her transition Roche wrote:

> I do not need to be seen as woman, as a trans woman, as being androgynous, or even non-binary. Simply, I am happy to be seen as a trans person, born trans with a trans body capable of fluidity and change… For me, being transgender is not a stepping stone, a spare room between being a "man" and becoming a "woman"… Trans can be a destination itself… Seeking safety, but safety on our terms; unjudged and accepted without needing surgery to fit a prescribed mould that we know is harming everyone, trans and cis.[100]

Others, such as Shon Faye, have suggested that trying to trace the cause of trans at all is misdirected since it is not an illness that needs to be identified or a syndrome that needs to be diagnosed in order to access appropriate help and support.[101]

Of course, socialists should stand fully in solidarity with all trans people against transphobia, whatever their take on gender and identity.

For everyone, trans and cisgender people alike, our gender identity is socially constructed in a dialectical relationship with our material circumstances (including our biological sex) and it is to some extent fluid. People's self-identification and self-description (including trans people's) can and does change and develop over time. There is a certain fluidity in this because our identities and sense of self are structured within given material, historical and cultural frameworks, in the last resort by the class relations dominant within a given mode of production like capitalism.

But how fluid is this identity? In social science the popularity of the "polar opposites" view — either innate or socialised — has been used as justification for particular medical/social practices, sometimes involving pretty unethical interventions.

However, there is a downside to the anti-essentialist position as well. Thus if we take the view that gender identity is entirely "caused" via social construction then we should not be surprised if those who advocate transgender "cures" (analogous to gay "cures") conclude that they can eradicate trans and gender-variant people's gender behaviour by "training" them, or in psychological terms reinforcing them, to behave differently (ie in more socially acceptable ways) in response to social mores and expectations.

At root here is a fundamental issue. In the search for a so-called cause of transgender identity and behaviour, both gender essentialism deriving from claimed brain differences and gender malleability deriving from social constructionism can lead to inhumane views and practices which are dangerous to trans people and deny validation of their existence — and can even lead to policies aimed at their eradication.

Attitudes of approval or disapproval and positive or negative policies are based on social and political assessments of people's various characteristics and are thus essentially political matters. Those who oppose oppression should know where they stand on such an issue in relation to trans people, just as they should know where they stand on matters of racism and sexism irrespective of the *cause* of people's skin tones or reproductive capabilities.

The reality is that trans people are unjustly and perniciously subject to transphobia in capitalist society and therefore need solidarity in fighting this oppression. Support for this should be unconditional and not dependant on what we think might be the explanation of being trans or non-binary.

I've argued above that biological sex has materiality, though it is nowhere near as binary or as purely biological as some people believe.

Yet in a (broadly) sexually bi-morphic, self-aware social species like human beings, sex is often both a biological prerequisite and a socially and historically influenced indicator of who bears children and who plays what role in the reproduction of the next generation of labour power. But how we are currently sex-assigned says little or nothing about who *could* nurture and socialise the next generation, *how* that might be accomplished, and for what purpose. These vary from one culture to another.

Biological sex as well as having materiality also has socially ascribed characteristics and values applied to it, including the ascription of detrimental values reflecting historically contingent societal sexism and misogyny — such as the objectification, devaluation and commodification of female bodies.

Some trans critics and transphobes do not recognise "gender identity" as a real category (for example, claiming it is just a "feeling") and this part of the debate therefore goes directly to how socialists do or do not recognise sex, gender and gender identity as being material.

Sexual orientation

It's important to make a clear distinction between sexual orientation (to whom we may be sexually attracted) and our gender identity (which gender we identify with and how strongly, if at all). In everyday conversations it's common for people still to assume that a trans person is gay, or that gay people are in some way gender variant. Such thinking finds its way into the slurs that imply that gay men must be effeminate, or lesbians must have "butch" tendencies. It is not that long ago that the medical profession, too, assumed such a conflation.

In fact all the evidence shows that trans people can be gay, straight, bisexual, asexual or pansexual. Conversely, homosexuality or bisexuality does not connote any incongruence between a person's biological sex and their gender identity. Most gay people are as secure in their gender identity as most heterosexual people.

Nevertheless, sexual orientation and gender identity are certainly intertwined. Thus some trans people will also be gay or bisexual and these matters of sexual orientation, and associated homophobia, will interact with the person's gender identity and associated transphobia.

Similarly, a trans person's sexual orientation will be regarded differently if they transition from whatever gender they were assigned at birth to another, assuming their sexuality does not change in the process. Someone who was perceived, pre-transition, as a gay man becomes, in society's eyes, a straight woman after transition. Similarly, someone perceived as a straight woman who remains attracted to men after transition, becomes perceived as a gay man.

In this sense sexuality and gender, while conceptually distinct, cannot be neatly and separately packaged in terms of societal perceptions and reactions. Homophobia and transphobia are thus co-related. The growing recognition of this was one of the factors that justified the development of collective campaigning and organising since the 1990s under the acronym LGBT — lesbian, gay, bisexual and transgender.[102]

Gender oppression

Gender can be understood as having two elements: it is both *socially* applied (ie as something which exists externally to the person — gender roles) and it is also an *internal* sense of self — gender identity.

Gender expression can vary enormously from one society to another, one historical period to another. But both elements of gender constitute factors in the social relations existing in class societies like capitalism. So, we might also think of social status, class consciousness and sexuality as part of the reality of capitalist social relations, all "determined by our social being", as Marx put it.[103]

Marxists therefore seek to understand sex, gender and

the oppression of women, and also gender-variance and non-heterosexual sex, through the lens of historical materialism and recognise that the relationship between them is a complex interaction — each affects the other reciprocally.

There is a constant tension within capitalism in that while certain rights and legal protections may be won in some societies by oppressed groups as a result of pressure from below (such as equal pay legislation, same-sex marriage or nominal equal rights for trans people) these are all historically and socially contingent and do not essentially undermine the capitalist mode of production's reliance on the subordination of women for bearing and raising the next generation of workers.

From this fundamental economic factor flow the social mores intended to control women's sexuality as well as the continuing dominance of the nuclear family structure which remains at the heart of capitalist society. And as part of the ideological adherence to "family values"also flows the oppression of alternative sexualities and gender-variant behaviour which carry the threat of undermining the capitalist nuclear family.

This means, as Judith Orr writes, that:

> Women and their bodies are battlegrounds for society's debates over moral and ideological values — whether that's about women's appearance and behaviour, their sexual activity or even clothes and alcohol consumption.[104]

Those battle lines have been growing more sharply defined. In the US under President Trump, attacks on abortion rights, effectively sanctioned by the White House regime, have been driven by the right, who describe themselves as defenders of family values and opponents of "gender ideology",[105] at the same time as moves to undermine LGB and trans protections at the state and federal levels have been stepped up.[106] Two examples of this, the "bathroom wars" in the US and the attacks on trans rights in Britain, will be discussed in later chapters.

Some writers have described the huge variety of ways many people have come to describe their sexualities and genders (gender fluid, gender pluralist, gender queer and so on — see Monro[107] for example) but the point is that these are situated within a wider social framework shaped by capitalism.

Given this context, how we identity and describe ourselves (certainly important for how people live their lives in society and who they identify with) and the *causes* of such identities, are far less important than the fact that women's sexuality outside the nuclear family, as well as non-heterosexual sexualities and expressions of non-binary gender variance, are subject to social, political and ideological disapproval and sanctions — in other words, sexist, homophobic and transphobic oppression.

The point is that for socialists these cannot be examined or fought against as discrete oppressions — they all derive from the fundamentals of the capitalist system and the drive to accumulate at the heart of it.

The nature of gender identity

Gender identity or our gender-self, like sexuality, is much more than a "feeling" as it is sometimes rather dismissively described in trans-critical and transphobic narratives. It is an outcome of interactions between the person's self-perceived body, their biological sex (including in some cases their deep unease about this), the social perception of their body in the eyes of others, social factors like gender values and expectations, and finally the person's development as a sexual being with sexual attractions and sexual needs (their sexuality).

Our gender identity or gender-self has a certain mutability or plasticity as a result of these dialectical interactions mutually influencing each other, but it also has a level of persistence in the face of social pressures which serve to constrain us within binary and sex-ascribed gender expectations on pain of hostility, disapproval, and even ostracism and violence.

Trans people need to have the right to make their own decisions about whether and to what extent they choose to transition or even (very uncommonly[108]) to de-transition or desist from support and treatment. Only by having such autonomy can individuals fully explore the implications of transition and what is most appropriate for the expression of their gender identity. At the moment, even in countries where there may be basic transition options available within the legislative framework, such decisions are constrained within a context of medical gatekeepers, funding arrangements and priorities, and the persistence of gender binary social mores and attitudes.

Gender essentialism

Some radical feminists and trans-critics take issue with the concept of gender identity itself and with the claim that trans women are women and trans men are men. They often explicitly promote an essentialist view of gender and say they want to maintain the long-held feminist distinction between sex as biology and gender as social construction.[109]

Some socialist trans-critics may reject identity theory in respect of women's oppression because of its focus on the primacy of identity categories and its disavowal of class and class struggle, but they may express opposition to the promotion of trans rights in what amount to essentialist terms — trans women cannot be women, trans men cannot be men, because of biology.

The influential Australian radical feminist Sheila Jeffreys has argued that:

> Women's experience does not resemble that of men who adopt the "gender identity" of being female or being women in any respect. The idea of "gender identity" disappears biology and all the experiences that those with female biology have of being reared in a caste system based on sex.[110]

The question of gender socialisation per se and trans/non-binary people will be discussed more fully in chapter 9.

However, contrary to Jeffreys' claim, being apparently biologically male or female does not automatically map onto the gender descriptors "man" or "woman". Even less does it map onto such descriptors as "masculine" or "feminine", unless you accept the view that biological sex straightforwardly determines gender.

The social and political contexts of debates and arguments like those put forward by Jeffreys and others are important.

Thus some feminists have been critical of what they claim to be the substitution of "gender" for "sex" by some trans activists, which they argue flies in the face of the commonly accepted definitions of "sex" and "gender" on the left and more broadly, in other words that sex is biological, gender is socially constructed.

For some feminists the long battle against women's oppression, obviously not yet won, has involved opposition to the gender constraints of masculinity and femininity — and they see transgender people as somehow reinforcing gender stereotypes and diluting or undermining a clear biological category, that of woman.

However, this essentialist approach is potentially quite moralistic — it can lead such feminists to effectively insist that trans women ought to continue to live in their ascribed sex and gender because to do otherwise is to caricature women or contribute to implicitly enforcing society's gender stereotypes. Such criticisms are not new to the LGBT+ or gender rights world. They have existed around drag, and also echo arguments within feminism about women who use make-up or have cosmetic surgery.

To assert on the contrary that trans women are women and trans men are men begs the question of what we mean by "woman" and "man". Put starkly, can a person who is biologically male-ascribed be a woman, and vice versa? Trans and gender-variant people answer yes to this question because they argue that gender is not limited to or bounded by biology but is the outcome of an interactive process involving social roles and expectations, social perceptions of others, and a person's sense of self, or gender identity. Biology is not destiny.

This view rests both on trans people's self-declared gender identity and on the basis of the way the rest of society treats them, including the fact that trans women who are perceived socially as women (who "pass") will experience sexism and misogyny.

Accepting this is not to imply any denial of the oppression faced by cisgender/natal women nor does it imply the erasure of "woman" as a category, another issue we shall discuss later in relation to proposals emerging from a government review of transgender lives in Britain.

To expand on that claim we might consider what actually goes on when we first meet or see someone.

When humans interact socially it is generally considered impolite to inspect their primary or secondary sexual characteristics for "comparative binary gender authenticity". Dogs may sniff each other's backsides or genitalia but people normally confine themselves to a handshake or a peck on the cheek, which doesn't tell you very much about what the person may have lurking under their clothes or in their genome.

People will either "read" a person they meet as the gender they are presenting through clothes, hair, voice and other signifiers (in which case the person's early life experiences will be *assumed* and — if the person is in fact a trans woman — they will automatically be assigned to the oppressed group "women"): or they will read that person as not quite "right", as trans or non-binary, and will react in ways that can vary from being supportive and respectful via neutrality to open expressions of hostility.

It is thus the social perception of the person as a man or a woman (or trans) that is the key determinant in interactions shaped by expectations driven by patterns of oppression in a society. Gender is not a simple match to biological sex, it is not merely the "social face" of biological sex.

Thus gender identity itself is also conceptually distinct from a person's biological sex, it is conceptually distinct from and more complex than merely constituting an internalised reflection of societal gender expectations. The term "woman" should therefore be inclusive and cover trans women, and vice versa for the term "man" and trans men.

"Gender identity ideology"

Some trans-critics who are critical of identity theory and who promote a (rather mechanical version of) historical materialism in understanding oppression reference the influence of "gender identity ideology" as a key reason to reject the notion that gender identity is a reality.

It is a problem, however, for anyone on the left referencing gender identity ideology in this way since there is a danger of giving credence to an unholy trinity of sexist and transphobic right wing tropes — "gender ideology", "gender theory", and "gender identity theory".

These pseudo-scientific mythical descriptors have a long history among right-wing ideologues and political movements often associated with reactionary Catholicism, evangelical Christianity and far-right traditionalist political parties strongly opposed to same-sex marriage, gender equality, abortion rights, reproductive rights, sex education and transgender equality.[111]

By deploying this terminology of opposition to gender identity and trans rights the opponents of these various human rights seek to frame their homophobia, sexism and transphobia in terms of the secular defence of family values and "the natural order of things". They seek to dress up their reactionary position in clothes that may appeal to the middle ground and not just the religious right. Thus these notions have underpinned reactionary and conservative movements in France, Hungary and elsewhere in recent years.

For trans critics on the left to endorse such concepts is to run the risk of providing left cover for alt-right attacks on diversity and equal rights.

Trans-misogyny

What is it about crossing gender lines, particularly crossing from male to female, that can attract considerable hostility, including from some feminists and people on the left? There appears to be a particular misogyny directed towards trans women.

Julia Serano describes trans-misogyny as, "how the existence of societal misogyny/traditional sexism greatly informs how people perceive, interpret, or treat, gender variant people who seemingly 'want to be female' or 'want to be feminine' (regardless of their actual identity)".[112]

Trans-misogyny understood in this way focuses on the particular hostility directed at those born biologically male who are driven to deny masculinity.

Serano rejects the generalised identity-based way that some trans people have come to use the term trans-misogyny to refer to any and all forms of discrimination targeting trans women. Crucially, this hostility stems from the same roots as the general anti-women misogyny (being demeaned, denied, diminished, dehumanised in respect to men) that is involved in the maintenance of women's oppression. Trans men are generally not subject to this form of hostility. Serano's understanding of the term helps us to focus on the common roots of women's and trans people's oppression.

Others have similarly picked up on this perceived gender trigger for explaining the hostility and violence of "gay bashing".

Vivian K Namaste argues that many homophobic attacks would often be better conceptualised as gender bashing.[113] She is critical of the ways in which, she claims, violence against sexual and gender minorities has often been conceptualised solely as anti-gay prejudice by lesbian and gay activists, the police and policy makers, ie focusing on the sexuality of the victim, thus effacing the experiences of transgender people and missing the gender component of much of this violence:

> Though scholars and community activists have increasingly addressed the issue of violence against lesbians and gay men, there remains very little reflection on the function of gender within these acts of aggression... I argue that a perceived transgression of normative sex/gender relations motivates much of the violence against sexual minorities, and that an assault against these "transgressive" bodies is fundamentally concerned with policing gender presentation through public and private space.[114]

Namaste refers to research suggesting that the perpetrators of violence in such attacks have relied on gender cues to decide on the person's sexuality. If a person seemed effeminate, for example, this could justify an attack.[115]

One study found that 39 percent of the men surveyed who behaved in a "feminine" manner had suffered attacks, whereas only 22 percent of those described as "masculine" and 17 percent of those described as "very masculine" had been attacked.[116] A study of anti-lesbian violence revealed that a number of lesbians who wore their hair short and dressed in trousers also suffered violence.[117]

Certainly, there has been strong evidence for decades that the social meanings given to bodies are structured by the dominance of implicit sexist and heteronormative expectations in society. In a classic study of 960 subjects by Suzanne Kessler and Wendy McKenna in 1978 subjects were shown various representations of human bodies.[118] The researchers found that the interpretation of sexed bodies was heavily skewed to masculine referents. So if there was a "penis" then subjects attributed the figure as male 96 percent of the time. On the other hand, for a figure to be attributed as female more than 95 percent of the time there had to be a "vagina" plus at least two other gender referents associated with femininity, such as long hair and breasts.

The researchers, and Namaste herself who discusses this study, infer from this that in our society genetic males who live as women will be among those at greatest risk of trans-misogynist violence if they are suspected or "unmasked" as being "not female". Most studies of violence against trans people do indeed find that trans women are more likely to be attacked than trans men.

Conclusion

The source of sexism, misogyny, women's oppression *and* trans oppression lies in the exploitative class relations that derive from capitalism's drive to appropriate and control labour power in order to accumulate surplus value, and in the dominant ideology of the nuclear family and its role in the socialisation, reproduction and provision of care for workers.

Everyone's gender identity is part of a deeply held sense of self which develops neither as an exclusive derivative of our biological sex nor merely as a response to the social norms and gender expectations that we encounter by virtue of being social beings. If it were simply one or the other, arguably there would not be transgender or non-binary people, either because our chromosomes would be all-powerful in forming our gender identity or because society's strong and pervasive gender binary oppression would lock us all irrevocably into one of the two hegemonic gender binary categories.

The bourgeois nuclear family model remains the standard and norm in capitalism, even if its boundaries in Britain and elsewhere have been expanded more recently to incorporate unmarried couples, single parent families and monogamous gay and lesbian relationships legitimised through marriage or civil partnership.

Some trans people who fit into the gender binary can probably also meet these bourgeois standards, particularly if they have enough money to access gender affirmation treatment privately and quickly without having to navigate the NHS.

Nonetheless, trans women in particular can be subject to the same oppression and potential risks as those assigned female at birth — objectification, sexism, gender inequity, sexual harassment, assault and rape — plus the particular aggression meted out by trans-misogynists.

Chapter 4
A brief history of trans

Our earliest ancestors do not appear to have been
biological determinists. There are societies all over the
world that allowed for more than two sexes, as well
as respecting the right of individuals to reassign their
sex. And transsexuality, transgender, intersexuality
and bi-gender appear as themes in creation stories,
legends, parables and oral history.[119]

Trans people in British history

What does the record tell us about the existence of transgender
people and gender variant behaviour in Britain's past? There
are many references to what we would now call transgender
behaviour and transgender people over hundreds of years in
Britain.

In 1395 John (Eleanor) Rykener was arrested dressed as a
woman while publicly engaged in a sex act with a man. While
some have doubted the validity of the records it seems likely
that he (she) was a transgender prostitute. She confessed to
many sexual liaisons with men, including priests.

In 1682 the singer and musician Arabella Hunt's marriage
to James Howard (Amy Poulter) was dissolved after her
husband was discovered to be a woman.

Catherine Coombes, born in 1834, lived as a man called
Charley Wilson for 40 years.

In 1865, after James Barry died having worked as an army
surgeon for many years, he was revealed to have been a woman.

People's reasons for cross-dressing or for seeking to live as another gender were no doubt many and varied. It would not be correct to assume that everyone who did so was expressing trans motivations. In some cases women cross-dressed to avoid unwelcome male attentions, or to gain independent employment, or so that they could join the armed forces.

Historian Katie Barclay has suggested that:

> In Ireland, where abductions of young women to force a marriage were common in the early nineteenth century, many a girl donned her brother's clothes to protect her from raiding parties who invaded homes during the night...for other women...cross-dressing marked their desire for other women, their affinity to a culture of like-minded women, and perhaps even suggested they wished to explore or challenge constructions of gender (like modern transgendering). Similarly in the eighteenth century dressing as women or behaving in effeminate ways began to be associated with some homosexual subcultures, and some men chose to live their whole lives as women. Yet men, like women, could have economic reasons for disguising themselves as women — a number of male thieves were found operating in female dress; there were male prostitutes who dressed as women, while men who wished to get access to a lover trapped by a family may seek employment as her maid.[120]

In many cases, women posed as men in order to live with a female lover, and men lived as women for similar reasons, or were part of a subculture focused around the theatre or music hall or homosexual clubs and societies.

It certainly seems that while cross-dressing women have tended to remain private or in private relationships, cross-dressing men were often found in clubs and social situations.

Court records and other sources indicate that there were many people in Britain who chose, or felt compelled, to spend all or part of their lives living as a gender different to that assigned to them at birth. It is also clear that traditions of gender variance have existed on these islands for many hundreds if not thousands of years, before Britain became Britain, as elsewhere finding their expression in a variety of folk and cultural traditions such as masquerade and carnival.

Some of these traditions have persisted into modern times. In the 1950s and1960s it was common at holiday camps, for instance, to hold a "topsy-turvy night"[121] where working class men and women swapped clothes. And today many British men (apparently heterosexual and gender invariant) seem willing, even enthusiastic, to crossdress given very little excuse for various social occasions.

Then there is the long tradition of British pantomime with its cross-dressed roles and gender ambiguity, and music hall with popular cross-dressed acts like Hinge and Bracket. Drag acts like Danny La Rue and Lily Savage were still going strong into recent times. Drag (dressed as a girl) and drab (dressed as a boy) were originally stage directions in theatre. Drag was necessary in order to portray women characters at a time when actors were all male and acting was a lowly profession.

Cross-dressing and the subversion of gender roles

In a 1988 article in *Shakespeare Quarterly* discussing cross-dressing in Elizabethan and Jacobean England, Jean Howard writes:

> That actual women of several social classes did cross-dress in Renaissance England is an important fact, but equally important is how their behaviour was ideologically processed or rendered intelligible in the discourses of the time. Specifically, what made adopting the dress of the other sex so transgressive that lower-class women were pilloried and whipped and merchant wives were harangued from the pulpit for doing it?[122]

She goes on to suggest that cross-dressing "opened a gap between the supposed reality of one's social station and sexual kind and the clothes that were to display that reality to the world".[123]

The state at the time regulated dress in early modern England in terms of who could wear certain fabrics like silk, or the colour purple, or adornments like daggers or jewels. To break these codes was to disrupt the social order and people's stations in life that were deemed predetermined and immutable. Likewise with gender and sex. At the time, women were seen as the inverse and inferior reflection of men ("incomplete men" rather than being the *opposite* of men) and to cross-dress was to flout and subvert this notion. "The stability of the social order depends as much on maintaining absolute distinctions between male and female as between aristocrat and yeoman," writes Howard.[124]

The social and political context at the time included concerns about political corruption and homosexuality in the court of James I on the one hand and growing support for Puritanism on the other.

Social mobility and consequent class tensions were increasingly important factors at the time, with the rapid growth of both a merchant class and a labouring class in emergent English capitalism. This threatened the social position of royalty, the aristocracy and the landed gentry. The threat became a reality in the successful English Revolution in the mid-17th century that decapitated Charles I and put the representatives of the merchant class in power after the English Civil War.

Cross-dressing in this period was a matter of heated public discussion and debate. In 1620, for example, two pamphlets were published on the issue, *Hic Mulier* (*The Man Woman, or female transvestite*), which attacked cross-dressing and women's rights more broadly, and *Haec-Vir* (*The Womanish Man*), which defended cross-dressing.

Aimed at the fashions among well-to-do London City wives and their enthusiasm for cross-dressing, *Hic Mulier* argued that these women from the "trade" classes and their ornate dress were encroaching on the privileges of aristocratic women. Just as shocking, or even worse, than transgressing class boundaries was the sense that their behaviour also transgressed supposedly immutable gender boundaries.

But these transgressions seemed quite different in character for men and women. Social disapproval of male cross-dressing focused on either a suspicion that the men involved were doing so to deceive others for money or sex, or that they were unworthy, not real men, as they chose to de-masculinise themselves. For women, however, cross-dressing was often seen as upstart behaviour by "monstrous" women attempting to invade male territory and privilege. This has resonances in today's attitudes to gender variant behaviour.

Passing women

Over the past few hundred years there have been many stories of women either taking on stereotypical male roles (soldiers, sailors and so on) or living together as man and wife.[125] Some accounts have suggested that they did so in order to escape the confines of the female roles assigned them, or to follow male lovers.

Rebecca Jennings notes: "Despite the fact that cross-dressing, as a form of fraud, was potentially a serious offence, popular ballads and autobiographical accounts from the period celebrated such women as eccentric adventurers".[126]

Jennings points to other examples which strongly suggest that taking on male clothing and behaviour by some of these women was motivated by wishing to live as a man and included assumptions about the sexual fluidity of the women concerned and their undoubted sexual relationships with other women. In some cases the women went beyond courting other women and married them, becoming "female husbands":

> Two entries in a Cheshire marriage register of 1707 and 1708 suggest that it might even have been possible for women to marry each other as women…[127]

> Elsewhere in Europe, women could be executed for passing as men or having sex with other women. In England, there were no specific laws against either sexual encounters between women or cross-dressing. However, some female husbands were prosecuted under vagrancy or fraud laws…[128]

> Many women may have escaped detection altogether and

successfully passed as men throughout their lives. This is particularly likely in the case of middle class women, whose social position may have assisted them in maintaining their disguise... Middle and upper class women might have been able to use the privileges of wealth and greater freedom to travel, to avoid detection.[129]

Detection, however, could lead to tragic outcomes. In one sad case Paul Dowling, a black farm labourer from Kent, was arrested in 1905 while looking for his wife on Blackfriars Bridge in London. He was revealed as a woman called Caroline Brogden and subsequently incarcerated in the City of London Asylum where he died about a year later.

Another noteworthy case was Colonel Sir Victor Barker DSO. Barker later turned out to have been born in 1895 as Valerie Barker. She apparently always wished she had been born a boy. In 1923 she left her common law husband and adopted the persona of Sir Victor Barker, marrying Elfrida Haward in 1932.

Sir Victor was unmasked when arrested and imprisoned for bankruptcy. He changed his name several times and sold his life story to the press three times, eventually dying in poverty in 1960.

Cross-dressing, revolt and class resistance

Various well-documented revolts and social movements from the Middle Ages up to the mid-19th century right across Europe saw men dressing as women when they carried out collective acts of resistance. One example was the movement in rural South West Wales by "Rebecca and Her Daughters" that reached its height around 1843, although it later re-emerged in 1870 in disputes about salmon fishing rights.[130]

Rhian Jones has argued that these cross-dressed resisters were very much a social movement involving whole communities of tenant farmers and labourers, men and women, who opposed a range of deeply unpopular measures.[131] Their actions, generally led by a single cross-dressed man referred to as Rebecca, proved to be very difficult for the authorities to suppress. Despite prosecutions and transportations of alleged ringleaders, their militant tactics, which included destroying toll booths, mass demonstrations, the invasion of the Carmarthen workhouse, arson, and physical attacks on landowners, bailiffs, gamekeepers, judges, employers and Anglican clergymen, often delivered victories for the insurgents. Their demands were as much political as socio-economic, and there is some evidence of Chartist influences on the movement.

Jones asks "*Why* had these men donned women's clothes to protest?" She writes:

> Previous studies have interpreted cross-dressing only as a method of disguise, or as an allusion to the social and community roles of women. However... The costume and behaviour of "Rebecca" in itself reflected the images of female power and agency which were available in south-west Wales. Additionally, attempts by Rebeccaites to oppose the New Poor Law, as part of which they upheld the rights of single mothers and illegitimate children, formed part of popular resistance to the Victorian state's attempts at imposing social discipline upon pre-existing cultural attitudes that had granted women greater rights and agency.

The Rebeccaites were just one example of such class revolts across England and Europe well into the 19th century. Other examples include the War of the Desmoiselles in the Pyrenees in 1829 against a new forest code; the White Boys in Ireland in the 1760s; the Lady Skimmington riots in Wiltshire in 1631 against the royal enclosure of forests; men in dresses and wigs who demolished tollgates in Somerset in the mid-18th century; and Madge Wildfire, who led cross-dressed men in the Porteous Riots in Edinburgh in 1736 against customs laws and union with England.

Many of these cross-dressed leaders and guerrillas in the Middle Ages were accused by Christian clergy of "consorting with faeries", in other words incipient paganism. Leslie Feinberg cites resisters in Beaujolais, France in the 1770s, male peasants dressed as women who attacked people surveying their land for a new landlord. When police agents came to interview their wives the next day the wives said they knew nothing, and the culprits were "faeries who came from the mountains from time to time".[132]

Such resistance movements suggest both the existence of more gender-fluid folk memories as well as the wish to disguise participants against the possibility of draconian penalties if caught. It is very unlikely that these cross-dressing rebels were all individually gender variant. Nevertheless, such examples may well tell us something about the persistence of more gender-fluid or gender variant attitudes that may have existed in pre-Christian societies and survived in these folk memories into later times.

Early trans and gay subculture: Molly houses

From the 18th century increasing religious, societal and state pressure had been brought to bear on what we might today regard as the trans and gay subculture, particularly the many Molly houses in London and other cities where trans women and effeminate gays of the day socialised.

These clubs provoked opposition from the establishment and polite society. In the first half of the 18th entury local Societies for the Reformation of Manners agitated for prosecutions of those frequenting Molly houses. Sometimes mobs were incited to attack the houses and the popular masquerade balls of the period.[133]

Right across Europe such balls and cross-dressing clubs had grown in popularity. Molly houses were often infiltrated by informants and agents of the authorities. Some participants were blackmailed and forced to turn on their fellow attendees. The exposure was frequent and drastic enough to cause some of those accused to commit suicide.

Reports from the time, including court records, show that those attending these clubs were mainly ordinary working class people — servants, cobblers, butchers, valets, coachmen and so on. Sometimes there was resistance to the police raids. In 1725 a raid on a London Covent Garden Molly house led to a riot when many of those present, in drag, resisted arrest and exposure.

In 1826 a famous raid on Mother Clap's Molly House in Holborn, London led to several arrests and prosecutions.

Although some of the party-goers were freed through lack of evidence, others were fined, imprisoned or pilloried, and three were sentenced to death and hanged.[134]

Church, state and local authorities were generally prepared to tolerate such cross-dressing on the stage, but cross-dressing in public, and its presumed (and often well-founded) link to same-sex sexual activity carried heavy penalties including long terms of imprisonment, being publicly paraded and put in the stocks, and capital punishment. People were still being executed for sodomy into the 19th century in Britain. Being put in the stocks could itself be lethal as those sentenced were left to the not very tender mercies of stone-throwing crowds.

Consequently, in this period transgender and gay people (though we should remind ourselves that these categories did not really exist in distinct forms at this time) were constantly under pressure to remain underground, or what later came to be called "in the closet". This was especially true of trans people unless they were able to pass convincingly, something which was much harder for working class people to achieve than those with wealth.

Nevertheless, some women and men managed to live much of their lives as the "opposite" sex and in many cases their birth sex was not discovered until after their deaths. One of these was a French spy, soldier and diplomat who lived part of his/her life in London. The Chevalier d'Eon de Beaumont (1728 — 1810) was a famous example long honoured by many trans people. Some named an early British cross-dressing organisation, the Beaumont Society, after their hero. So well-known was the Chevalier that people even made bets on what her true gender was. On her death it was confirmed that she was apparently biologically male.

The Chevalier Beaumont may have lived a long and famous life and died naturally but in the same period thousands of less famous gay and trans people risked death, disgrace and ruin for their "sins against nature" in order to socialise with similar others.

The creation of the homosexual
In Britain and elsewhere, as Weeks, Wolf, Stryker and others

have shown,[135] homosexuality became more heavily proscribed from the late 19th century. Given the general conflation of homosexuality with gender variant or gender transgressive behaviour at this time, this increasing discrimination impacted on what we might today regard as transgender or non-binary people as well as gay and bisexual people.

As part of combatting "licentious" and "undisciplined" working class behaviour and asserting greater control, as industrial capitalism and urbanisation rapidly developed in the 19th century, the capitalist class and its religious and social establishment attempted to extend greater and greater influence over the sexual behaviour of workers in general and women in particular.

The bourgeois ideology of the nuclear family and family values was a crucial weapon in this struggle.

This was true both in Britain itself and in the British Empire. The control of the sexual behaviour of colonised populations was an important element in controlling their labour power. Some of the legislation that applied in British colonies was not merely exported from Britain but was in fact initially adopted in those colonies before being imported back into UK jurisdiction.

For example, Section 377 of the Indian Penal Code, introduced during British rule of India in 1861, criminalised sexual activities "against the order of nature". It outlawed homosexual sex and sex with animals and was modelled on the British Buggery Act of 1533. It was punishable by up to life imprisonment. Similar legislation spread to many other countries of the British Empire and some still exists today. The highly repressive Section 377 was then repatriated to Britain in the form of the homophobic Labouchere Amendment, introduced in the wake of a famous trial which acquitted two cross-dressing actors, Fanny and Stella.

Fanny and Stella

In 1871 Fanny Park (born Frederick) and Stella Boulton (born Ernest)were arrested for public cross-dressing and for suspected importuning (prostitution). The pair had a stage act and were part of the London theatrical scene which was generally more tolerant of homosexuality and gender variance than the rest of British late-Victorian society.

Cross-dressing was not uncommon at the time in certain circles. There was a craze on the theatrical and social club scene for burlesques and pantomimes which often involved both male and female drag and cross-dressing and not a few same-sex dalliances. Male cross-dressing itself was not criminal, but homosexual sex was a crime under the anti-sodomy legislation. Stella was, it appears, having a relationship with a Tory MP, Lord Arthur Pelham-Clinton, at the time of her arrest and was therefore risking prosecution.

When it came to the trial, although everyone suspected that the two actors were having sexual relationships with men, the prosecution found this difficult to prove. Luckily also for the pair of them the testimony of Boulton's mother, who said her son had cross-dressed since he was six, helped convince the jury that he was not cross-dressing for sexual reasons.

They were also blessed with being middle class and having a good defence lawyer who argued that their cross-dressing was "just high spirits" and that no *real* sodomite would ever advertise themselves by parading up and down the Strand in ball gowns as Fanny and Stella did.

This all helped to win their acquittal after the jury deliberated for just an hour. After the trial Stella crossed the Atlantic to appear on Broadway as a popular female impersonator. Her career and fame did not last, however, and she died in poverty in London in 1904 aged 56.

Was Stella someone we would now regard as transgender? Playwright Neil Bartlett, who wrote a play about the case in 2016,[136] is quoted as saying, "For Stella, identity was never a destination — it was a journey, a constant transformation. And that's an idea we're now very open to".[137]

The acquittal was a great outcome for Fanny and Stella but it provoked an outraged reaction from the British establishment who took the view that if the law could not convict two pretty obvious "sodomites" as it stood then it needed to be strengthened. During the following years new homophobic statutes were introduced. Most notably in 1885 the Criminal Law Amendment Act was passed. This included the Labouchere

Amendment, named after Henry Labouchere, Liberal MP and arch-homophobe, who introduced Section 11 of the Act.

While the main Act concerned the protection of women and girls and the suppression of brothels, Labouchere's amendment was opportunistically tagged on it to criminalise "gross indecency" among men. Under this legislation, even if sodomy could not be proven, so-called evidence such as cross-dressing or the existence of love letters could suffice for a conviction.

The Oscar Wilde trials

Tragically, despite mixing in the most "cultured" and wealthy circles, Irish poet, wit and playwright Oscar Wilde did not have the good luck of Fanny and Stella. He became the most prominent victim of the Labouchere Amendment.

We should not underestimate the extent to which the trial of Wilde was a watershed moment in tightening the legal screws on same-sex behaviour in Britain. Wilde had declared himself a libertarian socialist in his 1891 essay, *The Soul of Man Under Socialism,* which helped contribute to his reputation as a subversive libertine and a danger to the British Victorian establishment both in his politics and in his personal life.[138]

In 1895 Wilde brought a libel case against the Marquess of Queensberry, the father of his lover Lord Alfred Douglas, when he publicly referred to Wilde as a "sodomite". Queensberry, John Sholto Douglas, was the originator of the Queensberry rules in boxing and reputedly a bad-tempered, obsessive and irascible man. He had been trying to break up Wilde's relationship with his son Alfred for some time by threatening to disown and cut off his son's allowance. In June 1894 Queensberry, accompanied by a prize-fighter, had shown up at Wilde's Chelsea house. An altercation followed, ending when Wilde, according to his account, ordered Queensberry to leave saying, "I do not know what the Queensberry rules are, but the Oscar Wilde rule is to shoot on sight."

Queensberry accused Wilde of being a sodomite and Wilde felt he had no alternative but to sue for libel despite friends advising him against doing so.[139] Wilde and the lawyer who led the prosecution, Edward Carson, had been student contemporaries, and rivals, at Trinity College, Dublin. Carson was an effective opponent in court and the libel trial went badly for Wilde, forcing him to drop the case for fear of its collapse. Despite being in shock at the turn of events he refused to flee the country before his subsequent arrest on charges of gross indecency and sodomy.

The civil trial was followed by criminal charges. The first criminal trial, during which Wilde made his famous eloquent speech about "the love that dare not speak its name",[140] ended in a deadlocked jury. It was followed by a second trial energetically lobbied for by his tormentor Queensberry. Even Edward Carson at this point urged the government to let up on Wilde.

Wilde was convicted of gross indecency at the second trial and sent to prison with hard labour for two years. The experience broke Wilde's health and led to his premature death three years later in 1900 aged just 46.

In the immediate aftermath of the trials a number of Wilde's friends and other homosexuals fled the country for fear of the same thing happening to them. More generally the outcome marked a significant upswing in the persecution of gay men by the police and courts. Over the next eight decades many thousands were imprisoned or chemically castrated and many thousands more had their lives blighted or killed themselves as a result of the vicious oppression and persecution. People routinely lost jobs, friends and family.

Enter the sexologists and the socialists

In the late 19th century a new category of person, "the homosexual", began to be recognised. Increasing social oppression fed into new legislation in counties like Britain and Germany but also generated resistance to homophobic oppression. This began to coalesce around the modernist scientific approaches of people like Havelock Ellis,[141] who was friends with Eleanor Marx; the gay British socialist pioneer Edward Carpenter, and the German Social Democratic Party member Magnus Hirschfeld. From the late 19th century it was the left, socialists and progressives, who first argued for the need to fight the oppression and subordination not only of women but also of homosexuals.

Havelock Ellis's book *Studies in the Psychology of Sex*, published in six volumes from 1897 to 1928, was the first medical textbook on homosexuality published in English. In Britain the censors were keen to stop people reading the book and prosecuted a bookseller who stocked it. This resulted in a trial during which the judge called claims for the book's scientific value "a pretence, adopted for the purpose of selling a filthy publication." Later volumes had to be published in the United States, where the censors restricted its distribution to those with a medical degree, fearing that its general availability might corrupt vulnerable minds.

After the cases of Oscar Wilde and Fanny and Stella, homosexual and what would later be called transsexual people, had increasingly started to seek help from doctors. In Britain, Havelock Ellis after 1920 was the first to draw a distinction between homosexuality and trans, which he called "Eonism" after the Chevalier d'Eon. He was aware of Magnus Hirschfeld's work in Germany on the same issues. Hirschfeld had been the first to come up with the term "transvestite" in 1910 in his book *Transvestites: The Erotic Urge to Cross-Dress*.[142]

Hirschfeld had visited England in 1905 and met Oscar Wilde's son, Vyvyan Holland. He attended a secret ceremony of gay Cambridge students who wore Wilde's prison number, C33, and read aloud his poem, *The Ballad of Reading Gaol*, which profoundly moved him.

In 1896 Hirschfeld had helped found the Scientific Humanitarian Committee dedicated to carrying out research to defend homosexual rights and overturn the infamous German anti-gay Paragraph 175. The committee gathered signatures (including those of Albert Einstein and socialists Eduard Bernstein, Karl Kautsky and August Bebel) on a bill for the German parliament to repeal the law. The bill was introduced by August Bebel in 1898 but it failed to win support outside the ranks of the Social Democratic Party (the German Marxist party of the time).

Hirschfeld went on to found the Institute for Sexual Research in Berlin in 1919, during the more liberal period of the Weimar Republic which followed the First World War and the German Revolution of 1918.

The revolutionary upsurge in Germany between 1918 and 1923, while successfully overthrowing the emperor, failed to overthrow the capitalist class, thanks to the murderous counter-revolutionary efforts of right wing Social Democrats.[143] This was a disaster for the German working class. On 15th January 1919 the counter-revolution murdered the two best known and most effective revolutionary leaders, Rosa Luxemburg and Karl Liebknecht.

However, the struggle did result in some improvements in general democratic rights and it opened up an unprecedented period of sexual experimentation in Germany. For example, as Laurie Marhoefer has noted, "The Revolution of 1918 and the advent of democracy opened up a space for a greatly expanded and more public subculture of women who sought romance with other women".[144] This greater space also applied to male homosexuals and, for the first time, transgender people. "The public spaces and print media culture of the Weimar Republic also proved hospitable to a movement of transvestites... one of the first examples of public activism by and for trans-identifying individuals anywhere in the world".[145]

A private surgeon, Gorhbandt, had performed a version of sex reassignment that essentially involved removal of the sex organs from 1921, but Hirschfeld's Institute was a pioneer in the field during the Weimar period. The first documented male to female full sex reassignment operation at Hirschfeld's Institute took place on Dorchen (Dora) Richter. Richter underwent castration in 1921, followed by penectomy (removal of the penis) and construction of an artificial vagina (vaginoplasty) in 1931.[146]

While Hirschfeld did suggest the term "transvestite" and distinguished such people from homosexuals, the term was a very vague one. Marhoefer notes that there were disagreements over "whether it denoted people who only wanted to dress in the clothing of the other sex, people whose true sex was not their birth sex, and who had transitioned to their true sex or wanted to do so, or both of these groups. By the 1950s, sexologists considered the former 'transvestites' and the latter 'transsexuals'. But in the 1920s people disagreed and used 'transvestite' to describe a variety of states of being".[147]

Treatment and "cures" for LGBT+ people

Havelock Ellis, like Hirschfeld, did not regard homosexuality as immoral, or a disease, or worthy of consideration as a crime. As a progressive reformer he was interested in examining forms of sexuality and gender expression sympathetically as social and medical phenomena.

He was certainly progressive for his time on matters of sexuality but like many progressives and some on the left at that time he was also a fan of eugenics and he became President of the Eugenics Society. His attitudes towards ethnicity and race would today undoubtedly be regarded as racist.

The considerable downside to this emerging medical approach promoted by the sexology movement in the first quarter of the 20th century was that it spawned repressive psychological theories and treatments meted out to gay and transgender people to "cure" their presumed sickness. This notion of curing homosexual/transgender sickness persists today in some medical and religious circles.

Transgender and gay people have been fair game for doctors and psychiatrists to attempt all manner of dangerous and unethical quack remedies. Until at least the 1970s trans people could be incarcerated and drugged against their will in asylums and mental institutions (often by their families) and had little power to resist these treatments.

For example, in the US in the 1950s, under the California Sex Deviates Research Act of 1950, Karl Bowman, a former president of the American Psychiatric Association who had previously researched homosexuality in the US military, studied the "causes and cures of homosexuality" in experiments that involved castrating male sex offenders and administering sex hormones.

Other so-called cures varied from Freud's relatively humane psychoanalytic talking therapy, aimed at uncovering and coming to terms with subconscious motivations, up to the growing popularity of behaviourist techniques.

Behaviourism, deriving from the Russian biologist Ivan Pavlov and the American psychologist John Watson in the early years of the 20th century, promoted a variety of aversion therapies purported to cure homosexuality and gender variant behaviour.

One method of aversion therapy was to show transgender people pictures of cross-dressed people, or "other gender" clothes, or get the patient to cross-dress, then administer emetic drugs which caused violent nausea, diarrhoea and vomiting. As part of creating the learning necessary to effect the cure, patients could be left in their own vomit and excreta for hours. This torture was supposed to create a visceral association, based on notions of classical conditioning, between cross-dressing and nausea and so extinguish the undesirable behavioural traits.

A different and decidedly inhumane treatment for LGBT+ people was to use electro-convulsive therapy (ECT). Having been originally developed by Ugo Cerletti to treat schizophrenia and manic-depressive psychosis in the 1930s, ECT was first used in 1938 on transgender people.

A surge of electricity between electrodes on either side of the brain induces seizures which can erase short term memories. Just as with homosexuality, there is no hard evidence that these techniques achieved anything beyond causing further harm, distress and guilt in those unfortunate enough to have suffered them.

Yet more barbaric was the use of lobotomy — the physical destruction of part of the brain's frontal lobes — to suppress various forms of behaviour deemed undesirable or damaging. Other treatments included being forced to take various drugs and male or female hormones, depending on the person's ascribed birth sex.

LGBT+ rights after the Russian Revolution

The general homophobia and pathologisation of homosexual and transgender behaviour in capitalist societies in the early 20th century was in marked contrast to the attitude of many socialists at the time. They recognised the oppression suffered by lesbians and gay men and believed that they deserved support and solidarity and should not be persecuted or prosecuted.

The attitude of the Bolshevik Party in Russia to oppression was a crucial factor in the party being able to win mass support in the 1917 revolutionary period. Lenin argued in *What Is To Be Done?* that the model for socialist activity, "should not be the trade union secretary, but the tribune of the people, who is able to react to every manifestation of tyranny and oppression, no matter where it appears, no matter what stratum or class of the people it affects".[148]

The Bolshevik attitude to the oppression of women and minorities (national, religious, Jewish or otherwise) was humane and supportive. Bolsheviks fought for solidarity between oppressed groups and for the unity of the working class. The behaviour and policies of the Bolsheviks after the successful 1917 Revolution show that this was not mere sloganising. They quickly put into practice their support for oppressed groups such as women and national minorities after the Russian working class won state power in October. For example, one immediate application of the principle of the right of self-determination for national minorities against national oppression, as argued for by Lenin before the Revolution, was to grant Finland independence from Russia within weeks of the October victory.[149] Independence had been consistently and violently opposed by the Czarist autocracy before 1917.

Similarly with women's rights. Women workers and peasants had played active and leading roles in the 1917 revolution. The new Soviet government understood that little progress would be made towards women's liberation until the drudgery of housework and privatised childcare could be addressed. In extremely difficult circumstances, including invasion, civil war and Western blockades, they took enormous steps to address this question.

Led by Alexandra Kollontai as Commissar (commissioner) for Social Affairs, the revolutionaries granted full citizenship rights for women, civil marriage, easier divorce, abolition of the distinction between legitimate and illegitimate children, maternity leave and protections at work for pregnant women. They also began to encourage communal laundries and other collective measures to relieve women's domestic burdens.[150]

Dan Healey, author of *Homosexual Desire in Revolutionary Russia*, writes that:

Kollontai's association in the 1920s with the World League for Sexual Reform (based in Berlin and inaugurated by Magnus Hirschfeld) would link her to campaigns in Western Europe for homosexual emancipation. Yet her published works never directly addressed "homosexuality", concentrating on love "between the sexes" and on the problems of women workers coping with maternity.[151]

Transgender people in Russia were also direct beneficiaries of this new approach to gender and sexuality, although as pointed out above, the conceptual distinctions between transsexual and transgender people (and homosexuality) did not really exist at the time in Russia as in the West.

Healey points out that in Russia in the early 20th century:

People who wore the clothing of the opposite sex, people who presented themselves in public (by cross-dressing, using specific manners, or forging identity documents) as a member of the opposite sex, those who wished to change their sex, people whose public gender performance veered towards the margins of respectability (effeminate men and mannish women), and hermaphrodites are the chief examples of sex and gender dissidents who were often identified in this language [ie the language and thinking of early 20th century Russians] as homosexuals.[152]

Revolutionary Russia rejected the bourgeois underpinnings of the previous legal codes. They were replaced with codes based on human rather than bourgeois values. In other words, the revolutionaries did not simply take over the Czarist legal codes and appoint their own judges and lawyers. Instead, they addressed the assumptions and the class basis of former Czarist legislation and found it wanting.

Using contemporary archive material Healey has examined in detail the process by which male homosexual sexual activity came to be decriminalised in post-revolutionary Russia. He writes that, "The trail of evidence leading from the potentialities of 1917 to the first Soviet Russian criminal code of 1922, which decriminalised sodomy, is rather unclear".[153]

However, he then refers to archive documents in the People's Commissariat of Justice and suggests that, "While these documents do not discuss the sodomy statute in detail, they do demonstrate a principled intent to decriminalise the act between consenting adults, expressed from the earliest efforts to write a socialist criminal code in 1918 to the eventual adoption of legislation in 1922".[154]

The archive documents suggest there was a general view that homosexual sex was to be a personal matter between consenting adults and not a matter for the state to interfere in except where force was used or when imposed on children. Nor were there to be arbitrary age limits for consent: instead, the ability to consent to sexual acts (and the new codes were gender neutral on this matter) would be judged on the basis of the person's maturity, to be determined on a case-by-case basis.

The legal codes which eventually became law on 1 June 1922 were, as Healey comments, "minimalist formulas" in which "the general conception of sexual crime as a violation of the individual's right to 'life, health, freedom, and dignity'" was enshrined. "Sodomy and incest were not named at all in the new code".[155]

Healey concludes: "The repeal of this ban [on sodomy] was a real political advance, and Soviet Russia was the most significant power since revolutionary France to decriminalise men's same-sex love, while sentences for similar 'crimes' ranged from five years (for 'unnatural vice') in Germany to life imprisonment (for 'buggery') in England."

However, "The medicalisation of sexual offences that accompanied the ambitious new legislative regime nevertheless offered police, jurists, and medical officials opportunities for the continued regulation of sexual and gender dissent".[156]

Nevertheless, the decriminalisation of homosexual behaviour marked a huge step forward both in Russia and internationally for LGBT+ people, an historic advance achieved many decades before anything similar was achieved in most of the rest of the world.

Totalitarian homophobia

Periods of class struggle and revolutionary upheaval wax and wane. Tragically the revolutionary wave at the end of the First World War waned after the defeat of the German revolutionary movement in 1923.

While the victory of the Russian Revolution was a beacon for socialist movements around the world the subsequent defeat of the international revolutionary insurgency made possible the growth of fascism, first in Italy with the ascendancy of Mussolini and his Fascist Party in 1922, and then most horrifically in Germany with Hitler and the Nazis gaining power in 1933.

Without the lifeblood of further international revolutions to sustain a fragile and isolated Soviet government, weakened by years of civil war and numerous imperialist military interventions, the Russian Revolution was unable to flourish. Stalin gained a grip on power after Lenin's death in 1924, and he went on to crush all opposition and turn back the social gains that the Revolution had won.

The Stalinist regime increasingly venerated the "traditional" family and motherhood, giving awards for women who had the most children. Homosexuality and gender variance, of course, did not fit this new orthodoxy. Consequently, gays were increasingly persecuted and homosexual acts in Russia were eventually re-criminalised in 1933, punishable by up to five years hard labour. Many gays ended up dead or in the gulags. The Stalinised communist parties in other countries who modelled themselves on Moscow generally parroted the same line.

In Germany the rise of the Nazis meant the banning of the gay clubs in Berlin and other cities, which had flourished during the Weimar period. Hirschfeld's Institute was closed and ransacked by Nazi students on 6 May 1933, just four months after the Nazis came to power. Its extensive library was publicly burned four days later. Hirschfeld himself, as a Jew and an advocate for LGBT+ people, was forced into exile. Hitler had described him as "The most dangerous Jew in Germany".[157] He died from a heart attack on his birthday in Paris in 1935.

Paragraph 175 — the piece of legislation first adopted in 1871 that outlawed male homosexuality — was broadened by the Nazis in 1935 and used to arrest tens of thousands of gay men. They were vilified and abused, imprisoned or thrown into concentration camps. Club membership lists were used to arrest more suspected gays and blackmail or threaten them into implicating others.

In the prisons and even more so in the camps gay men were seen as the lowest of the low, as sub-human, and they were identified with a pink triangle (political prisoners had red triangles, Jews had yellow stars).[158] As many as 50,000 gay men died in Nazi prisons and concentration camps.

After the war in the newly-formed West Germany (the Federal German Republic or FDR) Paragraph 175 remained in place, as did other Nazi legislation which was used to attack the left. Many gay men remained in West German prisons well into the 1950s. Paragraph 175 was not finally rescinded in the FDR until 1994 by which time around 140,000 men had been convicted. In East Germany (the German Democratic Republic or GDR), part of Stalin's Eastern Bloc, all the Nazi legislation including Paragraph 175 was rescinded after the war, but gay men were still often incarcerated in mental health institutions and subjected to "cures".

Conclusions

The criminalisation of (mostly male) homosexuality and its link to the policing of gender at the end of the 19th century and into the 20th created its own opposition. The naming of a new category of person, "the homosexual", a term which originally included both sexual- and gender variant people, facilitated the legal and social persecution of such people. Nevertheless a movement in defence of gay people, primarily gay men, also began to emerge and subsequently began to bring out of the shadows other oppressed groups such as lesbians and trans people.

There was a powerful link between the socialist move-ment and the notion of sexual liberation, as illustrated in the homosexual advocacy of such figures as Edward Carpenter,[159] Havelock Ellis, Magnus Hirschfeld and Alexandra Kollontai. The revolutionary wave across Europe at the end of the First World War brought some of this to life, particularly in Germany and Russia.

Tragically this link was ruptured by the defeat of those revolutions and the rise of Stalinism and fascism. The smashing of independent trade unions and socialist organisations in many countries, both East and West, in the 1930s meant that there were virtually no political organisations left that could or would advocate for homosexual and trans people after the end of the Second World War.

This also meant that the very memory of socialist and Marxist advocacy of free sexual relations or the acceptance of different sexualities and gender expressions was very largely lost, forgotten or denied both by the Stalinised communist parties at that time and by reformist socialist parties in the West.

This period can aptly be described as the nadir of gay and transgender visibility, and trans lives. In the next chapter we will examine how LGBT+ activism and visibility began slowly to re-emerge and gain momentum in the post-Second World War period.

Chapter 5
From post-war repression to Stonewall

And right up front, leading the cheers all along the sixty-block route, was Sylvia [Rivera]. "Gimme a G!" she screamed over and over. "Gimme an A ... a Y ... a P ... an O ... a W ... an E ... an R ... Whadda we want? Gay Power! When do we want it? Now!"[160]

Leitsch noted that most of the remarkable examples of physical courage he saw during the [Stonewall] riots were done by the more effeminate men, the real "queens": "It was an interesting sidelight on the demonstrations that those usually put down as 'sissies' or 'swishes' showed the most courage and sense during the action".[161]

The long haul
During the Second World War in Britain many women joined the auxiliary organisations attached to the navy, army and air force, or the Women's Land Army, who replaced conscripted male agricultural workers. Conscription for women in Britain was introduced in 1941. Many women worked in engineering and munitions factories. For women and men, relatively free from family influences and earning independent wages, this was a heady time, offering opportunities for socialising and even new relationships, including lesbian and gay relationships.

Post-war repression and propaganda, however, sought

a return to "normality", and this included attempts to push women back into the home and family. This ideological pressure ran up against capitalism's need for a growing labour force as the post-war economic boom accelerated into the 1950s. This demand was increasingly filled by women working both full-time and part-time while also being responsible for housework and caring duties. Nevertheless, the ideology of the nuclear family and family values bore down both on women and on any evidence of same-sex sexuality or gender variant behaviour. Military and industrial demobilisation therefore provoked mixed emotions for many LGBT+ people and for many heterosexual women too.

In the context of the state's attempts to impose bourgeois heteronormative orthodoxy from the late 1940s, being gay or gender transgressive was largely relegated to underground or niche expressions. Such people were regarded as undermining family values, as "queer", a stinging pejorative term of abuse at this time and for decades afterwards. Nevertheless in Britain, North America and elsewhere lesbians, gay men and transgender people sought company and support in an emerging subculture of underground gay and lesbian clubs, bars and pubs.

Outside the clubs the prevailing heteronormative ethos meant that gender variant people found they had virtually no-one to turn to for support. The vast majority of LGBT+ people on either side of the post-war Iron Curtain had little option but to remain in the closet. Long-term relationships were difficult — gay men and women who lived with partners had to maintain a fiction that they were housemates or friends rather than lovers. Gay men especially lived their lives constantly fearful of exposure, arrest, blackmail and police set-ups.[162]

For many gay and gender variant people this sort of denial plus the threat of general ridicule and hostility was enough to slam shut the closet door for decades. For some, their desperation could mean that suicide often seemed the only way out — although attempting suicide was itself illegal and, perversely, a failed attempt could result in prosecution. Suicide was the tragic outcome for the celebrated mathematician, Enigma code breaker and father of computer science Alan Turing. Having reported a break-in in 1952 he was subsequently convicted of gross indecency, forced to undergo hormone treatment and lost his security clearance.[163]

Despite this repressive atmosphere, by the early 1950s there were the beginnings of homophile organisation intended to break out from the secretive clubs and bars and begin to campaign for human and legal rights for homosexuals. Allan Horsfall, a headteacher and councillor in Bolton, set up the North Western Homosexual Law Reform Society in 1958 after a group of local men were convicted and this later became the Campaign for Homosexual Equality.[164]

Subsequent moves to de-criminalise homosexuality were generally predicated on what Jeffrey Weeks has called "a substantial medico-moral tradition, going back to at least the early nineteenth century, linking beliefs about health and disease to notions of moral and immoral sex, dangerous sexualities. The linkage of AIDS with homosexual lifestyles evokes a rich tradition that sees homosexuality as itself a disease".[165]

Allied to this hostility to homosexual or other "deviant" lifestyles was the notion that homosexuals were deficient in some way,suffering from a mental illness, and should not be blamed because of it — the predominant medical view at the time. However, the dominant approach at this time and for the following decades was for the medical profession to find cures for homosexuality and ways to make the mind fit the body and fit society's mores rather than accept the legitimacy of alternative sexualities and gender expressions.

In this context most early homophile advocates felt that any campaigning against homophobic legislation should therefore be discrete and well behaved, to try to minimise perceived threats and emphasise gay people's acceptance of society's values.

It is interesting, however, that despite the broken links between the left and LGBT campaigning as summarised in the previous chapter, in some cases such organisations were initiated by individuals who had their political roots in left wing organisations. One of these was Harry Hay who helped found the Mattachine Society in 1950 in the United States.[166] The name "Mattachine" probably derives from a group of medieval French masked players and was chosen to represent the "masking" of homosexuality.

Hay's roots were in the American Communist Party. He joined in 1934 and remained a committed activist over labour and anti-racist issues until the early 1950s, although he disagreed with the Party's belief, slavishly reflecting that of the Russian Communist Party at that time, that homosexuality was a "bourgeois deviation".

Hay went on to join the Gay Liberation Front in the wake of the Stonewall riot in 1969, was a founder member of the Los Angeles GLF, and then founded the Radical Faeries (a gay spiritual movement) as he became disillusioned with the declining radicalism of GLF. He remained an active anti-racist and gay rights campaigner until his death in 2002.

The pace of change for lesbian, gay and trans people quickened somewhat into the 1960s, but from a very low base. At the same time political opposition was growing to the Vietnam War, Black Civil Rights were moving centre stage and opposition to school segregation was developing, particularly in the United States. In Britain the Campaign for Nuclear Disarmament (CND) was attracting mass support.

Despite the newly emerging homophile organisations in this period, transgender people remained almost invisible and were often particularly isolated because there were (and are) far fewer trans people even than the marginalised lesbians and gays.

Trans and the medical profession

Initially, serious interest by the medical profession in lesbians, gays, bisexuals, trans and intersex people was very much on the fringes of medicine and support groups were almost nonexistent. A very early transgender support group, the Cercle Hermaphroditos ("to unite against the world's bitter persecution") was formed in America in 1895, but it did not last. In Europe some trans people had gravitated to Magnus Hirschfeld's institute and one or two other private physicians before the Second World War, but in Britain and elsewhere there appears to have been virtually nowhere for trans people to turn after the war in what was a very dark period of LGBT+ oppression.

In such a situation, and even today, there are examples of trans people resorting to self-mutilation in their desperation to find ways to make their bodies better conform to their gender identity. It was only after the war that a handful of doctors and surgeons began to be genuinely prepared to listen to and help transsexual people.

In 1945 two plastic surgeons, Harold Gillies and Ralph Millard, carried out Britain's — indeed the world's — first female-to-male gender affirmation operation on Michael Dillon. This involved a phalloplasty, the surgical construction of a penis. Gillies had performed similar operations on injured service personnel in the Second World War.

Gillies also performed Britain's first male-to-female gender affirmation operation on racing driver Roberta Cowell in 1951.

Dillon had already been having male hormone therapy (testosterone) since 1938 and later had a double mastectomy. Between 1946-49 he had 13 operations to create a phallus performed by surgeon Harold Gillies. In 1951 Dillon himself qualified as a doctor and later performed an orchidectomy (removal of the testes) on the racing driver Roberta Cowell, an operation which was illegal at the time.

In 1958 Dillon's past was exposed in the press. He was listed as the male heir to his older brother's baronetcy in one of the posh people's family tree books, *Debrett's Peerage*, but listed as a sister called Laura Maude in the other posh person's book of genealogy, *Burke's Peerage*. Having been outed, he fled to India where he became a Buddhist monk, writing and studying there until his death in 1962 aged just 47.

In 1946 Dillon had published *Self: A Study in Ethics and Endocrinology* in which he described people who we would today call transgender as "inverts" and wrote the radical assertion that, "Where the mind cannot be made to fit the body the body should be made to fit, approximately at any rate, to the mind". [167]

This statement summed up the stark divide between the recognised medical psychiatric approach at the time, which was to make the transsexual's mind fit their body through psychoanalysis and other techniques, and the transsexual's desire to create a body that better fitted the mind.

This dichotomy exists today. The "make the mind fit the body" approach is arguably a minority view held either by those who persist in believing that gender diversity/transgender is a form of illness that requires treatment and cure, or by those who accept essentialist notions of sex and gender. They insist that a person cannot "change sex" and that those who want to do so are victims of "gender identity ideology", an ideology that also, they say, amounts to child abuse when indulged or encouraged in those under the age of maturity.

Harry Benjamin and the *Transsexual Phenomenon*

In 1960 there were notable advances for transgender people in Britain. First, April Ashley, widely recognised as a transsexual pioneer and still a trans advocate today, had her gender affirmation surgery.[168] Second, Georgina Somerset (previously George Turtle) managed to get the gender marker on her birth certificate changed from male to female. It seems likely that she was intersex rather than trans. Her sex was not clear at birth but she was assigned male. However her gender identity was female and she had gender confirming surgery in 1957. She married and practised as a dentist in Hove until 1985, dying only quite recently in 2013. Having married in 1962 she became the first known woman to marry in a church having officially changed sex. She wrote two books about her life experiences including a memoir in 1962.[169]

So by the mid-1960s it looked like progress was being made for and by transgender people. In 1966 the Beaumont Society was formed. This was also the year that Harry Benjamin, who was born in Germany and had known and admired Magnus Hirschfeld, published his highly influential book *The Transsexual Phenomenon*.[170] Benjamin had moved to the United States in 1914 where he built up a successful medical practice over several decades. This was the first book dedicated to and sympathetic to the transsexual people who were referred to him in New York. Benjamin challenged the dominant psychoanalytic approach to addressing matters of sexuality and gender variance, arguing that it did not cure people but just drove them into isolation and miserable lives.

In the 1950s Benjamin had helped found the Society for

the Scientific Study of Sexuality. He had become convinced of the validity of distinguishing between transsexuals and transvestites on the one hand and homosexuals on the other after the sexologist Alfred Kinsey published his reports on human sexuality, including data on trans people, from 1948.[171]

It was also in 1948 that Kinsey referred a transsexual child to Harry Benjamin. Benjamin was sympathetic to the child's situation and prescribed the female hormone Premarin (Premarin first became available in 1941, extracted from the urine of pregnant mares) to alleviate the child's acute distress at being "the wrong sex".

Until the mid-20th century, for most sexologists, doctors and campaigners, gender variant behaviour had remained essentially undifferentiated from homosexuality. Someone who expressed the desire to "change sex" was most often regarded as a homosexual unable to face up to their homosexuality — a "self-denying homosexual". Many in the medical profession have continued to worry about how to distinguish between the "true" transsexual who may be worthy of medical intervention, from the "pseudo-transsexual" who may be "deluded", and many in the psychoanalytic tradition have regarded trans people as self-denying homosexuals in any case. Many Freudians persisted in that and similar views for decades after the notion of "the transsexual" became distinguished from "the homosexual". Despite the very difficult history of relations between psychoanalytic theory and gender variant activists and theorists, many psychoanalytic therapists continue to insist that the approach has developed useful tools to apply to any subjectivities involving what are theorised as repressed or unconscious drives, including trans subjectivities, as long as it can distance itself from its pathologising, normalising, heterocentric and transphobic/homophobic past.[172]

Transsexual as an established category

The term transsexual did not really emerge as a medical or social category, or a self-identification in more general use, until after the publication of Benjamin's book.

The Harry Benjamin International Gender Dysphoria Association was set up in the 1970s (now known as the World

Professional Association for Transgender Health). In 1979, it published *The Standards of Care for the Health of Transsexual, Transgender, and Gender Nonconforming People*, a set of non-binding protocols outlining appropriately supportive treatment for those who wish to undergo hormonal or surgical transition.[173]

Intended as a guide for health care professionals and to promote sympathetic, supportive and effective interventions,the *Standards of Care* (SOC) are still influential. The latest version, version 7, was published in 2012.[174] Many trans people criticised earlier versions for having too limiting or too restrictive criteria for treatment in particular the SOC's persistence in advocating quite lengthy "real life tests", that is, living full time in the preferred gender role to determine whether a person persists with their intentions. In version 7 this period has been reduced to a recommended 12 months for irreversible interventions. The current UK Gender Recognition Act still insists on a two-year "real life test".

1966 was also a watershed year because it was the year that the first gender identity clinics (GICs) were founded. One was at Johns Hopkins University in the United States, initially in conditions of secrecy under Dr John Money. The other was at Charing Cross Hospital (the Tavistock Clinic) in London.[175] The latter involved a former colleague of Money's, the American Richard Green, and the British psychiatrist John Randell. It was Money who popularised the term "gender" as applied to intersex and transsexual people. The term "gender identity disorder" was originated by Richard Green in 1974 and made its first appearance in the *Diagnostic and Statistical Manual* edition III, published in 1980.[176]

In the 1960s the Tavistock Clinic was seeing just a few dozen cases a year. In the 1970s this had increased to a hundred or so annually. In later years several more GICs were opened in Britain (there are now eight), although huge gaps in provision remain to this day — there is still no clinic in Wales, for example, despite promises.

Both the original clinics initially worked mainly with intersex patients and considered transsexual cases to be very rare.

The medical profession's model of early surgical intervention for intersex patients later came under intense public criticism from the 1990s, including from many patients themselves who rejected the dominant "normalising" medical model in favour of an approach that might address psychosocial factors and patient autonomy more effectively.[177] The medical model, they argued was also predicated on the relative convenience of medical technology at the time which has meant that a large majority of children with "disorders of sexual development" (DSDs) involving ambiguous genitalia were assigned female. Susan Stryker makes the point that:

> surgeons find it far easier to remove "excess" tissue than to build up new body structures for genitals deemed insufficient for a normal male appearance. This fixation on penis size, coupled with a cultural devaluation of the feminine that already conceived of women as "lacking" what men have, conspires to inflict unnecessary surgeries on intersex children.[178]

John Randell and the Tavistock Clinic were initially reluctant to recommend gender reassignment surgery for their trans patients, particularly not for those transsexuals who they considered did not "pass" sufficiently well. Most patients were male to female trans people and the criteria for passing were very gender stereotypical in terms of how the person presented — their dress, mannerisms, voice and outlook would be rigorously assessed and the person rejected if deemed not "feminine" enough. John Randell's rather autocratic, demanding and demeaning approach to his patients can be seen in his conversations with trans woman Julia Grant (who sadly died in January 2019) in the 1979 programme series *A Change of Sex*, the first time such a topic had been aired on British television.[179]

Where clinicians in more recent times have been criticised for being too ready to surgically intervene with intersex people, in the early days of the Tavistock Clinic clinicians were criticised as being too reluctant to authorise clinical and surgical intervention with transsexual people, since they accepted the established medical orthodoxy that transsexualism was essentially a psychiatric matter. Criticisms of long waiting times for appointments, staffing pressures, cancellations and other problems have continued to emerge from Tavistock service users despite changes of personnel and the practice ethos.[180]

The case of Christine Jorgensen

One of the trans people who persisted to a successful outcome was Christine Jorgensen, an ex-US marine. She later wrote about her trailblazing search for help with her gender transition from the early 1950s.[181]

Jorgensen became a household name based on claims that she was the first person to undergo gender reassignment surgery. In fact, as we have already noted, several such surgeries had taken place in Germany in Hirschfeld's Berlin Institute during the 1920s and early 1930s, before it was destroyed by the Nazis.[182] Perhaps the most famous case in the pre-War period was that of Lily Elbe[183] who had her operation in 1930 in Dresden, Germany, under Dr Gohrbandt, having been referred to him by Hirschfeld. Sadly, she died of complications in 1931. In Europe, such operations were being carried out in Copenhagen at the time and there were clinics in Belgium and Norway.

A number of "sex-change" operations had already been carried out in secret in the United States by Los Angeles urologist Elmer Belt, a friend of Harry Benjamin, long before the Christine Jorgensen case hit the newsstands. This progress in the US had stalled in 1949, however, causing more delays and difficulties for trans people, when an influential legal opinion in a court case caused doctors and surgeons to fear that they might find themselves subject to criminal prosecutions for "mayhem" — performing operations that involved the "wilful destruction" of healthy tissue.

Jorgensen was, however, a crucial role model for many trans people, being the first American to openly and publicly report on her transition. She may well have also been the first to combine gender reassignment surgery with hormone therapy, using recently available female hormones.

Jorgensen became an actress, singer and writer. There was a 1970 biopic film of her life, *The Christine Jorgensen Story*, directed by Irving Rapper. She is reported to have said in 1989, shortly before she died, that her transition had given the sexual revolution a "good swift kick in the pants".

Case law precedent — April Ashley

In 1971 a family law divorce case was decided involving April Ashley and her husband Arthur Corbett. The judge's ruling in this infamous Corbett vs Corbett case[184] would set back transgender legal rights by several decades.

April Ashley was in many ways Britain's equivalent of Christine Jorgensen. Having been born into poverty in Liverpool and having struggled with her gender identity from earliest times (resulting in several suicide attempts) the soon-to-be April Ashley developed a career as a performer in a famous gay club in Paris, Le Carrousel, working with female and male impersonators like Coccinelle and Bambi. The Paris scene and atmosphere were very different to the post-war austerity of smoggy London pockmarked with bomb sites, its rationing that lasted into the 1950s and its tight licensing laws.

Encouraged by her friends April had gender affirmation surgery in Casablanca in 1960 and quickly developed a successful modelling career back in Britain. However, she was outed by the *Sunday People* in a hostile transphobic article in 1961 which badly damaged her career.

In 1963 she married the minor aristocrat Arthur Corbett, who was fully aware of her background. The marriage broke down and in 1967 Corbett sued for divorce on the grounds that April was male and therefore the marriage was illegal.

April Ashley contested the case and asked for maintenance. In February 1970 Justice Ormrod ruled that the marriage should be annulled on the grounds that April Corbett was still legally a man despite having had gender affirmation surgery.

Gender psychiatrist John Randell, by this time regarded as the go-to expert on such issues, unhelpfully stated in court that April was "properly classified as a male homosexual transsexualist" while other court doctors preferred the description "castrated male." In light of such grossly transphobic opinions Justice Ormrod (who was himself medically trained) created a medical "test" and definition to determine April Ashley's legal sex status. She was subjected to intrusive and distressing medical examinations.

April, of course, along with other trans women, could never pass this biologically based test. In fact Ormrod's ruling would also logically exclude many other women — infertile women, women without ovaries or uteruses, many intersex women and so on — from being regarded as women. Nevertheless, the legal impact was to set a precedent that a person's sex could not be changed from that registered at birth.

This tragic and discriminatory legal position lasted for over thirty years until the passage of the Gender Recognition Act in 2004 allowed a person to obtain a gender recognition certificate and, subsequently, a new birth certificate under certain circumstances. Until then a transgender person constantly risked exposure if they had to show their birth certificate, or if someone happened to check it.

The setback due to this ruling was particularly unfortunate because in the 1960s transgender role models were beginning to emerge, giving confidence to others to seek gender transition. Thus a few years after this case in 1974 an early British transsexual, Jan Morris, published *Conundrum*, the story of her life and years of gender transition from well-known "male" journalist and mountaineer James to travel writer Jan.[185] The book has since become a classic of the transgender autobiography genre.

Such role models as Jorgensen and Ashley, early support organisations like the Beaumont Society, and the first gender identity clinics generated hope among trans people that things might be changing. But in Britain after 1970, as a result of the Corbett vs Corbett case, their very limited legal rights seemed to be going backwards rather than progressing.

This rather pessimistic legislative scenario was, however, offset in a spectacular and unanticipated way by the impact of the extraordinary Stonewall Rebellion that had erupted in New York in June 1969.

Stonewall: "We were not taking any more of this shit"

Some months before the Corbett vs Corbett ruling , a raw rebellion on the streets of New York resulted in trans and gay people taking a giant political leap forward.

The Stonewall Inn on Christopher Street, New York, was a seedy mafia-run gay bar where gay men, lesbians, drag queens and young trans people hung out. Many were street kids who made a living hustling or through the sex trade. It was from this unlikely seedbed that the Stonewall Rebellion exploded, marking the birth of a radical, revolutionary current in the fight for sexual and gender liberation.

By the middle of June 1969, the hippy peace and love era of the flower power year, 1967, was well and truly over. In early 1968, the Tet offensive by the Vietcong had profoundly undermined the view that US victory in Vietnam was inevitable. Civil Rights leader Martin Luther King was assassinated and Black Americans had rioted in dozens of cities.

The police had used heavy violence against anti-war demonstrators outside the Democratic Convention in Chicago.

The reality of the US state (and other capitalist states) was exposed in all its barbarity and propensity for violence against challenges at home and abroad. People were asking, "who makes the rules — and by what right?"

In May 1968 a huge revolt by students and the biggest general strike in history up to that time forced President Charles de Gaulle to, at one point, flee the country in panic. The events of May 1968 badly dented the confidence of ruling classes around the world, not just the French establishment. The revolt inspired radicals and socialists across the world, demonstrating that strikes and uprisings had the power to change the world.[186] As Chris Harman put it:

Every so often there is a year which casts a spell on a generation. Afterwards simply to mention it brings innumerable images to the minds of many people who lived through it — 1968 was such a year.[187]

Kickbacks, high kicks, and kicking back

In 1969 the mafia who ran the Stonewall Inn were handsomely paying off the local precinct police. Monthly police raids were tipped off to the bar owners in advance. Normally the police would turn up, harass people generally but only arrest those who had no ID, or who were cross-dressed, or some or all of the employees. Raids were timed for early evenings and by later in the night it was back to business as usual.[188] On Friday 28th June this cosy arrangement broke down.

Some have suggested that what happened was because the payoff had not been made, or the police were pushing for more money having discovered how lucrative the venue was. Another explanation was that the raid had been planned by federal agents of the Bureau of Alcohol, Tobacco and Firearms who had discovered that bootlegged liquor bottles were being used at Stonewall, and that the local police were being paid off. They deliberately notified the local police too late for the bar staff to be warned in advance by them. The raid took place at 1:20am, much later than normal, when people were well into enjoying a night out.[189]

As the police processed people in their usual aggressive and insulting way, a crowd gathered outside the bar. Accounts vary in some details but it seems the riot erupted either when a lesbian, Tammy Novak, objected to being shoved and started swinging at a cop, or when a cross-dressed lesbian who'd been arrested inside the club for wearing clothes of the "wrong" gender was pushed and hit outside the club by a cop trying to get her and some of the queens into the paddy wagon that had arrived. She jumped out of it and others tried to rescue her, and all hell broke loose.[190]

Sylvia Rivera was there that night. Sylvia was a Latina American LGBT+ activist, who identified at the time as a drag queen.[191] She reported that her boyfriend tried to persuade her to go home and get a change of clothes. Her response was emphatic: "Are you nuts? I'm not missing a minute of this — it's the *revolution*!"[192]

The original eight cops of the raid retreated into the bar and the crowd celebrated its control of the street. The beleaguered police called in the Tactical Patrol Force, the riot police. One eyewitness, Robert Bryan, recalled watching the face-off between the rebels and the police and being amazed by the young people's courage:

The queens — they were extremely effeminate young

men — formed this kicking line all across Christopher Street, and started to do a Rockettes kick. And singing, "We're the Stonewall Girls, we wear our hair in curls, we don't wear underwear" ... as it went. And the police started moving ahead, moving towards them... And the queens did not move: they just continued to kick and to sing as the police moved closer and closer and closer; and you just wondered how long are they going to keep this up before they break and run? The police got closer and closer to them with their clubs and their helmets and their riot gear and the whole thing; and I thought, it was just very inspiring, their bravery, like Bunker Hill or "Don't fire until you see the whites of their eyes".[193]

When the queens' line did break they simply ran off around the block, came out behind the police and started pelting them with stones and rubbish. This happened over and over again, to the cops' frustration as they realised they were dealing with hundreds of angry and determined people, not just a couple of dozen drunken "faggots".

The comment from Dick Leitsch, one of the participants on that fateful night, continues in the same vein:

The most striking feature of the rioting was that it was led, and featured as participants, "queens", not "homosexuals". "Homosexuals" have been sitting back and taking whatever the Establishment handed out; the "queens" were having none of that. The "butch" numbers who were around the area and who participated peripherally in the action remained for the most part in the background. It was the "queens" who scored the points and proved that they were not going to tolerate any more harassment or abuse... Their bravery and daring saved many people from being hurt, and their sense of humour and "camp" helped keep the crowds from getting nasty or too violent.[194]

Eventually two hours later, after much fighting, some serious injuries and a number of arrests, calm was restored.

But, as it turned out, only for that night.

The next night thousands of people appeared on the streets to celebrate the previous night's victories. Confrontations with the angry and humiliated police, including mounted police, inevitably flared. Once again, the resistance was led by the local queens and trans youth. Although some of the local gays and lesbians who had links with left wing groups had implored them to come down to the Stonewall to support the rebellion, they were disappointed that none of the recognised left organisations or straight radical feminists like the Redstockings responded positively.

While a few individuals from established homosexual rights organisations like the Mattachine Society may have celebrated the rebellion, many of the older gays feared for their public image. Carter reports that the New York Mattachine chapter put out a flier calling for "peaceful and quiet conduct on the streets of the village", and Mattachine officials came to the Stonewall Inn to stop people protesting.[195]

Martin Duberman writes:

> In this confrontational context of anger and defiance, the assimilationist civil rights goals of NACHO, the national homophile planning conference, and NACHO's characteristic tactic of petitioning for the redress of grievances, seemed old-fashioned — just as their long-standing insistence that homosexuals *were* an oppressed minority and *had* legitimate grievances suddenly seemed in harmony with the newly widespread resistance to traditional authority. Most younger gays and lesbians who sympathised with the New Left's broad agenda for ending inequality at home and interventionism abroad, joined not NACHO — which struck them as hopelessly bourgeois — but Students for a Democratic Society, or one of several organisations enlisted in the struggle for black empowerment.[196]

The new radicals were clearly going to have to do things for themselves.

Many of the young gay and trans activists explicitly saw

themselves as part of these movements and as revolutionaries. Trans people like Sylvia Rivera, Marsha P Johnson and their friends, drag queens and other gender variant people, played a central role in resisting the police at Stonewall from the night of 28 June 1969 out of which a new movement was born. Sylvia was a member of the Puerto Rican Young Lords and founder with Marsha Johnson of the Street Transvestite Action Revolutionaries (STAR), offering practical support to young homeless trans people.

In an interview with Leslie Feinberg in 1998 Sylvia said of the Stonewall riots:

> We were not taking any more of this shit. We had done so much for other movements. It was time... All of us were working for so many movements at that time. Everyone was involved with the women's movement, the peace movement, the civil rights movement. We were all radicals. I believe that's what brought it around... I was a radical, a revolutionist. I am still a revolutionist... If I had lost that moment, I would have been kind of hurt because that's when I saw the world change for me and my people. Of course, we still got a long way ahead of us.[197]

As in so many riots, rebellions, strikes and revolutions, being part of the Stonewall rebellion itself, or even experiencing it vicariously, changed people's consciousness and perspectives.

The peace campaigner and radical poet Allen Ginsberg visited the Stonewall Inn a couple of days after the rebellion, talking and dancing with those who had fought the police. Walking back home with a friend afterwards Ginsberg talked about what being gay used to be like and contrasting it with the new mood of the young gay and trans people after Stonewall. He concluded, "You know, the guys there were so beautiful — they've lost that wounded look that fags had ten years ago".[198]

The Gay Liberation Front
In the political ferment after Stonewall the 1970 manifesto of

the Gay Liberation Front[199] explicitly described itself as a revolutionary movement formed to fight for gay liberation alongside other oppressed groups against an oppressive capitalist system.[200]

It was young gay radicals dissatisfied with the conservative and inward-looking strategies of the existing gay and lesbian support organisations who in July 1969 came up with the name Gay Liberation Front, paying homage to the liberation struggles going on at that time in Algeria and Vietnam.[201] They needed a name to call and sponsor a demonstration they were planning in support of members of the Black Panther Party who were being held in the Women's House of Detention. The Mattachine Society and others had refused to be associated with the Black Panther Party.

Within a few months, however, some had split away from GLF and set up the Gay Activists Alliance (GAA). This was initially the result of a disagreement over a motion to give a substantial donation to the Black Panther Party which some activists objected to because of the homophobic comments of some leading members of the Party.[202]

The GAA insisted on focusing on one issue — gay rights — to the exclusion of other radical causes, although this was to be achieved through more militant action than the old homophile organisations were prepared to consider. Mario Mieli, an Italian gay activist writing in 1980, described the GAA as "reformists, disposed to a politics that was showy but cautious" and "who were against the gay movement giving support to other liberation struggles".[203]

The GAA organised a series of audacious "zaps" aimed at homophobic individuals and institutions. Between them, though, the GLF and GAA put gay power on the map in the post Stonewall period.

It was the GLF, the GAA, ECHO (East Coast Homophile Organisations) and others who organised the first gay pride march in the world, in New York on 28 June 1970, the first anniversary of the Stonewall Rebellion. It was supported by around 20 gay organisations. On the day people at first joined it hesitantly but eventually 2,000 people marched through the streets shouting "Gay power" and "Out of the closets and into the streets".

Sylvia Rivera and Marsha P Johnson marched on that fateful day and were enthusiastic supporters of both the GLF and the GAA for several years although they often suffered marginalisation and transphobia from lesbians and gay men in both organisations. Jim Fourrat was one of Sylvia's defenders who argued that "her instincts were always correct":

> Even when she was screwed up on drugs or booze and being abrasively loud, Sylvia had, to Jim's mind, a gut-level understanding of oppression and a willingness to speak her mind that more than made up for her "incorrect" vocabulary, her brazen, bullhorn voice, her inability to shut up... When attacked by a GAA man — who, in trying to liberate himself from traditional ridicule about being a surrogate woman, could be impatiently moralistic about cross-dressing "stereotypes" — Sylvia *would* attack back; she would remind him how tough you had to be to survive as a street queen, how you had to fight, cheat, and steal to get from one day to the next.[204]

Despite trans people being heavily involved over the five nights of the Stonewall revolt the event later became more synonymous only with a gay and lesbian revolt. Trans people's involvement was largely forgotten for decades. It was only much later that Sylvia's role, and that of other trans people in the riots, was recognised by Duberman in his classic book about the events.

Sylvia was one of six leading activists of that period whose recollections form the core of Duberman's book but she left the gay liberation movement in 1973 after an argument about whether she, as a trans person, could speak at the gay pride march that year. Having had to fight her way onto the platform against the opposition of organisers who wanted to ban "transvestites" she gave a spine-tingling, impassioned four minute speech in which she attacked the transphobia of the emerging gay, mostly male, movement's leadership for their willingness to sideline trans issues in their pursuit of limited gay rights.

The argument was symptomatic of the growing marginalisation of trans people in the gay liberation movement.[205]

The Compton's Cafeteria Riot

Stonewall was not the first organised and militant resistance involving trans people. The spirit of rebellion had been growing among young trans people well before Stonewall erupted and there had been militant local campaigns against trans exclusion from social venues. As early as 1959 there was a campaign by young trans people, who as we have seen tended to self-identity as queens at that time, against exclusion from Coopers Bar in South Side Los Angeles.[206]

In her *Transgender History* Susan Stryker describes other examples. In 1965 in Philadelphia Dewey's lunch bar refused to serve young trans people. Three trans people who refused to leave were arrested. Gay and trans people quickly set up a week-long picket until the owners backed down.

There was often overlap between gay and trans activism in working class areas. Their circumstances forced them to support one another and organise collectively to fight back. In just trying to live their lives, in trying to keep body and soul together, sometimes through sex or domestic work, they risked arrest, strip searches, being forced to have oral sex with corrupt cops, humiliation in (male) cells and having their heads forcibly shaved.

Sometimes rebellions and revolutions happen not during the severest period of repression but as things begin to liberalise. Often this is what gives some of the most oppressed and marginalised groups hope that things may improve and the determination to resist attempts to roll back even small beginnings.

This was almost certainly a factor in the Stonewall Rebellion and in the Compton's Cafeteria Riot three years earlier in San Francisco. The story, popularised by Susan Stryker and Victor Silverman in their EMMY award-winning documentary film *Screaming Queens*[207] showed that the riot itself erupted, again much like Stonewall, as a result of heavy-handed policing.

But the riot was also a result of contradictory pressures — on the one hand, growing access to information and support for trans people, for example through the work of the Glide Memorial Church and the Council on Religion and the Homosexual, radical Methodists who advocated for trans rights and offered support to trans people. In addition the new, if still difficult to access, availability of transsexual surgery through the gender clinic at Johns Hopkins University provided trans people with a sense of hope.

On the other hand, Compton's Cafeteria was a congregating place for young trans people and drag queens because they were not welcome in the city's growing gay bar scene.

Compton's was an all-night café, which suited the needs of young trans people seeking refuge after a long night hustling or engaging in sex work. The owners would regularly call the police — and drag queens could be arrested for the crime of "female impersonation". There had been ongoing harassment and a number of arrests by police through the summer of 1966.

One night in August a trans woman who was facing arrest threw her coffee in the face of the police officer, and "all hell broke loose". It was reported that "drag queens beat the police with heavy purses and kicked them with their high heeled shoes".[208] And, as with Stonewall, the protests continued for several nights.

Their courage ultimately led in San Francisco to trans people at least formally being entitled to recognition as citizens with rights and with entitlements to access services and legitimate employment opportunities.

Fragmentation, reformism and accommodation
In a period of rapid expansion, such as during the post-Second World War economic boom, capitalism could afford to incorporate some of the growing demands for greater equality in terms of race, gender and sexuality coming from the mass movements which developed during the 1960s and 1970s.

Paradoxically, that room to manoeuvre also tended to encourage a variety of reformist theories and strategies among many anti-oppression activists.

The period of radicalism and increased strike action peaked in the late 1960s and early 1970s. Increasingly many activists and former revolutionaries began to turn away from class struggle approaches and the fight for liberation in favour of the fight for better rights that they believed could be gained through reformist strategies.

Getting representatives elected to city councils and campaigning to win gay-friendly legislation, better funding and more civil rights became ends in themselves rather than useful and necessary reforms along the road to the kind of root and branch transformation of society that was, and still is, so desperately needed.

Within a relatively short time after Stonewall splits emerged in the movement for gay and trans liberation. In its early days the movement included trans people and trans aspirations. Very quickly, however, these were seen as an impediment to the achievement of gay rights advances within the system. Increasingly the movement split into "safe" LGBT+ activists and those deemed to be unrealistic and too radical.

San Francisco's first Pride in 1972, which celebrated the Compton's Cafeteria riot and welcomed drag, ended in fighting between the organisers and a lesbian separatist group. In 1973 there were two Prides, one of which banned trans people and drag.

The notion of "homonormativity" (that gay people's goal should be acceptance and accommodation within capitalist society) began to dominate among activists. The fight for liberation and the transformation of society that many of the early activists aspired to had become anathema. The new direction was more about winning friends and allies in national and local government, progressing LGBT+ friendly legislation and statutes, and aiming to convince society in general that gay men and lesbians, at least, share the same family values as heterosexual people. Trans and non-binary people find themselves on the margins of this accommodationist orthodoxy by virtue of the challenge they inherently represent to widely accepted binary norms in capitalist societies.

The revolutionary socialist and gay activist Mario Mieli wrote about this process, flagging up the gender transgressive element of unacceptability and outrageousness:

Society attacks transsexuals or those who might appear

as such with special violence: the butch lesbians, the fags, and the "effeminate" homosexual bear a greater brunt of public execration and contempt, and are frequently criticised even by those reactionary homosexuals who are better adapted to the system, the "straight gays" who have managed to pass as "normal" or heterosexual. These reactionary homosexuals (these homo-cops) insist that outrageous queens and transvestites "trash the gay scene and the image of homosexuality in the eyes of all". For our part we outrageous gays see them as queens disguised as straight, as disgraced people who are forced to camouflage themselves, to act a "natural" life in the role imposed by the system, and to justify their position as consenting slaves with ideological arguments.[209]

In this process of capitulation to the capitalist status quo the trans movement, which had much less potential for incorporation in the post-Stonewall period and tended to retain a more radical ideology, quickly lost its alliances with both the gay liberation movement and the emerging women's liberation movement.

Even from the early 1970s trans women began to be excluded from the women's movement by some radical feminists.[210] Various militant movements of the 1960s and early 1970s were disastrously fracturing along perceived differences of identity. Among women's movement activists, notions of radical separatism and political lesbianism, and a complete rejection of working with men (and trans women) or involvement in the class struggle, gained in strength.[211]

The shifts, retreats and incorporation of some gay aspirations in the following decades, theorised within the subjectivism and relativism of emerging postmodernist theory in the 1980s[212] has had serious long-term implications for class struggle politics and the discussion of strategies for the liberation of oppressed groups because underlying this was the rejection of the notion that it is the unity of the oppressed, and our potential power alongside organised workers, that bring hope of winning real advances.

Nevertheless, the impact of struggles against homophobia and transphobia in the late 1960s, in particular the Stonewall Rebellion, have been far-reaching but we should note how quickly they faced conflicting interpretations and competing reformist political strategies. Such strategies sought to blunt and edge out the revolutionary and liberationist zeal and promise of those early years.

Birth of the modern trans movement

In the early 1980s another vicious round of homophobia erupted, initially in the United States but quickly followed in a range of other countries.

The growing Aids epidemic, which impacted trans people (particularly trans women, and particularly poor trans women) as well as gay men, gave rise to high levels of homophobia and public hysteria enthusiastically fanned by the tabloid press. *The Sun* newspaper, for example, described Aids as a "gay plague" in February 1985, a term which became widely adopted.

Initially the disease hit gay men, but as it progressed quickly to haemophiliacs, intravenous drug users, as well as women and transgender people, especially those engaged in the sex industry, it became obvious that it was transmitted through exchange of body fluids and was not something to do with being gay or restricted to those in same-sex sexual relationships.

Myths about the "gay plague" persisted, though, and governments, including the British government, were very slow or reluctant to act in terms of practical help and advice to those infected or at risk of infection. Research funds were de-prioritised or even cut (as happened in the US under Ronald Reagan). Advice when it did come was universally poorly-informed, crass and inherently homophobic. Blaming gay people and sex workers for their own illness and death was commonplace.

LGBT+ people had to organise their own support organisations (like the Terrence Higgins Trust in Britain, formed in 1982 after the death of an early Aids victim Terry Higgins) and organise their own agitation in the face of generalised, and in many cases, paranoid homophobia.[213]

It was not until the late 1980s that joint political campaigning against HIV/Aids, as well as the struggle against Section 28 in Britain, began to lead to a pooling of resources and energy by the groups affected to fight for medical help, support and justice.

In the United States Ronald Reagan's administration had inflicted very damaging funding cuts that had set back Aids research and support programs in the 1980s, but in the 1990s as a result of vigorous campaigning more funding became available to combat the epidemic. This followed the development of a number of quite militant campaigning and support organisations, such as ActUP, Transgender Nation and Queer Nation, but also Riki Wilchins' Transexual Menace.[214] Wilchins went on to form the trans advocacy organisation GenderPAC. These developments in turn promoted the obvious need for closer cooperation among LGBT+ people who were commonly impacted by the suffering and mortality of the epidemic and the rampant homophobia and transphobia of the period.

It was also around this time that intersex people began to organise for recognition and lobby for changes to the medical abuse they had been regularly subjected to. As mentioned above, the first intersex organisation formed was the Intersex Society of North America, founded by Cheryl Chase in 1993, to help those people born with ambiguous genitalia or with genetic or chromosomal conditions (DSDs) which impact their biological sex and/or gender identity. This was followed in Britain by the formation of the UK Intersex Association[215] and Organisation Intersex International.[216]

This growing activism coincided with the development in academia of queer theory, which was critical of the compromising and accommodating strategies adopted towards the predominantly heterosexist, binary culture by the lesbian and gay movement since the mid-1970s. Queer theory's target, as Stryker put it, was to disrupt the smooth functioning of the heterosexist state.[217]

It was around this time that the more inclusive acronym "LGBT" gained popularity — a reflection of the need to address the previous rifts between gays, lesbians, bisexuals and trans people and encourage campaigning unity. By the 1990s, while there was still anti-trans suspicion and hostility from a minority of radical feminists and lesbians involved in the lesbian and gay movement there was also much more willingness by many, particularly among the newer generation of activists, to be trans and bi-inclusive.

Trans activism has continued to face hostility and opposition from many quarters, however. There continued during this period to be debates and disagreements among LGBT+ people about whether, or the extent to which, transgender phenomena could be adequately incorporated within queer sexuality.

But by the late 1990s many organisations which had been active around sexual orientation issues were adding the "T" to their organisation's acronym and beginning to include gender identity issues as core concerns. The currently preferred terms "transgender" or "trans" also became widely adopted at this time. The term transgender was popularised by Leslie Feinberg, among others, in hir writing during the 1990s. Some organisations addressed this shift more quickly than others. The UK-based gay advocacy organisation Stonewall, for instance, had resolutely excluded advocating on trans and saw itself as exclusively dealing with matters of sexual orientation but it decided to appoint a Trans Advocacy Group in 2015 and since then has consistently addressed trans issues.[218] This has not been without criticism from some, however, and in October 2019 there were reports of a split, subsequently denied by Stonewall CEO Paul Twocock.[219]

By the early 2000s the developments towards more inclusivity for trans (and bisexuality) was widespread, including in the trade union movement where, thanks to the efforts of many activists, increasing numbers of trade union "gay and lesbian" support groups became "LGBT" (now more often LGBT+) support groups.[220]

Some critics, however, including Susan Stryker, have suggested that this has often amounted to a mere tokenistic name change that actually:

represented a retreat from the more radical alliance, resistance, and rebellion by different groups against the same oppressive structures in the dominant culture and the adoption instead of a liberal model of minority tolerance and inclusion — sometimes amounting to little more than a "politically correct" gesture of token inclusion for transgender people.[221]

It is clear that the gains for LGBT+ rights in the 30 years after the end of the Second World War were achieved through the courageous self-organisation of LGBT+ people often in the face of widespread indifference and hostility. For trans people the fight necessitated resistance and resolve in the face of societal ignorance and lack of understanding, repressive medical orthodoxy, political isolation, heteronormative social assumptions and, by the mid-1970s, an accelerating process of incorporation of lesbian and gay identities (though not bi and trans) into capitalist society and its institutions.

We should never forget that it has been mass acts of militant resistance, most notably the Stonewall Rebellion, that have most progressed LGBT+ rights, not the generosity and social liberalism of particular governments.

Chapter 6
Trans voices around the world

Hatred, bigotry and hostility towards those who are transgender, gender variant, gender queer, gender fluid or gender non-conforming — essentially anyone perceived as being "gender abnormal" and outside the man/woman binary — remains widespread in the 21st century.[222]

Nevertheless, in some parts of the world there has been sufficient political and economic space for pressure from LGBT+ activists since the post-Stonewall period to achieve some meaningful reforms, at least in formal, legislative terms.

In many other places recent decades have seen a neoliberal economic agenda go hand-in-hand with a far from liberal social agenda. This has often flowed from the promotion of "traditional" family values by religious and right wing, reactionary forces and has resulted in restrictions on LGBT+ rights.

In some cases, the impact of Western military intervention has massively disrupted or even destroyed a number of some-times already socially conservative societies in recent decades — Iraq, Syria, Libya and Yemen, for example — and this has had the effect of strengthening homophobic and transphobic social attitudes and legislation.

Iraq is one example of this dynamic. After an estimated one million deaths and millions of refugees created by the wars and invasions launched by the US, Britain and other allies, homophobia and transphobia have been very significantly ramped up. LGBT+ activist Amrou Al-Kadhi wrote in the *Independent* in July 2017 in response to the brutal murder of the Iraqi actor Karar Nushi, that between 2004 and 2009 alone, 680 people were murdered in Iraq due to gender and sexual non-conformism. Karar Nushi was stabbed to death in Baghdad in July 2017. It seemed that his "crime" was not only that he might be gay, but he also received death threats due to his "transgressive appearance", particularly his long blonde hair.

Al-Kadhi describes how:

> Violence against LGBTQI people in Iraq has escalated dramatically since the Western invasion of 2003, and it's not a coincidence. Just as the far right use LGBTQI rights as a way to brew racism, ISIS exploit LGBTQI people as a tool to fuel anti-Western hatred. Disdain for the West is potent on Iraqi soil — what did we expect after destroying a civilisation for no actual reason?[223]

In Turkey and in many countries in Africa, Asia and South America, nationalists and right-wing ideologues and bigots are quick to tag homosexuality and transgender expression as decadent Western imports which offend against traditional values. Some have claimed, in the face of overwhelming alternative evidence, that homosexuals and transgender people were unknown in their "traditional" cultures. In fact, what has been imported from the West is not homosexuality but LGBT+phobia. Despite their anti-Western rhetoric some of these same regimes have been happy to ally with right-wing reactionary Western religious (usually Christian) groups in pursuit of their bigotry.

In the necessarily brief and incomplete examination below I have selected widely varying societies from around the world to examine the situation for transgender people. They all involve strikingly similar forms of transphobic oppression, but they also involve examples of *resistance* to transphobic oppression and solidarity between trans people in such countries and trans people and their supporters in other countries.

In most of them courageous campaigning and support organisations fight to change attitudes, offer practical support to trans people and try to keep the world informed of what is happening in their country, often at very real risk to their own lives and liberty.

Turkey: "Don't be silent, shout, trans exist"

On 12 August 2016 the raped, burned and mutilated body of well-known 23 year old Turkish transgender activist and sex worker Hande Kader was found in a forest near a middle class area of the town of Zekeriyakoy. She had last been seen getting into a client's car some days before. Some reports said she had been gang raped before being murdered. Her body was so badly disfigured that her flatmate Davut Dengilur could only subsequently confirm her identity by her prosthetics.

Hande was murdered just a few weeks after the beheading of Muhammad Wisam Sankari, a gay Syrian refugee who had only been in Turkey for a year. Having fled the killing fields of Syria, he fell victim to homophobia across the border in a supposedly safe haven.

Hande's brutal killing was the latest in a long line of trans murders in Turkey. The manner of their deaths, like Hande's, was often particularly vicious, including throats cut, savage beatings, shooting and sometimes genital mutilation. In the past, Hande herself had been beaten and stabbed.

Recent statistics demonstrate that Turkey is the worst country in Europe for trans murders and ranks ninth in the world.[224] A fundamental problem for trans people is that those who commit these murders and assaults know that they stand every chance of getting away with their crimes. While some forms of hate crime *are* recognised in Turkey those related to sexual orientation or gender identity are not.

Some Turkish government ministers have fanned the flames by making widely reported homophobic and transphobic comments that undermine the human and civil rights of LGBT+ people. Such comments have rarely been criticised by the government or in the media.

In 2010, for example, the former State Minister for the Affairs of Women and Families, Aliye Kavaf, stated that she believed: "homosexuality is a biological disorder, a disease… something that needs to be treated".[225]

Not only are the police usually reluctant to investigate attacks but the Turkish judiciary offers loopholes to perpetrators in the very few cases where convictions might be achieved. Thus in the Turkish legal system judges are allowed to reduce sentences if the perpetrator may have been subject to "unjust provocation." While we might consider this a possible recognition of the principle of self-defence by a victim of hate crime, in practice it has been used to undermine criminal cases against those accused of crimes against LGBT+ people.

On February 26, 2014, for example, a man who killed a trans woman was given an "unjust provocation" sentence reduction from life to 18 years. According to the verdict, the "unjust act" was the victim "being a transvestite".[226]

Asli Zengin, an LGBT activist and visiting professor at Brown University's anthropology department, describes the situation in Turkey thus: "There's this constant emphasis on one nation, one religion, one ethnicity. Everything is consolidated around this uniformity of what it means to be a Turkish citizen who deserves to live."[227]

Violence and insecurity are experienced as a way of life for trans people in Turkey. In an interview with a journalist, trans sex worker Kemal Ordek, who uses the gender-neutral pronouns "they/their", said they were "lucky" to survive an attack in their home: "There are very few trans individuals who die of natural causes — nearly none." And they concluded, "When you are pushed into sex work, it's not possible for people to reach old age. They are killed. I don't know how I survived. That's the sad part".[228]

As if to emphasise their words, in the weeks following Hande's murder, Azize Ömrüm, a trans sex worker in İzmir, took her own life. In 2015 another sex worker, Eylül Cansın, had done the same. They both said in their suicide notes that they could not deal with the oppression and discrimination any longer.[229]

Trans people in Turkey face particularly marginalised and difficult situations, a transgender Catch 22. The gender transition process, which many would like to pursue, can take five or six years and until this has been completed the person is forced to keep using their gender-inappropriate identity — making legitimate employment, education, housing and access to health care difficult, if not impossible. Until 2018 identity cards were based on sex assigned at birth and were colour coded blue for male, pink for female.[230]

Until 2018, the Turkish state demanded proof of surgical sterilisation in order to sanction recognition in a new gender — there is no option of self-identification. Since military service is compulsory in Turkey for men, for transwomen to avoid conscription as men they can effectively be forced into painful, expensive and difficult procedures and surgery which many might not choose otherwise to undertake. Similarly gay men, considered to be suffering from a psychosexual disorder and therefore unfit for military service, have to have someone vouch for their homosexuality. For gay and trans people it is common for families to refer them for so-called cures.[231]

Even so, many still feel that they cannot or do not wish to undertake it. Gender transition surgery and hormonal treatment are expensive. Very few Turkish surgeons or clinics will undertake it and consequently many trans people are forced into sex work to find the money to fund it or even just to pay rent and buy food.

Hande Kader had been prominent in helping to organise trans rights events such as Trans Pride and in offering support to other marginalised trans people. Her murder was protested by hundreds of supporters in towns and cities across Turkey, despite the state of emergency implemented after the June 2016 attempted military coup.[232] Many thousands of people worldwide followed the case on social media demanding changes in the country's laws that would help protect LGB and especially trans people. At the time of writing no-one had been arrested or charged with her murder.

Some Turkish MPs supported the protests which promoted slogans like "Trans murders are political" and "Hande Kader is here, where are the murderers?" Many activists hoped that the solidarity and protests expressed at Hande's vicious killing could begin to turn the transphobic and homophobic tide in Turkey, and it is certainly the case that the LGBT+phobic backlash in Turkey has been met by growing organisation and resistance with hundreds organising Pride events in other towns and cities and hundreds prepared to defy bans.

One of the problems they face, common to many oppressed groups, is a largely disinterested national media. There is a widely used photograph of Hande at the 2015 Turkish Pride march in Taksim Square, Istanbul. The march had been banned by the authorities. Angry and frustrated at the actions of the state and the police she said to journalists there, "You take pictures, but you do not publish them. No-one is hearing our voices".[233]

The situation for LGBT+ people in Turkey, after many years of campaigning and activism, had begun to look a little more optimistic. Until 2014, Istanbul's Trans Prides had been growing in size and confidence. In 2013 around 10,000 people marched, boosted by the prominent role that trans women in particular had played in the 2013 Gezi Park protests.[234] Their way of life and opportunities to make a living, often from sex work, would also be hit by closure of the park, and they had joined soccer fans, left organisations, anarchists and others trying to keep the park open in the face of state attempts to close it down. They fought back shoulder to shoulder against police attacks on the mass protests.

However, Trans Prides since 2015 have been banned by the Turkish state. When LGBT+ people tried to march and read out a statement in 2016 the police attacked them with water cannon, rubber bullets and pepper spray. The police also failed to prevent harassment by groups of fascists and bigots.[235]

The ban was repeated in June 2017, using the excuse of potential public disorder after threats by far-right groups to break up the parade. Nevertheless, hundreds of protestors turned out and tried to march but were attacked by police with batons and water cannon. In June 2018, Istanbul Pride was banned by the Mayor at the last minute, shortly after Prime Minister Erdogan's victory in the general election and his assumption of vastly strengthened state powers. The ban was repeated in 2019, with police attacking those who defied the ban with teargas.[236]

The statement that trans activists in 2016 tried to read at the banned protest was politically sophisticated, determinedly internationalist, and made common cause with minority nationalities and other oppressed groups in Turkey and beyond.[237] The first part said:

This argument that began with the excuse of disrespect for the month of Ramadan shows us where those who are not Turkish, Muslim, Sunni, and male will stand in this nonsensical New Turkey. This sensibility that imposes their own norm on the totality of society and targets those who do not abide by this norm will bring nothing but a massacre for the Kurds, Alevis, Armenians, Greeks, Roma, LGBTIs, women, labourers and workers.

It went on to condemn the growing authoritarianism of Prime Minister Erdogan's AKP (Justice and Development Party) government:

While every critical opinion about the President expressed on Twitter draws house raids, arrests, and detention, open calls to attack are disregarded and the complaints of rights defenders remain unprocessed.

Within this reality, the situation of trans society is in an even worse state. Trans individuals who cannot camouflage themselves in social life are turned into targets and are deprived of all their fundamental rights...

The statement condemned the unconstitutional harassment and discrimination meted out to transgender people:

The Republic of Turkey, which defines itself as a social state, usurps our right to life, housing, education, health, and movement, forcing us to live in oppression that has not been seen before.

We, the children of the rainbow, shout out once again: We are the owners of these lands and the guarantors of a bright future!

And it ends with a defiant cry of resistance:

We will continue to fight for an equal, free, and democratic world. We bow with respect to the memory of our friends massacred in Orlando and promise a world without homophobia and transphobia!

Don't forget Orlando, don't let anyone forget! Despite hate, hooray life! Hate crimes are political!

This all took place a couple of months before the failed military coup of June 2016 in Turkey.

Since the 2016 attempted coup Prime Minister Erdogan's government has arrested tens of thousands of alleged dissidents, sacked tens of thousands of state employees, and sought to suppress freedom of the Press, and freedom of expression and assembly under the guise of "restoring order".

Despite this trans and LGBT+ organisations in Turkey continue to fight back.

Malaysia

Discrimination against lesbian, gay, bisexual, and transgender people is pervasive in Malaysia. Article 377A of the penal code criminalizes same-sex activity between men with punishments of whipping and up to 20 years in prison. Public agencies have been set up to "protect" people from being "tainted" by homosexuality.

Transgender people in Malaysia (the Malaysian male to female transsexual community is called the Mak Myahs) had for centuries enjoyed a relatively high level of acceptance. Malaysian texts from the 15th to 19th centuries document periods of much greater acceptance of transgender people within a majority Muslim society. Joseph Goh, a PhD candidate in gender and sexuality studies at Malaysia's Monash University, notes:

> Trans* persons have long been important figures in the landscape of the Malay Archipelago. In the 19th century, the manang bali or Iban shamans who dressed as women were respectable curers and local leaders. Right up to the 20th century in the archipelago, many transwomen were royal courtiers. Transwomen village performers were also favourably treated by the Sultan of the state of Kelantan in the 1960s.[238]

However, from the 1980s onwards the situation became worse for trans people in the context of a government that wanted to crush growing dissent and promote much greater control over people's bodies, their sexual behaviour and gender expression, particularly through the promotion of Sharia law. In 1994, the Malaysian government banned gays, bisexuals and transsexuals from appearing in the state-controlled media, and in 2010, film censors ruled that the depiction of homosexual characters was only permissible if the characters "repent" or die.

Sex reassignment surgery, which was once available in Malaysia, is now effectively prohibited following a 1989 fatwa declaring it haram (forbidden) and no doctor will perform it.[239] Trans people wanting such gender affirmation treatment have to travel abroad. Currently in Malaysia transgender people cannot get identity documents which reflect their gender identity, even if they have obtained hormones and gender affirmation surgery abroad. Consequently they are at constant risk of exposure. They can only get jobs if they dress "appropriately", and so many find they have no alternative but to engage in sex work. Some are entertainers, but they receive very little general recognition. Trans people have become progressively criminalised and marginalised. Politicians, state officials, and religious figures frequently use transphobic rhetoric, making discrimination and violent assault more likely, and anti-LGBT+ propaganda is promoted in education and religious institutions.

A Human Rights Watch report in 2014 documented ways in which the religious (and civil) police arrest, harass, extort, violently assault and deny basic civil rights to transgender people.[240] Some have been arrested on multiple occasions and sent to prison for between four months and three years. This direct discrimination extends to the denial of education and housing, being sacked from jobs and being refused access to health services. The report does point out, however, that resistance to the ramping up of trans oppression in Malaysia has been growing:

Despite the challenges they face, transgender people in Malaysia are not passive victims of their circumstances. A vibrant transgender movement has developed, with trans people increasingly speaking out and demanding that their rights be respected. The Kuala Lumpur-based organization, Justice for Sisters, seeks to raise public awareness about violence and persecution against transgender women, and supports legal challenges to the state Sharia "cross-dressing" laws. The "I AM YOU: Be A Trans Ally" multimedia campaign aims to promote positive images of transgender people and allows transgender people an avenue to share their stories. Civil society organizations ranging from the Malaysian Bar Council to the Muslim feminist group Sisters in Islam have taken public stances in support of transgender rights.[241]

Justice for Sisters published a report in 2019 that set out how trans people in Malaysia are impacted by state-sponsored LGBT+phobia, including widespread conversion therapy:

In Malaysia, LGBT people are criminalised through many federal and state laws. There are also multiple government-initiated anti-LGBT programmes, overseen by the Prime Minister's Department and JAKIM [Department of Islamic Development Malaysia] since 2011, most of which focus on rehabilitation and conversion of LGBT persons.[242]

In 2014 the Justice for Sisters had won an important victory in the Court of Appeals which found that a state's application of Sharia law was unconstitutional and discriminatory. Unfortunately the ruling was reversed a year later in the Federal Court.

A British *Unreported World* TV programme in early 2016 investigated the severe discrimination and harassment experienced by trans people in Malaysia.[243] This is particularly true of Muslim trans people affected by Malaysia's parallel legal codes of civil and Islamic law.

The programme documented how the Federal Territories Islamic Department (JAWI — the religious police) regularly carry out night time raids of hotels and clubs looking for people in unmarried "liaisons" or involved in other religious transgressions such as being cross-dressed. When transgender people are arrested by the religious police they can also be forced to wear gender-(in)appropriate clothes or sent to special camps to be "cured."

State repression of political dissent in Malaysia had been growing after resistance emerged to the right-wing coalition National Front government which had been in power since independence was gained from Britain in 1957. The country has been run since then by the dominant party in the coalition, the United Malay National Organization (UMNO).

Government ministers, far from recognising the difficulties faced by trans people in Malaysia, have fanned the flames of prejudice by stating, for example, that being transgender is to reject God's wisdom in creating two genders, or that the existence of LGBT+ people is related to mental disorder and HIV/Aids.

The 2014 Human Rights Watch report said:

> in 2013 Deputy President Muhyiddin Yassin referred to the LGBT rights movement as a threat to Islam, backed by "foreign influences". In December 2013, an UMNO [ruling party] delegate who was chair of the Johor Islamic Religious Committee stated that, "LBGT exists in the West so that bad people (orang jahat) can be purged, leaving behind only the good people to inherit the earth." He specifically claimed that transgender people "do not live long".[244]

In the elections of 2008 and 2013 the governing party only barely beat the opposition coalition and as a consequence has been ramping up the scapegoating of minorities, such as LGBT+ people and Shia Muslims.

In 2018 the opposition parties won the national elections which led to hopes that the situation for LGBT+ people might significantly improve, but according to Human Rights Watch's Asian director Phil Robertson it has not done so, and things may even have got worse because the new government ministers do not want to appear to be soft on LGBT+ issues in the "New Malaysia" while under political attack from the former government parties.

Thilaga Sulathirey of Justice for Sisters said that the new

government's policies were, "a continuation of the previous administration's policy, which had introduced a five-year government action plan to address some 'social ills' [including LGBT identities]."[245]

Russia

There was a time just after the 1917 Russian Revolution when Russia led the world in LGBT+ rights. Those advances were extinguished during the rise of Stalinism in the later 1920s. The situation worsened following the collapse of the Soviet Union in 1989 and the severe economic shocks and disruption of the 1990s.

In October 1991 Boris Yeltsin, the Russian President, announced sweeping market reforms which amounted to shock therapy. The neoliberal policies adopted — liberalization of the economy and privatisation of state enterprises and resources as part of the transition to a market economy — were essentially a capitulation to the Washington consensus as set out by the International Monetary Fund and the World Bank.

The impact on ordinary Russians was devastating. The end of price and rent controls, combined with mass redundancies and hyperinflation meant that poor people, pensioners and workers saw their savings and pensions wiped out and their incomes plummet while bureaucrats and Communist Party bosses grew fabulously wealthy on the corruption and rich pickings on offer, becoming virtually indistinguishable from criminal elements like the Russian mafia.

World Bank estimates showed that whereas prior to 1991 around 1.5 percent of the population lived in poverty as defined by an income of less than $25 per month, by mid-1993 between 39 and 49 percent of the population were living in poverty. Per capita incomes fell by another 15 percent by 1998, according to government figures.[246] Life expectancy also fell in those years. 1998 marked another severe financial crisis, with only a partial recovery before the world financial crisis of 2008 hit.

In the absence of strong left wing and working class resistance, various minorities have borne the political brunt of the backlash. There has been rising racism, the growth of nationalist and fascist organisations, the resurgence of the very conservative Russian Orthodox Church and the institutionalisation of political corruption along with attacks on democratic rights, such as the right to protest.

Formally, transgender Russians had been able to legally change their gender on identity documents since 1997, although this depended on proof of genital surgery. But in 2014 new legislation was passed in the Russian parliament, the Duma, banning trans people from holding driving licences on the grounds that they suffer from a mental illness.[247] Such legislation also obviously serves to legitimise the activity of homophobic and transphobic gangs who in parts of Russia today hunt down, beat and terrorise LGBT+ people.[248]

This retrograde law followed President Putin imposing a "gay propaganda law" in 2013, as part of his moves to simultaneously crackdown on dissent and suck up to the Church. This claimed to protect minors by banning the circulation of information which might promote non-traditional sexual relations such as homosexuality because it contradicts "traditional family values".[249] There are echoes here of Britain's notorious Section 28, which was only repealed in 2003.

Another source of homophobia and transphobia in Russia is the growth of fascist and right wing populist organisations, drenched in machismo, a phenomenon common to other former Soviet and Eastern European countries like Hungary and Poland, where attacks have increased on Pride marches and LGBT+ people generally. Indeed some European LGBT+ activists at the 2019 conference of ILGA-Europe (International Lesbian, Gay, Bisexual, Trans and Intersex Association) have suggested that in terms of LGBT+phobic hate crimes and institutional hostility, 30 years after the collapse of the USSR there is still an Iron Curtain running across eastern Europe.[250]

Russian authorities have refused permits for Pride parades, arrested activists and condoned ignorant and dangerous homophobic comments from public figures. ILGA-Europe has ranked Russia as the least protective country in Europe for its LGBT+ citizens, 49th out of 49.[251]

Russian LGBT+ activist Elena Grigoryeva was stabbed and strangled to death in July 2019. Like many other Russian LGBT+ people her name was on a far-right hit list and she lived in constant fear.[252]

These are life and death issues not only because people face physical attacks due to their sexual orientation or gender identity but because such discrimination, harassment and marginalisation can only accelerate the rate of suicides, especially among young people, in a country where the suicide rate is already three times higher than the global average.

With great bravery, LGBT+ people are fighting back in Russia against these attacks, but it can be difficult to organise protests when LGBT+ support groups are prevented from operating openly, when even online support networks are heavily monitored and trolled, and when the police show little interest in responding to attacks.

The situation is even more difficult due to the absence of any serious independent trade union movement. Marches and protests are often banned, and protesters are atomised by having to stand fifty yards apart even when they are not banned from protesting completely. This has been part of the clamp down on all political protest and dissent under Putin's regime.

In one of Russia's satellite states, Chechnya, the pro-Russian government has been promoting a vicious anti-LGBT+ campaign including arresting and kidnapping suspected LGBT+ people and incarcerating them without trial in what amounted to a concentration camp where, by late 2017, reports suggested that at least three people had died. LGBT+ activists mounted an international campaign to raise funds to set up an "underground railroad" to help persecuted LGBT+ people get out of the country.[253]

India

Indian law since 2014 has recognised transgender people, including the traditional trans and intersex community, the Hijras, as a third gender after similar laws were passed in Pakistan, Bangladesh and Nepal.[254] The new legislation is supposed to allow quota-based access to government jobs and education but most Hijras still find greater security, safety and financial support by living in Hijra communities organised by a guru or mother figure.

Despite the 2014 legislation the ruling Indian party, the Bharatiya Janata Party (BJP) announced in 2018 that it intended to reintroduce the misleadingly named Transgender Persons (Protection of Rights) Bill (TPPR) which would in practice legitimise violence and discrimination against transgender, intersex and gender non-conforming people in India. If the TPPR is passed it will undermine the right to gender self-determination in the 2014 Act.

Colonial legislation like the 1871 Criminal Tribes Act (CTA) criminalised and persecuted "eunuchs" — the pejorative colonial term used to label Hijras — by labelling them as "reasonably suspected" of sodomy, kidnapping and castration. Part II of the CTA required the police to keep a register of Hijras. This law applied in the North Western Provinces. It was intended to cause the "extinction" of the "eunuchs" and was repealed in 1911 when the colonial authorities felt they were close to achieving their goal. However, in reality the Hijras had become adept at avoiding the register or had moved to other Indian states. In any case, despite the repeal many of the colonial era attitudes and proscriptions remained in post-colonial practices and policing in the Indian subcontinent, and still do today. Laws exist which outlaw hate crimes and harassment of trans people in India but the police are often reluctant or slow to take up cases.

Jessica Hinchy of Nanyang Technological University, Singapore, has described the situation for Hijras under British colonialism as:

India's British colonisers viewed Hijras as a multi-faceted threat to colonial authority — as a population that was ungovernable in manifold ways. Misgendering feminine Hijras as men, colonial officials viewed Hijras as"professional sodomites" who challenged the colonial legal system, which was based on heterosexual, reproductive sexuality and the family. In the colonial view, Hijras were an "obscene" public nuisance that undermined the order of public space — a discourse that ignored the cultural significance of Hijra badhai (donations collected at births and weddings) and performance.[255]

Hijras have existed for around 4,000 years and have links to Indian cultural traditions and to Hinduism, appearing in various religious texts, rituals and stories. Under the Muslim Mughals in the 16th to 19th centuries Hijras held important positions in court and administration. They also held religious authority and offered blessings, particularly during weddings and religious ceremonies.[256]

Today the Hijra community is very marginalised compared to 300 or 400 years ago. While they are sometimes still sought for blessings and performances, they are mostly forced to make a living through begging or sex work. Consequently, they are a high risk HIV group. HIV prevalence among transgender people in India was estimated to be 3.1 percent in 2017, the second highest prevalence among all key populations in the country.[257] The HIV rate among Hijras in Mumbai is 18 percent compared to a background rate of 0.3 percent.

Section 377 of the Indian penal code was introduced in 1861 and criminalised "unnatural offences" such as "carnal intercourse against the order of nature with any man, woman or animal" and carried a maximum sentence of life imprisonment. The law stemmed from British colonial legislation, which was, in turn, based on the English Buggery Act of 1533.

The Indian High Court had dismissed Section 377 in 2009 but in 2013 the Supreme Court overturned that ruling. India thus controversially re-joined seventy other countries where homosexuality was illegal. However the High Court again ruled in August 2017 that LGBT+ people had a fundamental right to express their sexuality and a right to privacy under the Indian Constitution and gay sex was finally decriminalised by the Indian Supreme Court on 6 September 2018.[258] Nevertheless LGBT+ campaigners describe how difficult it remains to be open in India where social attitudes and conventions remain very conservative, especially in rural areas.[259]

Nevertheless, LGBT+ people argue that social attitudes are shifting and growing more accommodating towards gay and gender variant people, especially among the young. Yet this new major world power has a very politically and socially conservative government under the BJP and right wing Prime Minister Narendra Modi.

It is based on right wing Hindu nationalist ideology which is generally hostile to minorities such as LGBT+ people and celebrates a virulent masculinity and the oppression of women. The party formally believes that gay people can be cured and is keen to marginalise and suppress gay and gender variant people. Its militants have been involved in gang rapes of women and attacks on Muslims.[260]

Pakistan

"We have been considered only fit to sing and dance at weddings, and that's it".[261] Trans people generally in Pakistan are forced to eke out a living through dancing at festivals and weddings or through sex work. Transphobic violence and discrimination are common. In May 2016 a 23-year-old Pakistani transgender activist, Alisha, was shot eight times and died after delays in treatment. Hospital staff reportedly taunted her and could not decide whether to put her in a male or female ward, according to her friends.[262]

The wars and Western intervention just over the border in Afghanistan, in which the Pakistani military and intelligence agencies are deeply involved, have created tensions in a society where poverty and ethnic conflict, particularly impacting the Pashtun minority, are endemic.

In 2012, Pakistan's Supreme Court declared equal rights for transgender citizens, including the right to inherit property and assets.[263] They were also granted the vote in 2011.

Bindiya Rana, who was the first transgender woman to stand as a provincial political candidate in Pakistan, was quoted in 2014 as saying that previous changes in the law, which came into effect in 2012, had not been enough to change lives:

> In Pakistan we are recognised and there are some jobs — mostly on three-month contracts or with NGOs — but not across the employment sector... The government have not supported us — they haven't implemented the law. I had more opposition when I fought in the election from politicians than I did from the public. Society in Pakistan is more understanding, more accepting and supportive of us than the government is. We have

claimed our space in the law, but we are not protected by it.[264]

In May 2018 Pakistan's parliament passed legislation guaranteeing rights for transgender citizens and proscribing discrimination by employers and private businesses. Despite this, as in India, the gap between the limited rights of the official position for trans and LGB people and the reality on the ground remains wide.

The new law gives people the right to self-identify as male, female, or a blend of genders and to obtain passports, driving licences and other official documents in their chosen gender. According to reports, people will have the right to express their gender as they wish, and their gender identity is defined as "a person's innermost and individual sense of self as male, female or a blend of both, or neither; that can correspond or not to the sex assigned at birth".[265]

The change in the law followed a fatwa or ruling by a group of fifty leading Muslim clerics in 2016 which declared that transgender people who have "visible signs" of one gender or the other can legally marry someone with "visible signs" of the other and should not be discriminated against or disinherited by families. However, those with visible signs of both genders would still be banned from marriage.[266]

Thus, marriage between trans people, or trans and cisgender people, would be possible in some circumstances but would still remain strictly regulated.

TransAction, a transgender advocacy organisation in Pakistan, welcomed the new law.[267] Veteran transgender activist Rana said, "I thought this would never be achieved in my lifetime, but I am fortunate to have seen my own parliament pass this bill."

TransAction has suggested that there are around half a million transgender people in Pakistan, and pointed out that 45 trans people had been killed in 2015/16 in one Pakistani province alone (Khyber Pakhtunkhwa), where they estimated there were around 45,000 trans people.[268]

The legal advance was welcome in that it could begin to change attitudes towards trans people in a country where being transgender usually means being driven to the margins of society, unable to find employment and often being excluded from their families. Trans people generally in Pakistan are forced to eke out a living through dancing at festivals and weddings or through sex work.

Bangladesh

"The few of us who haven't left the country are too afraid to get organized".[269]

In Bangladesh, with a population of 163 million, trans rights groups estimate that although there are only around 10,000 officially registered Hijras there are close to half a million trans people. For the first time in 2019 Hijras were allowed to register to vote, and the first openly Hijra candidate (Pinki Khatun) in a local election was elected as vice-chair of a town council.[270]

As elsewhere, the Hijra tradition stems from ancient times but today's Bangladeshi Hijras remain similarly marginalised to others on the Indian subcontinent. Despite official state recognition as a "third gender" passed in 2013 they continue to face discrimination, harassment and sometimes violent attack.[271]

There are no laws in Bangladesh to protect trans people from such harassment, and same-sex sexual activity is punishable by fines and sentences up to life imprisonment.

Human Rights Watch reported in 2016 that:

The third gender status [in 2013] came with no official definition but could ostensibly accord hijras education, health, and housing rights. However, the decree did not indicate any process by which legal recognition as a third gender should be conferred. In December 2014, a group of 12 hijras were selected for a government employment scheme, and in early 2015 they were subjected to invasive and abusive exams as part of the hiring process. The hijras said they were asked humiliating questions about their bodies, and some reported that the physicians in charge of the exams called them "disgusting" and then instructed hospital janitors and security guards to conduct physical exams, which included touching their genitals. Shortly after the medical exams, the hijras' names were exposed in a newspaper article that declared them impostors because they were "really men". The 12 were denied their employment positions and report increased harassment from neighbours.[272]

As elsewhere in the subcontinent, transgender people in Bangladesh normally find themselves disowned and excluded from their families and having to resort to odd jobs, petty crime, begging and sex work to get by. Despite this, 1,000 Bangladeshi transgender people held the country's first ever Pride March through the streets of the country's capital, Dhaka, in 2014 demanding equal rights and protesting transphobic violence.[273]

Prominent LGBT+ activists have been murdered. On 26th April 2016 Xulhaz Mannan, the editor of Roopbaan, the only LGBT+ magazine in the country, was hacked to death with machetes along with Tanay Mojumdar for their activities in fighting for the LGBT+ community. He had co-organised the Bengali Rainbow Rally held in 2014 and 2015 on the Bengali New Year.[274] Police banned the rally in 2016 claiming security threats.

Four days after the murders, Ansar al-Islam (a Bangladeshi armed group claiming links to al-Qa'ida and Islamic State in the Indian subcontinent) released a statement claiming responsibility. There has been little official sympathy or action, reinforcing the fear and distrust of the police commonly felt among LGBT+ activists in Bangladesh.

An indication of the official attitude was the comment by the Home Minister Asaduzzaman Khan Kamal who said: "[o]ur society does not allow any movement that promotes unnatural sex." As in the cases of secular bloggers who have been killed since 2013, government officials implied that activists had brought the situation on themselves. Despite Bangladesh's secular constitution homophobic fanatics took it upon themselves to target and brutally murder those who have criticised religious intolerance and argued for women's and LGBT+ rights.

In April 2017, a year after the murders, Ta, a Bangladeshi

LGBT+ activist, wrote in an Amnesty International article from which the quote at the top of this section is drawn:

> Foolishly, I thought that the murderers would be arrested within six months. Instead, very little has happened. On 10 January 2017, police missed their ninth deadline for filing an investigation report into the killings. As a community, our activities have all but stopped. The few of us who haven't left the country are too afraid to get organized.[275]

Africa

"We will fight these vermins called homosexuals or gays the same way we are fighting malaria-causing mosquitoes, if not more aggressively".[276]

In most African countries transgender people are an almost invisible despised minority subject to violent oppression. In several countries vicious homophobic and transphobic laws have been passed or strengthened in recent times and now carry even heavier sentences.

Amnesty International data shows that same-sex activity is prohibited in around seventy counties of the world, including thirty-four out of fifty-five African countries.[277] In four of these it is punishable by death. This can affect trans people too, of course, not just because of the same-sex sexuality of some but also because it encourages widespread discrimination within general healthcare and sexual health services. The medical and social attitudes towards trans people as "sick" or "mentally ill" further reduces the potential for vital access to services since people are effectively forced to disclose their gender status.

This reactionary process has been driven by religious fundamentalism (often linked to US-based Christian groups), political opportunism and cultural conservatism, as well as myths about the past.

The situation in Africa was not always so hostile. Leslie Feinberg gives a number of examples of transgender figures from Africa's pre-colonial past. One example was Nzinga, king of Angola from 1624 until 1653, a woman who ruled as a king. She dressed in male clothes and led armies in warfare against the Portuguese.[278] Feinberg writes:

> African spiritual beliefs and intersexual deities and sex/gender transformation among their followers have been documented among the Akan, Ambo-Kwanyama, Bobo, Chokwe, Dahomeans (of Benin), Dogon, Bambara, Etik, Handa Humbe, Hunde, Ibo, Jukun, Kimbundu, Konso, Kunama, Lamba, Lango, Luba, Lulua, Musho, Nuba, Ovimbundu, Rundi, Shona-Karonga, Venda, Vili-Kongo and Yoruba.[279]

The great carve up of African countries and societies by Western imperialisms (Britain, Germany, France, Belgium) in the 18th and 19th centuries meant the wholesale export of laws, proscriptions and missionaries to the new colonies to convert and subjugate whole populations so that the imperialist rulers could get their hands on abundant African natural resources for rapidly expanding capitalist industries, as well as slaves and cheap labourers for mines and plantations.[280]

Traditional cultures and belief systems that might have had more recognition of trans people were suppressed, trashed and sometimes eradicated so that today the very folk memories of these earlier times may be completely denied by those whose interests lie in maintaining their dominant positions by scape-goating such vulnerable minorities.

In Egypt, according to the online LGBT+ organisation AllOut, in late 2017 forty-three people were arrested and charged with "promoting sexual deviancy" after film of someone waving a rainbow flag in solidarity at a concert where one of the bands' lead singers was openly gay was circulated. Many were sentenced to six years in prison for the crimes of "habitual debauchery" and "inciting immorality".[281]

The crackdown followed the brutal military coup against the Muslim Brotherhood government headed by Mohamed Morsi. Thousands of Brotherhood supporters and others were killed and jailed. The current dictatorship under Abdel Fatteh al-Sisi is actually more repressive towards independent trade unions, the left and LGBT+ groups than the Mubarak regime toppled by the popular uprising of 2011.

Nigeria, one of most populous and modern African societies, is also another example of a hostile country for LGBT+ people, as are Gambia and Uganda.[282] In 2014 Nigeria's President Goodluck Johnathan signed into law the Same Sex Marriage Prohibition Act which carries sentences of up to 14 years for some sexual acts.[283] Also in 2014, Gambia's President Yahya Jammeh announced: "We will fight these vermins called homosexuals or gays the same way we are fighting malaria-causing mosquitoes, if not more aggressively".[284]

Another notorious example was Uganda's Anti-Homosexuality Act, strengthening the already oppressive colonial-era anti-LGBT+ laws, which was passed in February 2014. A new version was passed in 2018 which extended the maximum sentence from seven years to life and for the first time included those accused of "promoting" homosexuality.[285]

Evidently Simon Lokodo, Uganda's Ethics and Integrity Minister and architect of the new homophobic law, cannot imagine kissing a man, comparing doing so to coprophilia: "I think I shall die," he said in 2014. "I would not exist. It is inhuman. I would be mad. Just imagine eating your faeces".[286]

In Uganda the mainstream media fan the flames of generalised homophobia and transphobia. In the run up to the passage of the anti-gay legislation one tabloid paper in 2010 even published mugshots and other details of dozens of alleged gay men under the heading "Hang Them". Even after the murder of one of the named men the editor expressed no regrets.[287]

The small transgender community in Kampala, Uganda's capital, consists largely of young trans people driven out of their families and living a highly marginalised hand to mouth existence. They lack safe venues in which to socialise and are unable to go about in Ugandan society as their true selves. Isolated from general society they are also isolated from the gay community — itself under vicious attack.[288]

Today in many African countries LGBT+ people do not have the organisation or confidence even to hold a Pride event. In others, where such events are organised they are often met with state repression or attacks from bigots to which the police either turn a blind eye or are themselves involved.

The picture is not uniformly bleak however. In early 2019

Angola decriminalised same sex relationships following years of campaigning by the country's only LGBT rights advocacy group, Iris Angola.[289] This followed Mozambique, another former Portuguese colony's decriminalisation in 2015. LGBT+ activists had hoped that Kenya would follow suit in 2019 and ditch colonial-era anti-LGBT laws but instead the Kenyan High Court ruled to maintain them.[290]

South Africa

While the majority of African countries still criminalise same-sex sexuality and gender variance, South Africa appears to buck the trend. When the country's new constitution was adopted in 1996, as a result of the lobbying efforts of LGBT groups and the support of the African National Congress, it became the first country in the modern world to outlaw discrimination based on sexual orientation.

This was followed in 1998 by legislation intended to protect lesbian, gay, bisexual, transsexual and intersex South African citizens from employment discrimination, and legislation permitting same-sex marriage and civil unions was passed in 2006. The legislation has a get out clause, however, in that it allows individual civil servants and members of the clergy to decline to perform such ceremonies if they wish.

Under the former apartheid regime, male homosexuality had been punishable by up to seven years in jail, although female homosexuality was not covered, as had been the case in Britain and many former British colonial regimes.

An important victory for trans people in South Africa was the establishment of the first specifically transgender, gender diverse organisation on the continent, Gender DynamiX, in Cape Town in 2005.[291]

Despite the progressive legislation, however, LGBT+ people in South Africa point out that public attitudes have been much slower to change and much of the country remains very socially conservative, with strong religious underpinnings that continue to claim that same-sex sexuality and gender variant lifestyles are "wrong". There is a big mismatch between words and deeds, between the letter of the law and lived experience for many LGBT+ people. In some of the urban areas there are

LGBT+ clubs and annual Pride marches, but in rural areas hostility to homosexuality and gender transgression can be harsh and LGBT+ people live with the constant threat of violence.

Trans people in South Africa, as in much of the rest of the continent, often remain an almost invisible minority, even of the LGBT+ community, and few human rights organisations address this invisibility. At the very least this can discourage people from coming out of the closet.

The South African government has continued to resist calls to adopt hate crime laws to tackle homophobia. According to a five-year monitoring report the most discriminated against group in South Africa are the LGBT+ community, and 35 percent of all the hate crimes reported came from LGBT+ people.[292]

Despite equality legislation, there continue to be many instances of discrimination against LGBT+ people, including physical attacks. Many lesbians and trans men have been victims of so-called "corrective rape", often gang rape, fuelled by the deeply misogynist view that women must only be lesbians or bisexual because they have not had sex with men, or the right men.[293] It is thought that around 500,000 rapes occur annually in South Africa. "Corrective rape" of lesbians is mostly targeted at black lesbians, particularly in the townships, but rapes of males (particularly transgender men) are also thought to be quite common.[294]

Transgender people can also find it very difficult or almost impossible to access support for gender transition via the country's medical services. Minimal funding, particularly in the post-2008 financial environment, can mean waiting years for medical support for transition.

The Alteration of Sex Description and Sex Status Act 2003 allows transgender people to apply to change their gender marker in the birth register but this must be supported by medical evidence such as hormonal treatment. The evidence does not need to include gender affirmation surgery. However, access to especially male hormone therapy can be difficult due to short supplies and medical gatekeeping, and the waiting time for approval to change gender markers can run into years. In the case of one clinic (there are just four in South Africa offering trans-specific health care) the waiting list for gender affirmation surgery for trans women was 25 years![295]

Cyril Ramaphosa, elected President in 2018, seemed to have a more liberal record of support for LGBT+ people than his predecessor Jacob Zuma who was openly hostile to LGBT+ rights and refused to condemn anti-LGBT measures in other African countries. Along with vigorous campaigning by LGBT+ organisations — support, counselling, public marches, Prides and protests, outreach measures to help tackle high HIV/Aids levels in the country, and more — activists hope that the situation for LGBT+ people can improve to better match the formal position of equal rights.

South Korea

Despite a legal change in 2006 allowing trans people to transition and be legally recognised in their new gender there are still serious impediments to full recognition for transgender people in South Korea.[296]

While the law does not specify preconditions for changing gender the Korean Supreme Court set out the following conditions: the person must have no underage children, they must meet certain medical criteria like having a psychiatric diagnosis, and they must undergo sterilisation and gender affirmation surgery.

It is estimated that only around 13 percent of trans people undergo this demanding and expensive process. One judge even demanded that the applicant should produce a photo of their genitals as proof of sex affirmation surgery.

The cost of transition in South Korea is prohibitive for most trans people because most hospitals are privately owned and run, and national health insurance, which may cover most other eventualities, will not cover gender affirmation surgery or treatment.

A further issue related to formal transition is that it is not possible to change one's Resident Registration Number (RRN — equivalent to the UK National Insurance Number) without legal transition. This number is needed to vote, apply for jobs or even get a cell phone. The number also codes for the person's gender, presenting an obvious problem for trans people. Many trans people have had to give up having a cell phone, buying insurance or voting.

Unsurprisingly, trans people in South Korea suffer a high degree of job insecurity, even compared to other LGBT+ people (only about a quarter of trans people are in secure employment) and they earn significantly less on average. Many are forced to rely on working in the sex industry.[297]

In addition to state hostility, prevarication and obstruction, and transphobia from the political right, trans people in South Korea are increasingly facing transphobic arguments from trans exclusionary radical feminists and trans critics on the left who take much of their inspiration from British and American trans exclusionary radical feminists. There have been arguments and online debates on the relationship between feminism and trans issues.

Latin America

"Altogether I have been shot nine times".[298]

Latin America in general has a terrible record of trans murders, suicides and widespread transphobic violence and discrimination.

Colombia, however, stands out as not only having legislation permitting same-sex marriage (passed in 2016) but as the only South American country which allows self-declaration of gender. Transgender people have been able to change their names since 1998 and to change their official gender status since 2015. There is no legal provision for a third gender, however.[299]

There is not space to discuss in detail how this relative social liberalism in respect of gender relations and LGBT+ rights has developed in a country riven by decades of civil war but part of the context involved the peace deal negotiated in the watershed year of 2016 between the government and the main armed resistance organisation, the FARC-EP (the Revolutionary Armed Forces of Colombia — People's Army). Women's rights, LGBT rights, democracy and the peace process were all elements in these negotiations. Despite the initial setback of the rejection of a deal in a plebiscite of October 2016, a revised version was finally accepted two months later.[300]

Nevertheless, despite the peace process and the general fall in the country's murder rate, there is still widespread hostility to LGBT+ people and the number of mainly gay men and transgender women (according to the main LGBT organisation Colombia Diversa[301]) murdered annually is still running at around 100 per year.

Trans peoples in Colombia and other Latin America countries, as elsewhere, are often forced through economic circumstances into sex work where many face the constant threat of rape, violence and murder from clients and police in a culture dominated by traditional machismo, Catholicism and minimal reproductive rights for women.

There is considerable general hostility to LGBT+ people and especially to trans women. Nearly 80 percent of all recorded worldwide killings of transgender people in recent years took place in Latin America.

The largest and most populous South American country, Brazil, has one of the highest trans murders rates in the world. Stonewall noted that in the year to November 2018, 167 trans people were murdered, the highest number in the world. Indianare Siqueira, a trans woman activist and politician in Rio de Janeiro, explained,

Trans people in Brazil live in a context of total abandonment by a society that attacks and kills us. The Government does not have public policies including us and also mechanisms through Government departments that protect us.[302]

The election of Jair Bolsonaro, who took office on 1 January 2019, a man who had said he would rather his son died than be gay, was a huge boost to LGBT+phobia and the far-right in Brazil and the whole region after a decade and a half of left-of-centre government by the Workers Party. In the Stonewall article referred to, trans activists reported that at least four murders of trans women were directly linked to Bolsonaro supporters.

In January 2019 a man was arrested suspected of murdering trans woman Quelly Da Silva and cutting out her heart. Yet he could not be charged with a hate crime against a trans person because, like many countries, Brazil does not recognise hate crime against trans people, nor is it possible to charge perpetrators with "femicide" because the law describes femicide as the killing of a woman due to her "sex" not her gender.[303] Femicide carries 12 to 30 years imprisonment as opposed to 6 to 20 years for simple homicide.

In the wake of Bolsonaro's election trans organisations made appeals for solidarity from supporters abroad and even began discussing safe houses and emigration routes for threatened trans people.

Elsewhere in Latin America, an Avert report originally published in 2017, updated in 2019, highlighted one local transgender organisation in Honduras, Colectivo Unidad Color Rosa, that had six of its seven members murdered. A local specialist in public health and transgender rights in San Pedro Sula, Honduras, said:

> Altogether I have been shot nine times. There are witnesses but they are also afraid to make a statement. I myself have witnessed many other police attacks but I'm also afraid to report them. This is what the police call "social cleansing". According to them, it's because there are lots of complaints against transgender women doing sex work.[304]

In Guatemala between 2005 and 2012, 35 transgender women were murdered with just one person prosecuted. In Honduras there were 61 murders of LGBTI people between 2008 and 2011, with ten prosecutions. Turning to the authorities for help often proves to be fruitless — eighty percent of trans activists across Latin America reported violence or threats of violence from state actors such as the police. This is the dire current context in which LGBT+ and trans organisations there struggle for legal rights and to support one another.

HIV/Aids

Another huge source of mortality and risk of insecurity and poor life chances for transgender people right across the world is HIV/Aids. This is particularly true in Central and South America. A number of reports demonstrate the extent to which HIV/Aids infection is a constant threat for many LGBT+ people, especially trans people.[305]

These survey figures suggest that while the rates of HIV infection among transgender people vary greatly from country to country, globally an average of 19 percent of transgender people are infected, a rate roughly 49 times higher than the general population. Many of those infected are unaware as they cannot access testing and even if they can get tested they are often unable to access appropriate health care.

The HIV+ rate is generally higher among trans women than trans men, although much less is known about the situation among trans men. Sometimes the virus can be transmitted by sharing syringes used for injecting hormones or for the doubly dangerous practice of injecting cheaper industrial silicone straight into tissues for body shaping (a practice known as "pumping").

As we have seen, trans people in many places often have little option but to sell sex. In India an estimated 90 percent of trans people are in this situation, in Malaysia 84 percent, 81 percent in Indonesia, 47 percent in El Salvador and 36 percent in Cambodia.

The UNAIDS Gap Report in 2014 suggested that HIV infection was around nine times higher among transgender sex workers than genetic female sex workers.[306] Often knowledge about safe sex and the use of condoms is very limited among transgender sex workers.

The hostility, moralism and transphobia from health professionals which transgender people, and sex workers in particular, often face can make it harder to access health and advice services. State health care staff and health care insurers often ignore the needs of transgender people. Such stigma also makes it harder to insist on safe sex or condom use and often sex workers get paid more not to use condoms resulting in much higher levels of infection.

In some places, police have shut down organisations offering HIV prevention services on the grounds that they are complicit in illegal sex work. Failure to criminalise discrimination against trans people by most countries leaves people isolated and vulnerable.

As a result of their marginalisation, HIV testing rates are

much lower among transgender people and access to health care and HIV prevention schemes are much more limited and difficult. One source found that 61 percent of national HIV strategies did not include transgender people in their target audience.[307]

There are a few examples where initiatives do include trans people and employ trans people as staff, such as the Pehchan project in India, initiated in 2010. This has reached more than 433,000 people and infection rates have been reduced saving many lives.

As a result of campaigning by LGBT+ and transgender advocacy organisations other projects in El Salvador and Thailand have also been able to offer access to general medical and mental health services, HIV testing and counselling as well as communication on condom use and safe sex techniques. These struggles inevitably carry risks to the safety of campaigning trans advocates and their supporters.

Europe

The situation for transgender people in Europe can be summed up in one short sentence: "There is no safe country for trans people".[308] In 2019 the report pointed out that 16 countries in Europe and Central Asia still require people to be sterilised before their gender change can be legally recognised.[309]

This is despite a number of countries having seen greater civil and workplace rights and protections for LGBT+ people, even if these may not be applied consistently or effectively, or even at all in some cases. Thus several European countries — Britain, Ireland, France, Germany, Malta, Denmark, for example — have passed LGBT+ friendly legislation in respect of civil partnerships, same-sex marriage, hate crime and gender recognition in recent years.

On the other hand the widespread imposition of austerity measures in response to the 2008 crisis, rising inequality, the collapse of the political centre and rising support for far-right, fascist and populist right wing ideologies and parties, often working hand in glove with the Catholic Church or Orthodox Christianity, such as in Hungary, Poland, France and Russia, have seen some of these legislative advances come under threat.

Harassment and violence against trans people is often still as common in Europe as elsewhere in the world. Between 2008 and 2016 more than 100 murders of trans people were documented across the continent. Younger trans people, especially those engaged in sex work or those who are migrants and/ or black or Asian bear an even greater risk of discrimination, harassment and assault.

Only 13 European states explicitly prohibited transphobic violence. Thus, although Europe includes several states that have the most advanced legal rights for trans people in the world, the general picture painted, for example, by Transgender Europe's annual *Trans Rights Europe Index* is very variable.

In terms of gender transition and formal recognition, recent surveys have shown that both transgender surgery *and* sterilisation are required before legal recognition of gender reassignment/affirmation in 24 European countries including Russia, France and Switzerland. In these countries it is also not legally possible for a person to self-declare their gender.

In France campaigners are seeking to liberalise the situation for trans people but even the changes they are currently fighting for would leave many young trans people outside the provisions and adults would still need a legal ruling on changing gender from a judge. France therefore remains a long way from the principle of self-declaration and self-determination that most trans people and trans organisations aspire to.[310]

Elsewhere, proof of gender affirmation surgery is not required for official gender recognition in 15 countries, including Britain, Ireland, Sweden, Italy and Spain.

In July 2015 the Irish parliament passed a Gender Recognition Act very similar in its main provisions to the British one. The Irish law makes some provision for 16 and 17 year olds but the process is more complex and difficult than for those over 18 years old. Nevertheless, it is significantly more trans-friendly than the current British Gender Recognition Act in that it allows trans people to self-declare their gender status and obtain a replacement birth certificate in their new name.[311]

Some Scandinavian countries have also adopted relatively trans-friendly legislation. Thus after more than a decade of determined campaigning by activists and socialists Norway's parliament approved a law in mid-2016 which allows trans people to self-declare their gender status.[312] Norway, and now Belgium and Portugal in 2018, join only six countries in Europe, along with Denmark, Ireland and Malta, where the process for legal definition of gender identity has been separated from any medical (physical and/or psychiatric) interventions and assessment.[313]

However, much of Europe still lags far behind these few countries. Some have made virtually no progress from the bad old days. Thus gender affirmation surgery itself is not even considered legal in Hungary, Cyprus, Moldova and Albania, and Hungary and Albania do not recognise transgender in law.

Conclusions

These snapshots of life for transgender people around the world demonstrate that transphobia is endemic in modern capitalism although it varies in form and intensity from society to society and over time. A range of factors contribute to this — cultural and religious issues, economic factors such as crises and levels of wealth and poverty. A very common factor is how prejudice, discrimination and violence against trans people and others is whipped up as part of general repression of opposition to growing inequality and disparities of wealth.

Despite this, everywhere we have looked trans people continue to organise and resist as best they can and to support and protect one another, lobby for improved rights as well as protest at transphobic attacks, police indifference and state transphobia. Much of the time, they are organising under very difficult circumstances and many still pay with their lives for doing so.

Chapter 7
Trump, trans rights and the US bathroom wars

> A transgender Honduran woman died in ICE [United States Immigration and Customs Enforcement] custody...after coming to the US as part of a caravan of Central American migrants, including several dozen other transgender women fleeing persecution in their respective countries. Roxana Hernandez reportedly died from HIV-related complications following an alleged five-day detention in what's known by immigrant rights groups as the "ice box" — ICE detention facilities notorious for their freezing temperatures.[314]

Roxana Hernandez is just one of the victims of the xenophobia, homophobia and transphobia of US official policy towards migrants and refugees that has been heightened by the racist and anti-LGBT+ rhetoric of President Trump and his administration.

The shocking success of Donald Trump's presidential campaign in 2016 was a jolting example of the political volatility inherent in capitalism's systemic crisis in the second decade of the 21st century.

His rapid appointment of a rogue's gallery of bigots, multimillionaires, alt-right ideologues, corporate lobbyists and Trump family members to his administration signalled that attacks on women, Muslims, LGBT+ people, black and Hispanic people would not be long in coming.

After slashing funding and undermining women's reproductive rights and attempting to ban Muslim immigration to the US, in July 2017 the president signed an order banning transgender people from serving in the US military, citing the costs of their medical care and "disruption" as justifications.[315] To find themselves apparently Tweeted out of their jobs overnight will have been deeply shocking and disorientating to trans people in the military.

Later in the year, a court temporarily blocked Trump's ban but his Executive Order signalled which way the wind was blowing under his right wing administration and the attacks on trans and LGB people have continued. The ban on trans people in the military which came into force in April 2019 was a very serious but perhaps not surprising attack on an oppressed group following hard on the heels of his attempts to cut medical support for millions of poorer Americans in his assault on Obamacare. The fact that this was defeated seemed to enhance his vindictiveness towards minority groups.

His administration's attacks on trans people and encouragement for those wanting to roll back the clock on a range of LGBT+ rights sparked mass protests. Following his military ban hundreds of protesters carrying placards saying "Resist!" marched in New York and there were other protests in San Francisco and Washington.[316] The blows kept on coming and there were more protests in New York and elsewhere in October 2017 over the Trump administration's decision that transgender people were not to be included any longer in the 1964 Federal Civil Rights Act that bans discrimination at work. The Justice Department released a sweeping "license to discriminate" allowing federal agencies, government contractors, and even businesses to engage in illegal discrimination as long as they could cite religious reasons for doing so. The National Center for Transgender Equality published a long list of measures announced by the Trump administration and his appointees in 2019 as the attacks continued unabated through his term of office.[317]

The reasons Trump offered in justification of his ban on trans people in the military did not match the economic realities. Estimates of the number of trans people in the US military in 2017 varied from about 2,500 to 15,000 (out of 1.28 million active personnel plus 800,000 reservists). Clearly the cost of implementing a trans-inclusive military policy was not the real reason, given that the US Department of Defense spent around ten times more on the erectile dysfunction drug Viagra ($41.6 million annually) in 2016 than it would cost for transgender care (about $8 million between 2016-2018).[318] And it is a vanishingly tiny drop in the ocean of the total US military's health care budget of $50 billion or the overall military spending of $989 billion in 2019.[319]

When it comes to arms spending by the US government there seems to be no limit to the depth of the federal pocket. In April 2017, President Trump ordered the firing of 59 Tomahawk missiles at a government controlled Syrian airbase. Each of these missiles is worth around $832,000 and the cost of these 59 was over $49 million.

In spite of its role as the world's primary imperialist bully boy, the fact is that a lot of poorer Americans, including trans people, have traditionally joined the US military to get a job and training, and to have access to decent healthcare that they might otherwise be denied.

Part of the significance of the Trump ban has been that what the Trump administration would like to do to trans US military personnel today, transphobic individuals and organisations in civilian life will try to emulate tomorrow.

Trump ditched his previously more liberal position on LGBT+ issues (he had originally been pro-choice on abortion, too) and readily embraced homophobia and transphobia during his campaign as a means to shore up his right wing constituency.

Prior to Trump's election there had been a slow liberalisation in US society and in the military in respect of LGBT+ rights. In 2014, President Obama had issued an executive order prohibiting discrimination against transgender federal employees.

In 2016, the Departments of Justice and Education followed this with federal guidance indicating that transgender people in education should be treated as the gender to which they aspired and should therefore, for example, be able to use gender appropriate toilet facilities. However, on 26 July 2017 the Departments of Justice and Education withdrew this guidance and stated that future guidance should be issued at the state level.

In April 2018 a new ruling proposed by the Trump administration to allow medical staff to refuse treatment of any kind (not just related to gender identity, per se) on the grounds of religious objection was implemented.

The obvious problem with this is that it confers "freedom" on state and other legislative bodies (who vary greatly in their attitudes to transgender people) to make up their own state level and even local level laws and regulations. For example, it remains the case that some courts in the US will negatively take into consideration a parent's transgender status when deciding on child custody and visitation rights. Given the lobbying power of various well-funded right wing religious and "family oriented" groups, this was rightly seen as another huge red light for trans people in the US.

Trans tipping point in America?

Prior to Donald Trump's election it seemed that much of the media coverage of trans people and trans issues had been broadly more sympathetic and less sensationalist and prurient than it had been in the past.

Having been marginalised from the mainstream gay rights movement in the mid-1970s trans people found themselves the subject of vicious transphobic policies once again from the early 1980s.

An infamous report for the US government by Janice Raymond in 1980 was used as a justification for removing access to health care for transsexual people under the cuts implemented by the Reagan administration.[320] Its effect was to eliminate federal and state aid for indigent and imprisoned transsexuals. It forced incarcerated trans people to file federal court cases to get back trans related medical treatment that they lost as a result of Raymond's transphobic article.

Supervised in her doctoral studies by Mary Daly, another transphobic radical feminist who described trans people as "Frankensteinian", Raymond in her 1979 book, *The Transsexual*

Empire: The Making of the She-Male, wrote: "All transsexuals rape women's bodies by reducing the real female form to an artefact, appropriating this body for themselves... Transsexuals merely cut off the most obvious means of invading women, so that they seem non-invasive".[321]

Raymond's 1980 report was used as a pretext by private health insurance companies to follow the federal government's lead and deny or disallow services to trans patients for any medical treatment remotely related to being trans, including breast cancer or genital cancer. The cancer denials were held to be a consequence of treatment for transsexuality and trans people's rights under Medicaid and Medicare were abrogated for any sex reassignment surgery or any trans related care.

The situation was compounded by the HIV/Aids epidemic in the US in the 1980s and 1990s that had a devastating impact on trans women especially, forcing LGBT+ people to set up direct action campaigning organisations to fight for desperately needed health care, support and palliative care.

By the early 2000s the situation seemed to be improving as a result of such campaigning and the greater visibility of trans people. Various trans role models began to emerge. For example, the African-American trans actor Laverne Cox played the role of a prisoner in the acclaimed US series *Orange is the New Black.* She received the mainstream accolade of appearing on the cover of *Time* magazine in 2014 in a perhaps over-optimistic article entitled "The Transgender Tipping Point", suggesting that trans acceptance was now becoming mainstream.[322]

The same year another American celebrity, Janet Mock, wrote a book about her own transition, *Redefining Realness,* which received rave reviews in the mainstream media and won awards for its "honesty and bravery".[323]

Had some sort of tipping point really been reached? Studies suggest that while the struggles of recent decades have undeniably led to advances for trans people, transphobia remains a damaging, dangerous and sometimes deadly reality for most trans people, not least in the United States. The high visibility of a small number of rich, beautiful or famous trans women (trans men seem to have much less of a public profile) is a long way removed from the real life experiences of most trans people.

Findings from the National Transgender Discrimination Survey in the US in 2014 found that against a general population background suicide rate of 4.6 percent of lifetime suicide attempts, transgender respondents reported a 41 percent rate. The rate was 10-20 percent for LGB adults. The figure for trans men at 46 percent was slightly higher than that for trans women at 42 percent.[324]

Age, social class and poverty were important factors. Suicide attempts were highest among 18–24 year olds, at 45 percent. The figure was 54 percent among those in ethnic minority groups, 56 percent among American Indian or Alaskan Natives, and 54 percent among the poorest, defined as those living on less than $10,000 a year.

For most transgender people in the US and around the world not much seems to have changed since the middle of the 20th century or even earlier. Hatred, bigotry and hostility to LGBT+ people, and especially towards those who are transgender, remain widespread.

The mass murder at the Pulse club in Orlando, Florida in June 2016 was a particularly bloody and horrific outrage, just one of many attacks on LGBT+ people over the years.[325] In the Pulse shootings 50 people were killed and another 53 were injured by a gunman armed with assault rifles. At the time, some claimed it was the worst mass shooting in US history, although in fact that dishonour probably belongs to the massacre of Oglala Sioux people at Wounded Knee by the US cavalry in 1891. It was certainly the worst attack on LGBT+ people in US history. The vast majority of the victims were African-American or Latino people, and a number of them were transgender. This was not just a homophobic attack but also a transphobic one.

Being transgender in the US

Laws on sexual practices including sodomy in North American states were inherited from the British legal system and carried over after American Independence in 1776.

Susan Stryker in *Transgender History* points out that specifically transphobic prohibitions have a long history in the

United States, dating from at least the 1850s. She writes:

> The transgender movement for social change that emerged in the United States after World War II traces its roots to conditions that began taking shape about a century earlier. Starting in the 1850s, a number of US cities began passing municipal ordinances that made it illegal for a man or women to appear in public "in a dress not belonging to his or her sex". There is an even longer history of public regulation of dress — dating to the colonial period, ordinances have forbidden people from disguising themselves in public or wearing clothes associated with a particular rank or profession, and some also prevented white people from impersonating Indians or black people from impersonating whites — but the wave of local legislation in the 1850s represented a new development specific to gender presentation. We can interpret this as a response to the changing ways that some people lived their lives in cities.[326]

In San Francisco the relevant ordinance passed in 1863 allowed for a fine of up to $500 for violation, a huge sum of money at the time. Stryker points out that Enlightenment and "first wave feminist" ideas about women's rights, early campaigns for universal suffrage and votes for women, over property rights, and freedom to dress more comfortably were also likely factors in city fathers introducing regulations intended to block these early demands for gender equality.

Relaxation of gender specific social dress codes could be seen as undermining gender appropriate behaviour and thus as threatening the "natural order." During the gold and silver rush era in California in the mid-19th century there was much social comment by Euro-Americans about being unable to distinguish between male and female Chinese immigrants because they both wore their hair long and dressed in very similar pyjama-like garments.

Such ordinances on dress codes continued to be adopted into the 20th century, right up to those in Cincinnatti, Ohio in

1974. Historian John D'Emilio links these recent repressive measures to a reaction against the new possibilities for lesbian, gay and trans people.[327] Opportunities to socialise and live different lifestyles were growing as the numbers of Americans living in urban environments overtook the rural population in the 1920s. Elements of popular culture, particularly in music and theatre, offered new horizons.

Susan Stryker is one of the few writers to have begun to draw together the long history of transphobia among non-indigenous people in the US. However she does not examine traditions among First Nation or indigenous societies in the Americas which were often very different in their attitudes to transgender (sometimes called Two Spirit) people.

She has described this period as one in which both homo-sexuality and gender variance became increasingly patholo-gised and legally proscribed in the US. The laws which were passed in states such as California in the 19th century to enforce gender specific dress codes and even hair length persisted until quite recently and were used to criminalise, in particular, cross-dressing men. Wearing less than three items of "male" attire meant a man could be subject to arrest. These codes were used to harass gender variant people including drag queens and were one of the causes of the pent up frustrations and anger that triggered the Stonewall Rebellion and other acts of resist-ance in the 1960s.

While most states had removed anti-sodomy laws during the 20th century, homosexuality between consenting adults was not finally decriminalised in the United States until 2003. It had been declassified in the official *Diagnostic and Statis-tical Manual of Mental Disorders* (DSM) as a mental illness in 1973. For transgender people, the diagnosis of "gender identity disorder" was only dropped from the DSM in 2013 in favour of "gender dysphoria", defined as a condition of distress which trans people may feel about the mismatch between their gender identity and their bodies.

Transphobic violence

A Human Rights Campaign post in 2016 pointed out that in the period from 1 January 2008 to 31 December 2014, 108 trans people had been murdered in the United States.[328]

On 4 January 2018, Christa Leigh Steele-Knudslien, Miss Trans America, was found murdered in her home in Massachusetts. She had been repeatedly bludgeoned with a hammer and then stabbed. Her husband was later arrested and charged with her murder. She was the first trans person murdered in the US in 2018.[329]

The 27 trans people murdered in the United States in 2016 were almost all black or Hispanic. Some were killed by their own families.[330] As GLAAD (formerly the Gay and Lesbian Alliance Against Defamation) pointed out, in 2016 transgender people in the US were being killed at a rate of more than two per month.[331]

There are a number of glaring factors which can be unpacked from the figures for trans murders. Looking at cases of sexual and domestic violence, the figures showed black or Hispanic trans women constituted between 61 and 65 percent of the victims against a background figure of 41 percent of trans women generally. Figures for trans men also show high rates of susceptibility to violence and attacks.

Shockingly, the Human Rights Campaign reported that of the 53 transgender murders in the US between 2013 and 2015 *none* was prosecuted or reported as a hate crime. Not until the brutal murder of 17 year-old Mercedes Williamson by Joshua Vallum in 2015 was the 2009 Hate Crimes Prevention Act first used in the US to prosecute someone for a transphobic murder.[332]

Most of the recorded murders have been of trans women, but there are plenty of examples of trans men being attacked and killed as well. Perhaps the best-known US example is from 1993. Brandon Teena, a young trans man, was raped and later shot and stabbed to death by two male acquaintances on New Year's Eve 1993 having been "outed" by local police in Humbolt, Nebraska. The case was brought to world attention through two films: a documentary, *The Brandon Teena Story*, and a more fictionalised academy award-winning account in 1999, *Boys Don't Cry*, starring Hilary Swank.

Despite Brandon's open transgender identity, his stated intention to pursue gender transition and his repeated approaches to health services to seek gender affirmation surgery the final, tragic denial of his true identity and gender status by his family was his burial and headstone which referred to him as "daughter and sister."

Bringing murderers and attackers of trans people to justice faces additional obstacles. In the United States, as in many other countries, we have seen disturbing failures by the police and authorities to recognise or address transphobic hate crime. This is compounded by failure to properly investigate, charge or punish perpetrators.

Indeed, the legal defence of "trans panic" — where someone accused of killing a trans person claims they were overtaken by justified outrage and fell into an uncontrollable panic upon discovering that their victim was trans — has on occasion been upheld by courts in a number of countries including the United States. Such nonsensical and pernicious explanations are, not surprisingly, strongly opposed by LGBT+ and transgender organisations and since August 2013 also in the US by the American Bar Association.[333]

Chelsea Manning

Despite some courts recognising that medical intervention is necessary for the treatment of gender dysphoria, transgender people in the US still face major hurdles. Discrimination by medical staff and institutions is common. One trans person who faced this difficulty of accessing appropriate medical care, compounded because she was a member of the US military at the time and was incarcerated, was Chelsea Manning.

In July 2013 Manning, who as Bradley Manning had passed thousands of classified documents to Wikileaks in protest at US military operations in the Middle East, was sentenced to 35 years in Fort Leavenworth military prison following her conviction for espionage.

The day after sentencing Manning caused a media sensation by announcing that she had had gender identity issues since childhood and from now on wanted to be known as Chelsea. She intended to pursue gender transition. She faced many more difficult years in a US military prison and a long struggle to access medical support from an institution which was under no obligation to provide her with the medical care that a transgender person may need.

In September 2016 Chelsea announced she was not receiving any help in prison in respect of her transition and had begun a hunger strike in protest. She made two suicide attempts. As one of his last acts as US President, Barack Obama commuted and reduced Chelsea's sentence to seven and a half years, meaning that she was released in late 2017. As a legitimate whistle-blower exposing US state and military brutality and illegality many argued that she should never have been imprisoned in the first place. In early 2019 she was again jailed for contempt in refusing to comply with a grand jury subpoena demanding that she testify in an investigation into Wikileaks.[334]

Neoliberal contradictions

The motivations of the anti-trans bigots in the US encompass both right wing religious anti-diversity bigotry and neoliberal rejections of "regulation and red tape" governing matters of "conscience." We need to recognise the nature and impact of neoliberalism that has been the dominant transnational economic ideology since the 1980s. In pursuit of this economic orthodoxy, initially driven by the most powerful single capitalist economy, the United States, country after country has suffered wholesale attempts by ruling classes to shrink state provision, slash public services and welfare, privatise, marketise and casualise employment, and undermine trade union strength.

This has impacted very negatively on oppressed groups, including transgender people, in a range of countries. Racism, Islamophobia, the scapegoating of disabled people, the myth of "welfare queens" and hostility to single parent mothers have often been ramped up to try and divide opposition and resistance to austerity measures, corruption and growing inequality.

The impact on working class people in the US has been very detrimental. Most of the US population suffered falls in their living standards from the 1980s onwards. Many millions no longer feel that life for their children and grandchildren is likely to be better than theirs.

A country used to being top dog for decades now faces direct challenges for economic supremacy from emerging powers like China, now the second largest economy in the world. The squeeze on living standards has resulted in working class incomes declining in relative terms for decades. Historically, the US has been a deeply racist society towards Native Americans, African Americans, and Hispanic people, institutionalised in the violence of the police, the huge numbers of non-whites in the jail system, and the massive under-representation of black and minority ethnic people at all levels of society. Racism and Islamophobia are widespread and deeply entrenched.

The current fight to defend transgender rights needs to be seen within a wider context of resistance such as the emergence of the Black Lives Matter movement, challenging the outrageous numbers of black men killed by police, who are then normally exonerated or acquitted; the #MeToo challenging misogyny in public life; and the mass protests by Native Americans and others over proposed new oil pipelines in North Dakota in 2016 and 2017. Similarly, the fight takes place alongside the struggles of organised labour such as the Chicago teachers over pay and conditions and the campaigns opposing Trump's plans for the border wall with Mexico and the many thousands who organise to support refugees and migrants.

The bathroom wars

From around 2014 in the US the matter of who should be allowed to use public toilets became, bizarrely, a high profile political issue.

In 2015 trans people were banned from using gender-appropriate public toilets in North Carolina under an ordinance called the Public Facilities Privacy & Security Act or the House Bill 2 (HB2), despite the federal Equality Act opposing such discrimination. North Carolina is a state finely politically balanced between conservative rural areas and more politically liberal cities. Since the Republicans won control of the state a few years earlier it had been a political battleground.

HB2 was signed by Republican governor Pat McCrory and backed by the state Republican majority. It voided all local ordinances protecting LGBT+ rights, as well as banning transgender people from using their preferred bathroom, and it allowed businesses to discriminate against LGBT+ people on the grounds of religious belief.

The bridgehead achieved in North Carolina by anti-trans bigots predictably led to demands by reactionary campaigners in other states, often linked to right wing political and religious organisations, to introduce their own bans.

For example in Texas Republican Lieutenant Governor Dan Patrick was quoted in the *Texas Tribune* as saying: "Does anyone in here who has grandchildren, have a granddaughter who's eight or nine, want them to walk into a bathroom with a man?"[335]

By mid-2017 a number of bills had been filed (or carried over from 2016 legislative sessions) in Alabama, Kentucky, Minnesota, Missouri, Illinois, South Carolina, South Dakota, Virginia, Washington and Wyoming. The Wyoming bill was the first of its kind in the state, and it would make it a crime of public indecency to use a bathroom or changing facility designated for the opposite sex.

This all raised the tricky matter of who would monitor the enforcement of such measures on the ground. Would institutions station guards or police outside all the public toilets? That did seem to be what the Alabama Privacy Act proposed, to have attendants "stationed at the door of each rest room to monitor the appropriate use of the rest room and answer any questions or concerns posed by users".[336]

Some of these bills were already mooted before Donald Trump's election, but undoubtedly his ascendancy to the presidency encouraged anti-LGBT+ bigots in more conservative states in their plans to restrict LGB and trans rights.

It is important to be aware that such transphobic campaigning is not simply the expression of prejudice or the airing of mistaken ideas; it is politically orchestrated.

Organisations like Alan Sears' Alliance Defending Freedom, the American Family Association (AFA) and its offshoot the One Million Moms campaign employ highly paid lawyers and lobbyists to co-ordinate opposition to LGBT+ rights. They dig up legal loopholes in state or federal legislation to justify private or public bodies discriminating against transgender or LGB individuals. They have received a big morale boost with Donald Trump's election.

The hysteria in some quarters about the potential for trans people to undermine biblical strictures and the American way of life by wanting somewhere to safely urinate in a gender appropriate facility outside the home, might suggest that trans rights and protections have become deeply embedded in federal and state legislation. This is not the case, unfortunately. Despite the outrage expressed by establishment politicians and most of the media over the Orlando shooting, there remain over 30 US states that still have no anti-discrimination protection at all for trans people nor in many cases for gay men, lesbians or bisexuals.

Paper tigers

These right-wing attacks on trans toilet rights were mounted despite there being not a single recognised case of a trans woman using public bathroom access to attack cisgender (non-trans) women. On the contrary, those being harassed or bullied by police, store detectives and bigots have not only been trans women but also some of the very cisgender women the legislation supposedly protects from "predatory" trans women. Sometimes these women have even found themselves accused of being men, or at the very least, of not looking feminine enough.

In one example, cisgender woman Aimee Toms was verbally attacked in a Walmart toilet in Connecticut in 2016 while washing her hands by another woman who thought she must be transgender.[337] Aimee had short hair and was wearing a baseball cap.

She went on to post a YouTube video in which she compared the current fight for transgender rights to the Civil Rights Movement of the 1960s when black Americans fought for the right to occupy the same spaces as white people. She drew a parallel noting that trans people are simply trying to exercise their rights as human beings to safely live their lives the same way any cisgender person can.[338]

Inevitably, these attempts at bathroom prohibitions have also made gender-appropriate access even more stressful and dangerous for trans women. As a letter issued in 2016 by the National Task Force to End Sexual and Domestic Violence Against Women (signed by 250 organisations and campaigns) put it:

The efforts to ban transgender people from using public restrooms obscure the fact that all of us, including transgender people, are deeply concerned about safety and privacy in restrooms. Transgender people already experience unconscionably high rates of sexual assault — and forcing them out of facilities consistent with the gender they live every day makes them vulnerable to assault. As advocates committed to ending sexual assault and domestic violence of every kind, we will never support any law or policy that could put anyone at greater risk of assault or harassment. That is why we are able to strongly support transgender-inclusive non-discrimination protections — and why we oppose any law that would jeopardize the safety of transgender people by forcing them into restrooms that do not align with the gender they live every day... Discriminating against transgender people does not give anyone more control over their body or security. Those who perpetuate falsehoods about transgender people and non-discrimination laws are putting transgender people in harm's way and making no one safer.[339]

It is trans people who have been the primary targets of harassment and discrimination in such situations. This ought not to be hard to appreciate. It is a no-win situation. If a female-identified trans person needs to use a toilet and were to try using a male toilet in line with their birth-assigned gender, or a male-identified trans person vice versa, one can imagine the likely difficulties.

In North Carolina under HB2 businesses were not required to discriminate against LGBT+ people but they had legal backing if they chose to do so. Many consciously chose not to do so and some consequently faced pressure from religious and right wing groups to fall in line. When the US retailer Target changed its toilet policy to accommodate trans people, stating that it supported staff and customers who wished to use gender appropriate facilities, the American Family Association sought to organise a boycott of the chain claiming, without any evidence, that, "Clearly Target's new policy poses a danger to wives and daughters" and that the "policy allows a sexual predator that he could simply say he 'feels like a woman today' and enter the women's restroom…even if young girls or women are already in there".[340]

Some campaigners who sought to spread the North Carolina example were not above adopting terrorist tactics to try and bring dissenters into line. In June 2016 a small bomb was found in one Target store in Evanston, Illinois.

There was considerable resistance to HB2. Shocked at the North Carolina Republican legislators' action many joined the campaign to overturn it. There was a financial boycott of North Carolina during 2016, which was estimated to have cost the state hundreds of millions of dollars in lost revenue, investment and legal costs.

There was also a cultural boycott. A number of artists such as Neil Young, Ringo Starr and Bruce Springsteen refused to play there and singer-songwriter Cyndi Lauper pledged to donate proceeds from her appearances to LGBT+ causes. Steven Van Zandt (Little Steven), guitarist in Bruce Springsteen's E Street Band, described HB2 as an "evil virus" in explaining why the band cancelled a show in Greensboro, North Carolina early in 2016.[341]

Even other states joined the condemnation. More than two dozen cities and states, from Honolulu to Vermont, banned taxpayer-funded visits to North Carolina because of HB2, allowing state employees to refuse to travel on religious grounds to any states which had voided anti-discrimination laws.[342]

In September 2016 the Atlantic Coast Championship American Football game was moved out of the state to be re-scheduled in Orlando, site of the Pulse club massacre, on the grounds that the football club would not be able to guarantee the safety and wellbeing of its employees, students and fans under North Carolina's HB2 provisions.

Moreover, it would be wrong to assume that the North Carolina ban had majority support in the US. A CNN/ORC poll in May 2016 found that 57 percent of Americans did not agree with the ban. The figure was predictably higher among Democrats and independents than Republicans, but the poll found even Republicans were split 48/48 on the issue.[343]

Thankfully, in what amounted to a major victory for opponents of the bathroom bill, Pat McCrory lost his seat in the 2016 elections to Democratic Attorney General Roy Cooper, a vocal critic of the law, and the portion of the law regarding bathroom use was repealed on 30 March 2017.[344]

In accord with findings on other LGBT+ related issues, younger respondents were much more likely to support transgender rights than senior citizens.

Another US poll in autumn 2016 from the Pew Research Center showed that, while Americans were certainly divided on the issue, a majority of women actually supported trans people being able to use the restroom of their chosen gender, with 55 percent in favour and 40 percent against.[345] Men, on the other hand, were apparently more concerned about "women's safety" than women themselves, supporting discrimination against trans people by a margin of 52 percent to 40 percent. *Pink News* commented that: "It's almost as if women can see when they're being exploited as a political bargaining chip to attack a minority group".[346]

US trans rights since the bathroom wars

It is clear that Donald Trump's tenure as President greatly encouraged racists, homophobes and the far-right in the US and further afield. LGBT+ rights came under more determined attack from bigots and the far-right. For example, in June 2019 in Detroit an armed group of neo-Nazis were allowed to protest and harass Pride marchers while police protected their "free speech" and in July 2019 a report released by the Center for the Study of Hate and Extremism (CSHE) at California State University found that the surge in hate crimes in the US marked the steepest rise since 2015. This was not just a consequence of Trump's campaign and election since there had been five consecutive years of increase.[347]

In terms of transphobic attacks, in the first nine months of 2019 there were 15 murders in the US of trans women — all black or Hispanic. They included 17 year-old Bailey Reeves, shot to death in Baltimore, and 21 year-old Bee Love in Florida who was tied up, shot multiple times and set on fire in her car.

Attempts to roll back legal rights accelerated with Donald

Trump's election. His nominees to the Department of Justice pushed to legalize the right of organisations to sack people for being gay or transgender. There were attacks on LGBT+ rights in healthcare provision, housing, education, the prison system, the military and sports.

Meanwhile gay and trans conversion therapy (or so-called "gay cures") ranging from talking and behavioural therapies to electroshock, chemical and deprivation techniques, remains legal in around thirty US states.[348] These persist despite the well-documented negative effects of such techniques and being exposed as ineffective, unethical and damaging. They've been linked to higher rates of depression, suicidality and even to the subsequent need for treatment for PTSD and post-religious trauma.[349] Despite the American Psychiatric Association opposing conversion therapy since 1998 almost 200,000 trans people in the US — about one in seven — have been subjected to conversion therapy practices.

At the time of writing, the Trump administration was also pushing to redefine sex in an exclusively binary and essentialist way which would not only, in effect, erase trans, non-binary and intersex people's legal existence but would crucially give bigots the power to exclude them from same-sex facilities.[350] Trans people would face increased discrimination in hospitals and health care, prisons, refuges and shelters and more generally in employment, housing and education.

Court cases alleging discrimination against LGBT+ people in the US (two cases alleging discrimination against sacked gay men and one involving a trans woman sacked after coming out) were due to be heard in the supreme court at the time of writing and the outcomes of these could be far-reaching. A number of transphobic and anti-LGBT+ organisations, such as the radical feminist group Women's Liberation Front,[351] submitted hostile amicus briefs in these cases in their attempts to sway the courts towards more reactionary outcomes.[352]

Despite US courts having repeatedly affirmed that LGBT+ people are covered by Title VII of the Civil Rights Act of 1964 the Department of Justice now argues that sexual orientation and gender identity should be excluded under Title VII because "sex" narrowly refers to whether people are "biologically male or female."

The hostile briefs, in common with much of the scaremongering commentary around the proposed GRA amendments in the UK, frequently claim to reflect the "scientific basis" of binary sex. The claim is that science is "fact" and that "biology isn't bigotry". Yet, as we argued in Chapter 5, the biology of sex is a lot more complex and nuanced than the erroneous and simplistic beliefs being promoted by some. The claim that "biology isn't bigotry" is certainly wilfully naïve.

As Heron Greenesmith, a senior research associate with Political Research Associates in the US, points out: "Anti-trans feminists think they have science on their side. It is bananas how ascientific their rhetoric is, and yet literally they say, 'Biology isn't bigotry.' In fact biology has been used as bigotry as long as biology has been a thing".[353]

We only need think of eugenics, scientific racism, IQ testing, "proofs" of women's biologically-based inferiority to appreciate how false such claims are. Indeed Marxist biologists such as Richard Lewontin, Steven Rose and Leon Kamin have long debunked these ideas but like whack-a-mole they keep popping up from the political right.[354] The battle lines over LGBT+ rights have been clearly drawn in the US and as long as there is a populist right wing President like Donald Trump in the White House, with conservative religious and secular bigots urging him on, the attacks will continue and potentially escalate.

Yet despite the assaults on minority rights at both federal and state levels there is well-organised and popular resistance from oppressed people, including trans people, as we have seen with the marches and protests as each Trump measure has been announced. The experience of the mass campaign to defeat the North Carolina bathroom bill shows that mass resistance can be built, hearts and minds can be changed, and fighting back can win.

Chapter 8
Trans rights and transphobia in Britain

A man and a teenage girl have been arrested after a trans woman was found dead in a London hotel room. [Transgender woman] Naomi Hersi was found with knife injuries near to Heathrow Airport and pronounced dead at the scene 30 minutes later. The 36 year old, who lived in Mill Hill, north London, was described on social media as a "tennis lover, music junkie, film and TV addict". In a horrific twist, Hersi's final post to Twitter was a *Vice* article titled "Trans Women of Color Face an Epidemic of Violence and Murder".[355]

Trans as mental illness
Before 1967 not only was male homosexuality illegal in public or private in Britain but it was also internationally regarded as a form of mental illness. In the US, homosexuality ceased formally to be considered a mental illness in 1973 after vigorous campaigning by gays and lesbians but it remained a diagnosable mental illness right up until 1993 in Britain. People could be locked up and "treated" for being gay (or trans) for much of the 20th century.

Trans and gay people share similar histories of cruel and abusive so-called cures for their "conditions." Before her transition and fame, for instance, April Ashley, whose court case was discussed earlier, had been incarcerated in Walton Hospital in Liverpool after suicide attempts, where she was subjected to injections of the so-called "truth serum" sodium pento-thal, sessions of electroconvulsive therapy (ECT) and male hormones.

"Gender dysphoria" (GD) in the *Diagnostic and Statistical Manual of Mental Disorders* (DSM) — or in earlier versions "gender identity disorder" or GID — is the diagnosable mental illness or syndrome "suffered" by transgender people. It is analogous to the mental disorder allegedly suffered by LGB people until 1993 in Britain. Trans people, however, are still impacted by a "disorder" and this pathologisation of trans remains an objectionable aspect of medical orthodoxy.

While the claimed purpose of the authors of the DSM has always been to standardise the diagnosis of symptoms, it was, at least in part, a project to bolster psychiatry's reputation in light of critical social psychological studies in the early 1970s which exposed psychiatry's "impressionism" and the impact of labelling in generating false diagnoses.[356] The DSM has since become a psychiatric behemoth with rapidly multiplying diag-nosable conditions.

It has increasingly lent credence to what Iain Ferguson has called "the medicalisation of everyday life".[357] He makes the point that the DSM reflects an overemphasis on biological explanations for people's distress or problems and a down-playing of socio-economic causes such as living in poverty, loneliness and unemployment.

For transgender people it is trans oppression and the consequent hostility, marginalisation and invalidation of trans lives that create the distress, not being trans as such.

Medical access and treatment for trans people

The medical establishment is no stranger to transphobic atti-tudes. Having to deal with doctors, psychiatrists and other medical staff has traditionally been a source of great stress and distress for trans people, particularly working class trans people, who lack the financial resources to pursue privately the help they need, such as hormones or cosmetic and genital surgery.

In Britain today, for a trans person to have any chance of accessing NHS support, under current regulations she, he or they must convince psychiatrists and the relevant gender identity clinic that they have the medical condition "gender dysphoria." If they cannot access the NHS route to help with transition they face potential costs of many thousands of pounds. This can easily amount to £20–40,000 pounds for "top" surgery (mastectomy or breast augmentation), "bottom" or genital surgery, cosmetic surgery which might include facial reconstruction, plus many sessions of electrolysis or laser treatment for hair removal, and so on.

It is not hard to see the class issue here: if you are well off, like former boxing promoter Kellie Moloney, who claimed she paid for her £100,000 transition costs by disposing of part of her buy-to-let portfolio, then such support can be accessed quite quickly. The rest may be waiting many years and amass considerable debts.

Hormones and genital surgery are nominally available on the National Health Service but to access them requires a trans person to convince gatekeepers of the severity and endurance of their condition and to satisfy certain criteria, including spending a period of time during which they are required to undertake the "real life test." This can prove to be hugely difficult for the continuity of any employment, secure housing and personal relationships.

Problems for trans people in accessing appropriate health care don't just revolve around the matter of transition. Activist Pat Clinton has written that:

> You don't need to fly to the US bible belt to find a GP denying transgender people the most basic medical care: it's happening right here in the UK in 2017... Most of us within the community are accustomed to becoming our own doctors and having to educate experts on trans healthcare... A large factor is the lack of training for medical professionals on trans people's needs.[358]

One of the proposals put forward by the Women and Equalities Parliamentary Committee in 2017, as a result of its examination of transgender lives in Britain, was for much more systematic trans awareness training for NHS personnel in light of the widespread transphobia that trans people reported that they encountered from doctors and other health and care staff.

Trans people have over the years sought to raise awareness and understanding by bringing together trans activists and representatives of the medical profession. Between 1990 and 2004, for example, a series of biennial transgender conferences, the Gendys Conferences, were held at British university venues intended to foster better understanding of trans lives and to promote trans equality.[359]

These efforts to educate the medical establishment actually began much earlier than the 1990s. There had been two previous transgender conferences, the first in 1974 at Leeds University and then the following year at Leicester University. It seems that these were almost certainly the first in the world to try and bring together "transvestites and transsexuals" with "experts" and professionals in the field.

The 1974 conference seems to have been quite politically diverse and included people from the Beaumont Society and TVSG (the Transvestite Support Group) as well the Gay Liberation Front and a variety of lesbian and gay support groups and professionals. Some of the participants were already using terms like "gender alignment" and "trans-gender" to encompass both transvestites and transsexuals, terms which did not enter more general usage for at least another two decades.

There were certainly differences of political emphasis aired at these conferences which took place while the flame of post-Stonewall trans radicalism was still burning brightly. As one report of the conferences, written in 2007 by King and Ekins, put it: "Some of the more radical delegates wanted the [Beaumont] Society and its members to be less secretive and to follow the more aggressive and radical model of the gay liberation movement."[360]

There was also criticism of the Beaumont Society's exclusion of transsexuals, gay and bisexual cross-dressers, and those who cross-dressed for sexual reasons.

Towards a Gender Recognition Act
In 1991 the trans advocacy group The Gender Trust was

founded, followed a year later by the pressure group Press For Change. These were the key organisations that in association with the TUC and various trade union LGBT groups lobbied for legislation that would provide protections for transgender people in the workplace and in civil society.

Right at the end of the 20th century the Sex Discrimination Act, originally passed in 1976, was amended to include protections for transgender people on the basis of "gender reassignment." These were the Sex Discrimination (Gender Reassignment) Regulations 1999.

A major boost towards trans-friendly legislation in the UK was the 2002 European Court of Human Rights judgement in the case of transgender woman Christine Goodwin vs the United Kingdom. This found that the British government had violated Goodwin's human rights, specifically, the right to respect and family life, and the right to marry and found a family. The ruling paved the way for consultations on the need for a Gender Recognition Act (GRA) to address these violations.

The GRA that eventually became law in 2004 marked a huge step forward for transgender people in Britain, but also contained serious compromises and shortcomings which disappointed many.

At its heart is a legal process for permanent legal recognition of a person's gender. It allows trans people to apply for a Gender Recognition Certificate (GRC), which enables the person to obtain a new birth certificate and, importantly, makes it a criminal offence for anyone to disclose the person's former gender status.

However, it has been criticised by many trans people as it requires a psychiatric diagnosis of "gender dysphoria" and insists that the trans person must live in their acquired gender role for a period of two years to be eligible for the certificate. It also does not apply to those under 18, it costs a significant sum of money to obtain a GRC and, until the passage of the Marriage (Same Sex Couples) Act 2013, it debarred married trans people from obtaining a GRC. Married trans people can now receive a GRC without having to annul their marriage or divorce their partner.

The requirement for marriage annulment was a serious

anomaly that discriminated against married applicants and had knock-on effects for pension rights and other entitlements since the certificate was required as proof of gender identity when applying for these. A number of trans women in Britain found themselves refused pensions at the same age of eligibility as cisgender women because the state continued to treat them according to their former gender.

In June 2018 the UK government was found guilty of direct discrimination by the European Court of Justice (ECJ) for refusing to regard a married trans woman, "MB", as eligible for the state pension at 60. After a ten-year legal battle the ECJ concluded that UK legislation "constitutes direct discrimination based on sex" and is therefore in breach of European law.[361] At the time of writing the case has yet to be reconsidered by the UK Supreme Court, and the Department of Work and Pensions is also continuing to refuse to recognise its liability in respect to other trans women in similar circumstances.

The 2010 Equality Act

This important piece of legislation for the first time granted legal parity between transgender people and those with other "protected characteristics" such as women, BME and disabled people, and importantly the Act also included a commitment to *promote* equality.

Gender reassignment, one of the nine protected characteristics, provides people with legal protection from direct discrimination; indirect discrimination; harassment; discrimination based on perception (eg a person is perceived to have reassigned gender); victimisation and discrimination based on association (eg partner, parent, sibling or friend of a transsexual person).[362]

The Act introduced a Public Sector Equality Duty applicable to public bodies such as schools, colleges, prisons, the NHS and so on, meaning that any publicly-funded organisation must ensure discrimination against any of the protected categories does not take place, that they all have equal access to services and that good relations between groups are fostered.

Schools' obligation to end discrimination against transgender pupils and staff comes from their Public Sector Equality Duty.[363]

This intention to foster and promote equality has hardly seen the light of day, however. It was undermined when the New Labour government collapsed the various independent Equality Commissions, covering disability, race, etc, into one understaffed and under-resourced new body, the Equality and Human Rights Commission (EHRC).

The EHRC was set up in 2007 under the Equality Act 2006 and the serious impact of austerity, begun under the New Labour government in 2008, immediately contributed to undermining the necessary resources for LGBT+ people. Subsequent Coalition and Tory governments have continued cutting resources to the bone and beyond.

There are other anomalies arising from the confusing and sometimes inadequate language and terminology in the 2010 Equality Act. One of the general proposals put to the government in 2015 by the cross-party Women and Equalities Parliamentary Committee was to address these anomalies and create a specific new protected characteristic of gender identity.[364]

For example, there is a catch-22 situation that a number of trans people have fallen into, when they have been convicted of sexual assault for not making a sexual partner aware of their gender status, thus vitiating the person's consent.

British courts have convicted trans people living in "stealth" (ie those who choose to keep their gender history completely confidential) who have found themselves accused of sexual assault for engaging in sexual activity with a partner who was unaware of their background.[365]

This is a major inequality in the law for trans and non-binary people and appears to contradict the protected characteristic status of gender reassignment under the 2010 Equality Act. It is also horribly transphobic, suggesting that trans people must "out" themselves as transgender to every sexual partner or risk a criminal conviction.

Pressure from trans people and supporters around the perceived shortcomings and anomalies in the GRA, particularly in the light of subsequent legislation such as same-sex marriage equality, has generated proposals to amend the Act, in particular to de-medicalise and streamline the application process for obtaining a GRC. These proposals, and their transphobic backlash, will be discussed in more detail in the next chapter.

We should bear in mind that none of the advances for transgender people that have been won have simply been handed over without trans people organising to advocate, lobby and campaign for them. In many cases trans people have had to struggle even harder than some other LGBT+ people to try and ensure that trans rights are not relegated to the back of the bus.

Trans organisation — from small beginnings

From early support organisations such as the Beaumont Society around fifty years ago (still in existence today) there are now dozens of national and local self-help and support organisations in Britain either specifically for transgender and non-binary people (such as Mermaids or Gendered Intelligence[366]) or which are trans-inclusive (such as Stonewall[367]).

As Stephen Whittle put it in 2000, even before the GRA was passed:

> From the self-help organizing of a few transvestite networks of the 1960s and 1970s, there is now a plethora of groups catering for representative diversity on cross-gender behaviour and lifestyles. Many people have been involved in the running of these groups for over a quarter of a century.[368]

There are organisations which advocate on behalf of trans people, such as the Gender Identity Research and Education Society (GIRES) and Press for Change, venues for trans events, trans performers and now even specifically Trans Pride events as well as LGBT+ Prides. Imaan, an organisation for Muslim LGBT+ people, has a group for trans Muslims as well.[369]

Trans Pride Brighton has been running since 2013 and was the first Trans Pride march in Europe. Similar Trans pride events are held each year in Bristol, London and Manchester. For the first time in 2018 a Trans Pride march and associated programme of meetings, film showings and other events was organised in Leeds.

Such trans events often tend to be less corporate, more grass roots and sometimes more "political" than the general Pride events. Indeed there has been much criticism of various Prides — most notably London Pride — becoming over-dependent on corporate sponsorship and consequently downplaying political issues in favour of having a fun day. Trade union delegations and political campaigns, despite their important role in helping to achieve many of the limited gains so far, are generally allocated to the back of Pride parades and marches.

In protest, in 2016 a large contingent of more radical trans activists at the Manchester Pride march organised a protest over the treatment of trans prisoners, which had been a high profile issue during the previous year.[370] They wanted to block the Greater Manchester Police float from participating in the parade. The group was led by trans campaign group Direct Action for Trans Health, as well as No Prisons Manchester and the IWW Incarcerated Workers Committee.

The Trade Unions

In his 2017 book *Champions of Equality Trade Unions and LGBT Rights in Britain*, Peter Purton, a former Policy Officer in the TUC's Equalities and Equal Rights Department, wrote:

> There has been a significant problem... with the absence of protest from LGBT+ community leaders to recent austerity cuts. The economic crisis has been particularly felt by young LGBT+ people in the areas of mental health and homelessness — which are sometimes connected problems. The course followed by so many generations of young people leaving home — sometimes as a result of parental homophobia — for the big city has collided with a housing crisis. When this is combined with rapidly increasing poverty and homophobia, the recession has had a disproportionate impact on young LGBTs.[371]

Purton set out to fill the gap in British LGBT+ history left by the way in which the important campaigning role of the trade union movement has often been written out of the narrative.

He describes the role played by unions in the fight for LGBT+ rights and seeks to redress the balance. He tells the stories of the first strike in the 1970s in support of a victimised gay public sector worker, through to the solidarity and mutual support of Lesbian and Gays Support the Miners and the National Union of Mineworkers during the Great Miners' Strike in Britain in 1984/5, dramatised in the inspiring film *Pride*.

But the role of trade unionists went much further than this and he details various unions' involvement in campaigns to combat HIV/Aids, the struggle to set up lesbian and gay trade union groups, through to the TUC's financial support in 2012 for London Pride when key corporate sponsors pulled out.

Along the way, and after a great deal of lobbying by the various national trade union lesbian and gay groups, in 1998 the first TUC Lesbian and Gay Conference was held (after several initially unsuccessful attempts to convince the TUC to support it). This was renamed the TUC LGBT Conference in 2002 and trans delegates were formally included for the first time after that. The TUC annual conferences remain forums for debate and activism to support and protect LGBT+ workers, but they have only played a very limited role as springboards for active resistance to austerity.

The impact of cuts and austerity

Despite the occasional outbursts of workers' resistance since the onset of austerity, the TUC leadership has either failed to develop these or, worse, has sometimes actively blocked attempts to generate a mass fightback. Fine words at conferences mean little in the face of such failures of leadership.

It is not as if there have been no pretexts or opportunities to fight back. In just a few months in 2008 the British ruling class took £1.3 trillion from public coffers to bail out a series of banks. The situation has only deteriorated further since then. Billions have been stripped from public services, welfare and social services as well as workers' pay and pensions.

Working conditions have been driven down, house prices and rents inflated, and millions of people have been forced to use food banks. Libraries, swimming pools, playgrounds and other public facilities have closed and funding for third sector support bodies like LGBT+ organisations slashed.

It is no surprise that oppressed groups have generally fared worse in this process, and that reactionary ideologies have been used by the state, sections of the media, and those on the right to increase racism, Islamophobia, attacks on women's rights, homophobia and transphobia.

Rather than openly opposing austerity, the Lesbian and Gay Foundation, an umbrella body, wrote to the government before the Comprehensive Spending Review in October 2015 demanding that Equality Impact Assessments be carried out first and that the cuts should be "fair".[372] In 2014 the TUC produced a report on austerity and the LGBT third sector that detailed the impact and the particular vulnerability of such voluntary sector bodies.[373] Unsurprisingly such letter writing and reports cut no ice with a cabinet of millionaires determined to bash the poorest and most vulnerable in society in the interests of neoliberalism, and things grew considerably more difficult for such bodies in the following years.

Many organisations have been forced to slash staff and services for LGBT+ people. In light of NHS rationalisations, when Primary Care Trusts are reportedly making decisions not to carry out knee and hip replacement operations or cataract removals, how much harder does it become to argue for gender affirmation surgery for trans people?

These problems of access and allocation of resources have to be understood in terms of the human costs involved and the consequences of growing demand. Evidence submitted by GIRES, to the parliamentary inquiry into transgender equality in 2015 pointed out that of the estimated 650,000 gender variant people in the UK:

> So far only about 30,000 have sought medical help for gender dysphoria. Dutch research indicates that around a fifth of the 650,000 will do so, amounting to a further 100,000 people... Currently, referrals to NHS Gender Identity Clinics (GICs) are rising at a rate of 20 percent per annum. In the child and adolescent services (Tavistock Gender Identity Development Service) annual referrals are now doubling and predicted to reach 1200

a year in 2016. Recent reports indicate waiting times of 2-3 years for access to some of the adult clinics. The waiting time for genital surgery for trans women is 22 months; without additional services being commissioned, the predicted waiting time is 42 months by 2017 (NHS England). Plans to overcome this deficit, will still not achieve the 18 week rule for several years; it cannot be achieved, at all, for access to GICs.[374]

These are key services for many trans people because mainstream services often do not understand trans people's needs, which consequently are ill-served or even unrecognised by those providing affordable housing, physical and mental health support, and social care.

For example, domestic violence services will sometimes work only with cisgender women (although many others will accept trans women) and many LGBT+ people prefer to receive support from LGBT+ organisations. There is also the fact that LGBT+ people are often at increased risk of homelessness, violence, domestic violence and forced marriage. For example, one 2015 US survey of over 27,000 transgender respondents found that more than half (54 percent) of trans people experienced some form of intimate partner violence, including acts involving coercive control and physical harm.[375]

As Peter Purton pointed out in 2014, after five years of austerity:

Historically young LGB and T people have headed for the bright lights, confident of making a new life in the secure environment of an LGBT community. Except that in the age of austerity, this security is increasingly hard to find, and the support structures that were developed in urban areas during the last forty years are crumbling under the impact of cuts.[376]

A report published by NatCen Social Research in 2016 into the impact of austerity measures on LGBT+ people found that: "fears about the effects of public funding cuts reported in 2013 were seen as a reality for some LGB & T service users and service providers by 2016".[377] Reductions in public spending had resulted in reduced access to some mainstream services (eg GPs, mental health and sexual health) when LGB & T people had needed them. LGB & T service users and providers thought that cuts in public spending had a disproportionate effect on the LGB & T population compared to other groups through financial hardships; limited identity and support needs; feeling marginalised and invisible; and a sense that there had been reversal of gains for LGB & T people and increased in vulnerability.

The sustained funding reductions had left some LGB & T services focusing on survival, rather than delivering a high quality comprehensive service. Experienced and knowledge-able staff had been lost through redundancies and staff and volunteers were facing high workloads and stress due to trying to meet greater demand with fewer resources.

The monitoring problem

It is often difficult to access reliable data on the incidence of transphobic hate crimes and suicide since in many countries official monitoring of such incidents is minimal or entirely absent. Such data as there is has very often, out of necessity, been reported and collated by trans and LGBT+ support groups or NGOs and thus draws heavily on media reports and other unofficial sources.[378]

It is not always clear from raw data about attacks what the motivations of the attackers were. There is anecdotal evidence from LGBT+ people themselves that many attacks which might be recorded as "gay bashing" should be more accurately described as "gender bashing", but these are normally not distinguished or logged separately. Attackers, it is suggested, have often picked up on gender cues (the "masculine" woman or the man or boy who is not "masculine" enough) and so reports and statistics sometimes need to be carefully unpacked to get at the reality.

Britain does not have a great record on monitoring. The police did not even start monitoring hate crimes against transgender people until 2007.

It has been one of the demands of trans organisations for

many years that robust monitoring of hate crimes should be introduced by the police, local authorities and other institutions. Apart from the matter of obtaining justice for those attacked, it can be difficult to make a case that there is a serious issue of transphobia without appropriate data being available. Lack of monitoring is also an issue in the workplace, allowing some employers to claim "no problem here."

Consequently any appropriate policies intended to combat harassment and bullying of trans people in the workplace must include mechanisms for reporting and monitoring transphobic incidents. Like any monitoring of harassment, bullying, discrimination and violence, the absence of available and accessible routes for reporting incidents actively discourages people who have been affected from reporting them formally. And without a mechanism for reporting and dealing with them, workplace trade union reps often find it difficult to marshal sufficient empirical data to pursue cases, to organise support, and to hold managers and employers to account.

Lack of monitoring of oppressive behaviour in general can allow an employer to avoid implementing policies at all, or dodge demands from trade unions and others when they insist that staff should receive appropriate training.

Rising attacks

Many trans people are now increasingly concerned as it has become clear that a number of trans-critical individuals and organisations are seeking to roll back the protections that transgender people currently have under the 2010 Equality Act.

The 2019 Galop report on LGBT+ hate crimes in Britain made depressing reading.[379] It reported that: "Recorded anti-LGBT+ hate crime has doubled in the last three years."[380] The foreword of the report went on to say: "Young people polled tended to hold more negative views toward LGBT+ people than other age groups. This alarming finding warns of a generational pivot ahead and a bumpy road for those of us committed to challenging anti-LGBT+ violence and abuse".[381]

An extensive Stonewall survey in 2017 based on a YouGov poll of over 5,000 LGBT+ people had found that attacks on

LGBT+ people in Britain had risen by nearly 80 percent in the previous four years. Around half of trans children had at some point attempted to take their own lives and around 80 percent had self-harmed.[382]

An 2019 investigation into homophobic attacks by BBC Radio 5 Live found that while the number of reports of such hate crimes had risen across England, Wales and Northern Ireland from 5,807 in 2014-15 to 13,530 in 2018-19, the number of charges brought had stayed almost constant, meaning that the proportion of complaints leading to charges had fallen from around 20 percent to 8 percent.[383] In London the number of charges or summonses had fallen by around one third in this period.

At the end of May 2019 there was a vicious assault on a lesbian couple on a London bus that unusually made headline news and led to arrests. Less publicised attacks have included a 22-year-old gay man beaten by thugs in Preston, Lancashire in July; a group of teenage girls attacked by a homophobic gang as they were leaving Stoke-on Trent Pride in June; and a gay man attacked with a machete in London in July.

Studies by Schools Out and Stonewall among others have shown that, like homophobia, transphobia remains widespread in schools and involves bullying (in person and online), harassment, and verbal and physical attacks.[384]

Nor is the situation much better at post-16 level. An extensive 2009 report by the Equality Challenge Unit of UK Higher Education institutions showed that reported transphobia aimed at staff and students in British universities was even more prevalent than homophobia.[385]

Regarding trans hate crime specifically, the number of transgender hate crimes recorded in England, Scotland and Wales rose by 81 percent in 2018/19 compared with the previous year. In mid-2019 the BBC reported that in West and South Yorkshire hate crimes against trans people tripled over a three year period.[386] Some of the increases may indeed have been due to better reporting and monitoring but this could not mask the underlying rising trend in assaults and harassment. As a result, many trans people reported feeling unsafe to even leave their homes.[387]

This dangerous situation applies in workplaces as well. A Stonewall/YouGov survey of 870 trans and non-binary respondents published in January 2018 found that half of transgender people had hidden or disguised their gender identity or sexuality in the workplace, fearing discrimination. One in eight trans workers also reported being physically attacked at work by customers or colleagues during the previous year.[388]

Other reports, such as the *Trans Mental Health and Emotional Wellbeing Study*[389] and the TUC *Transgender Rights Report*[390] have highlighted the considerable prejudice, discrimination and harassment faced by transgender people on a daily basis.

The TUC report also found that just under a quarter (23 percent) of all LGBT+ respondents had been outed against their will, while almost a third (30 percent) of transgender respondents have had their trans status disclosed against their will. Only a third of respondents had reported the latest incident of harassment or discrimination to their employer, and only one in eight had reported it to the employer's human resources department.

Despite the situation illustrated by these reports very few organisations have trans-specific policies in place to address bullying and harassment at work, or support and protections in respect of workers who transition.[391]

The *Trans Mental Health and Emotional Wellbeing Study* found shocking levels of emotional stress and distress. Some 81 percent of the study's participants reported avoiding certain situations through fear. Half of these avoided public toilets and gyms and a quarter clothing shops and leisure facilities.

Nine out of ten reported having been told that transgender people are "not normal", 38 percent had experienced sexual harassment, and 6 percent had been raped for being trans, while 37 percent had experienced physical threats or intimidation, 19 percent had been hit or beaten up, and 25 percent reported having had to move house.

In terms of mental ill health and distress, 88 percent of respondents had experienced current or previous depression, with 58 percent so distressed at some time that they had sought urgent help. 53 percent had self-harmed, 84 percent had thought about suicide and 35 percent had attempted this at least once. 52 percent reported problems with work due to being trans or having a trans history and 19 percent reported being homeless at some point.

Despite this evidence that ought to highlight grave concern for the physical and mental wellbeing of trans people, in June 2019 the National Society for the Prevention of Cruelty to Children (NSPCC) cut its ties with trans activist Munroe Bergdorf who had just been appointed the first LGBT+ campaigner for Childline, after a transphobic social media campaign was mounted against her. This NSPCC decision prompted a letter from 148 staff members to the management criticising their capitulation to the criticism.[392]

The situation for trans people in prisons can also be desperate. There have been a number of deaths of trans prisoners in recent years. William "Billie" Evans, a trans prisoner in Full Sutton prison near York, hanged herself in July 2012 while seeking to undergo transition. There have been four more deaths of trans women kept in male prisons between late 2015 and early 2017 — Joanne Thompson, Vikki Latham, Nicola Cope and Jenny Swift.[393]

The existence of trans prisoners is an inherent challenge to the binary prison system. Regulations regarding the treatment of transsexual prisoners remain deeply problematic despite a British High Court ruling in 2009 in favour of a transgender prisoner who had been refused a transfer to a female prison. The Government published new guidelines in 2016 which accepted that prisoners should normally be accommodated in a prison that reflects their acquired gender. Prison Service Instruction 17/2016 stated that "all transgender prisoners (irrespective of prison location) must be allowed to express the gender with which they identify".[394]

However, following the deaths of several trans prisoners in 2017/18 a review of UK prison regulations in respect of the treatment of trans prisoners was conducted but this resulted in a disappointing step backwards in its insistence that only those prisoners who possess a gender recognition certificate under the GRA will be treated as their appropriate gender. Those trans prisoners without one will initially at least be sent to institutions matching their recorded birth sex. Trans organisations have condemned this as dangerous and demeaning. Some have also argued that it is counter to the spirit of the 2010 Equality Act.[395] The situation for trans people in custody is to be assessed on a case by case basis by a Transgender Case Board and the prisoner has to demonstrate evidence of living in the gender with which they identify.

The case of Karen White in 2018, a trans prisoner accused of sexually assaulting two women prisoners while on remand at New Hall women's prison in Wakefield, was used by those promoting anti-trans narratives as an example of the dangers trans prisoners allegedly pose in women's prisons.

White had a history of violence and sexual assault and was on remand accused of two rapes and violent assault. She was sentenced to life imprisonment in September 2018. However, despite the general anti-trans propaganda as a result of the White case, in fact this was an appalling example of the failure to take into account her violent record in assessing the risk she posed if transferred. In this case, there was a major failure of the process and the Ministry of Justice issued an apology for the failure. White's case should not colour attitudes towards all trans prisoners.

In March 2019 the Ministry of Justice opened the first unit for transgender inmates at a women's prison in South London.[396] The first inmates all had Gender Recognition Certificates, which begs the question why the Ministry felt that it was appropriate to segregate these trans women prisoners away from other women.

The surveys and cases discussed above show that as a consequence of continuing fear of harassment, violence and disapproval it remains immensely difficult and sometimes dangerous for many transgender people to come out to family, friends, neighbours and colleagues and live their lives openly. And as all LGBT+ people are aware, coming out is never a single event. It involves repeated episodes of coming out to new people around you.

Support for trans and non-binary school students
The Tory/Lib Dem Coalition government of 2010-15 took a serious backward step in dropping reference to gender

identity from the August 2013 National Curriculum document during Michael Gove's tenure at the Department for Education (DfE).[397] This was despite gender reassignment having been included for the first time as a protected characteristic in the 2010 Equality Act. The message this sent to teachers, teacher trainers and schoolchildren was a dangerous one.

Schools often avoid the issue of atypical gender identity development until they are faced with the potential transition of a young person, yet this should be included at all levels of the syllabus and be celebrated in the same way as other protected characteristics.

The numbers of very young children expressing gender questioning or gender variant behaviour in primary and secondary schools has increased rapidly over the past ten years so it is clear that information and reassurance needs to be given to them, their parents and the schools at the earliest stage.

Schools should be able to provide material for teachers and parents as well as pupils. Personal, Social and Health Education (PSHE) has been a compulsory element of the National Curriculum since 2000. Special attention to LGBT+ issues should be given within PSHE such as the bullying of vulnerable groups including young people who identify as lesbian, gay, bisexual or transgender, as evidenced by Ofsted in their 2012 report *No Place for Bullying*.[398]

As part of basic teacher training, all teachers should be made aware of how to support young LGBT+ pupils and to recognise and tackle transphobic bullying, including cyberbullying. The sources for appropriate information and guidance need to be carefully chosen, however.

In 2018 the transphobic website Transgender Trend produced such "guidance" which contained a number of misleading claims and dangerous advice. It advised schools to "be cautious" about giving transgender children the right to dress and be referred to as their chosen gender, to avoid giving transgender children time off school to attend medical appointments, and to sort children into PE groups based on "biological sex", all measures effectively denying or undermining the reality of the child's gender identity and likely to do considerable emotional and mental damage to the very children they purport to want to safeguard.

The organisation tried to promote this to schools. In May 2019 the *Times Educational Supplement* (TES) carried an article by a trans-critical supporter that referenced this guidance. In the wake of the article one of the TES's star columnists, Natasha Devon, resigned in protest citing her growing concerns with the publication's editorial line on trans issues.[399]

Genuinely supportive and helpful guidance for schools has been produced by a number of organisations such as the Mermaids Charity, Stonewall, the NASUWT and the Equality and Human Rights Commission that can be accessed via their websites.

The situation for students and staff in post-16 education is not much better. A 2011 study found that in Further and Higher Education 47 percent of LGBT+ students felt unable to talk to their tutors about concerns related to their gender identity or sexual orientation, and 19.1 percent complained about the "insensitive curriculum content".[400] Some 28.5 percent of trans students reported negative treatment from tutors and lecturers because they are trans. Other reports addressing the situation for LGBT+ students in post-16 education have found similar problems.[401]

A Statement of Needs

In the latter part of the 20th century and the early years of the 21st trans organisations in Britain increasingly sought to draw a clear picture of trans peoples' experiences and formulate specific demands to address the impact of transphobic attitudes, policies and practices. One example of these demands was the *Trans Community Statement of Needs*.[402]

Originally published in April 2011 (but since updated) this was developed from discussions and consultations among transgender organisations. In turn, the concerns were fed into the formulation of the 2010–2015 Coalition government's *Transgender Equality Action Plan* of December 2011.[403]

The *Statement of Needs'* Executive Summary reads:

> In employment situations, steps must be taken to reduce the risk of discrimination and abuse, both in

workplace and also in recruitment. This will require educating employers in their duties and trans people in their rights...

Education (covering primarily schools and colleges) has similar issues in terms of training teaching staff in their duties as well as supporting trans people (both pupils and staff)...

Existing legislation (primarily the Gender Recognition Act 2004 and the Equality Act 2010) needs to be clarified and revised, as there are several human rights issues that still need to be clarified...

There is real fear about pressures on NHS funding leading to the illegal withdrawal of health services to assist in the treatment of gender dysphoria. Additionally such treatment needs to be brought into standard NHS protocols ... This will require training of medical staff , such as GPs, as well as recognition that the "one size fits all" approach often seen needs to change.

Support and funding needs to be given to community groups...[404]

It was the government's review of the *Transgender Rights Action Plan* a few years later which gave rise to heated debate from 2016/2017 in respect of proposed amendments to the GRA in particular.

Conclusions

The legal and social situation for trans (and LGB) people in Britain, like other European countries, is contradictory. General improvements in social acceptance and attitudes to LGBT+ people sit alongside increased reports of physical attacks, bullying and harassment, widespread social and institutional homophobia, transphobia and bigotry, which can seriously impact the lives and wellbeing of gay, bisexual and trans people.

The general political background in the period between

2008 and 2018 has been of governments driving through neoliberal economic deregulation, privatisation and austerity in response to the financial crisis of 2008. This has fed the growth of racism and Islamophobia and led to considerable scapegoating of vulnerable groups of people, as well as assaults on organised labour and working-class living standards.

Governments have sought to pose as LGBT+ friendly through their support for some formal and legal extensions of civil rights for LGBT+ people, such as civil partnerships and same-sex marriage. But this toleration, essentially of "safe" gays, same-sex marriage in the form of the nuclear family model, and to a lesser extent toleration of stereotypical gender binary trans people, can be seen as the obverse of subversion, indeed as ideological reinforcement of capitalist social relations.

Those who fall outside the boundaries of the acceptable face of LGBT+ continue to be "othered", marginalised and mistreated. Refugee and asylum seeker support organisations point out that the British government's LGBT+-friendly face masks a situation in which from July 2015 to March 2017 Britain rejected close to 70 percent of the 3,535 asylum applications who cited being LGBT+ as one of the reasons for application, even returning people to countries like Nigeria where being gay or trans can carry the threat of long prison sentences or worse.[405]

Yet another source of concern for trans people has emerged or re-emerged in recent times, however. It is to this apparent convergence of criticism and attacks on trans rights both from some transphobic feminists and from "gender-critical" socialists and feminists that we will turn in the next chapter.

Chapter 9
Contested rights in Britain today

> You have opened my eyes to uncertainties I never
> dreamed existed and to heady vistas of the potential
> freedoms inherent in transgressing the binary, male-
> female gender identities around which my reality
> revolved. You tell me you want a society where, when
> you ask me what gender I am, the obvious response is:
> Why are you even asking the question?[406]

In October 2017 Linda Bellos, lesbian feminist and former
Labour leader of Lambeth Borough Council in the 1980s and
co-founder of Black History Month, was invited to speak to
students in The Beard Society at Oxford University. The invitation was subsequently withdrawn after she told them that she
wanted to question some aspects of trans politics in her talk.[407]

This was immediately characterised by commentators
on the right, and by some on the left, as an instance of unacceptable "no platforming" and an attack on free speech. It was
neither. It was in fact a decision by the Society to ensure a safe
space for their members. If the Beard Society decided, after
Bellos informed them what she intended to speak on, that they
did not want to provide an audience for her trans critical views,
it was surely their choice whether to withdraw the invitation
or not.

However, the incident was grist to the trans-critical and
right wing mill, given the wider context at that time. Some Tory
politicians, like the right in general, have been pushing a line

about the defence of "free speech". This is constantly invoked by those who in practice oppose restrictions on offensive language and behaviour and think people should be free to "say what they think." Tory governments in recent years have urged university administrations to pressure student unions to reverse "no platform" policies. These were originally argued for as a tactic to prevent fascists from accessing platforms on campuses.[408]

In December 2017 Tory Higher Education Minister Jo Johnson announced measures to fine universities for supposed violations of free speech and for allowing the use of no platform policies. He also put pressure on university administrations to block "undesirable" speakers or meetings from taking place on university campuses.

Far from being aimed at fascists and the far right this attack has in practice targeted the left — pro-Palestinian, anti-Zionist and anti-Prevent speakers and campaigners for instance — rather than those on the right.

Nevertheless, some on both left and right perversely regarded the Bellos case as an example of the malign influence of a sinister "transgender lobby" denying a platform to a well-known and respected black lesbian feminist.[409]

Following the Beard Society incident Linda Bellos took an increasingly prominent anti-trans rights position, appearing on platforms of the "trans-critical" group Woman's Place UK and even speaking at a right wing protest outside the US Supreme Court in October 2019 organised by supporters of the Trump administration in opposition to trans rights.[410]

The case (EEOC and Aimee Stevens vs RG and GR Harris Funeral Homes[411]) was the first ever concerning the employment protection rights of trans people to be heard in the Supreme Court. A lower court had already ruled in favour of the plaintiff, Aimee Stephens. The outcome of this case and two related cases involving gay men in the Supreme Court, as referred to in a previous chapter, could determine whether millions of LGBT+ people in the US are protected under federal workplace anti-discrimination legislation, Title VII of the 1964 Civil Rights Act. The ruling is expected in Spring 2020.[412]

Linda Bellos is not the only radical feminist to jump on the anti-trans bandwagon. She joins Germaine Greer, Julie Burchill, Julie Bindel, and Australian radical feminist Sheila Jeffreys, who have all been promoting openly transphobic narratives for some time.

One of Julie Burchill's columns for the *Observer* in January 2013 was headed "Transsexuals should cut it out". After an outcry, the *Observer* removed the article from its website. She now writes for the right wing Tory *Spectator*. She had described trans people as "shims", "she-males" and "bed-wetters in bad wigs".[413]

Sheila Jeffreys has written:

[Transsexual surgery] could be likened to political psychiatry in the Soviet Union. I suggest that trans-sexualism should best be seen in this light, as directly political, medical abuse of human rights. The mutilation of healthy bodies and the subjection of such bodies to dangerous and life-threatening continuing treatment violates such people's rights to live with dignity in the body into which they were born.[414]

Germaine Greer declared that a transgender person could not know their real gender identity, because "you don't know what the other sex is".[415]

Such views stand in the same transphobic tradition as those of Janice Raymond in her 1979 book *The Transsexual Empire: The Making of the She-Male.*[416]

The Gender Recognition Act and its discontents

On 24 September 2017 a number of trans critical feminists[417] in Britain published an open letter in the *Guardian*.[418] The letter claimed that politically motivated violence by trans people was being used to silence women and shut them out of discussions about proposed changes to the 2004 Gender Recognition Act.

The letter followed an altercation at Hyde Park Corner between a group of trans activists and some radical feminists who had been gathering for a meeting to discuss gender identity politics and the GRA. The altercation subsequently led to the conviction for assault of one of the trans protesters, Tara

Wolf.[419] Since then there has been a series of meetings, stunts, newspaper articles, blogs and online commentary attacking trans people, especially with regard to the proposed amendments and updates to the GRA.

Many trans people and trans advocacy organisations have been campaigning for years for changes to the application process for a Gender Recognition Certificate (GRC) — notably calling for the introduction of a self-identification process rather than the current requirements for medical/psychiatric diagnoses and a bureaucratic, lengthy and demeaning procedure.

In July 2018 a letter making similar allegations of violence and intimidation against trans-critical feminists, but which failed to mention transphobia or trans rights, was published in *The Morning Star,* immediately after the government announced that the long-awaited consultation on trans rights and proposed amendments to the GRA would go ahead.[420]

On 8 March 2018, International Women's Day, 300 feminists resigned from the Labour Party in disagreement with its decision to continue allowing trans women onto all-women selection lists.[421] Motions alleging that women were being "silenced and sidelined" on the issue and that trans women constituted a threat to women's rights and women's spaces have caused heated debates in some Labour Party and trade union meetings.

It should go without saying that violence between members of oppressed groups or trolling and online bullying from any quarter is unacceptable. The Hyde Park Corner events were an indication of the degree to which "the trans issue" had already generated a toxic and febrile atmosphere by late 2017.

The atmosphere has grown more febrile since these events. Trans-critical articles have continued to appear in sections of the mainstream media[422] and there have been attempts to commit some trade unions to opposing self-identification or self-declaration under the GRA. For example, a trans-critical motion moved by supporters of Woman's Place UK was tabled at the University and College Union Annual Congress in May 2019 that in effect called for opening up campuses to trans-critical/transphobic organisations like Woman's Place UK under the guise of "free speech" and academic freedom. The motion painted feminist academics as victims but failed to even mention the hostility that trans and non-binary people face.

The background to the GRA proposals

The backdrop to these events was the government's response[423] to the Women and Equalities Committee Report on Transgender Equality and the announcement in July 2017 of their intention to consult on proposals to update and amend the 2004 Gender Recognition Act.[424] In Scotland the devolved government pressed ahead with a consultation on proposals to amend the GRA, and transphobia in the Scottish press was minimal.

In England and Wales, however, sections of the press and other media have mounted a hostile transphobic campaign against the proposals. Sadly, a minority of trans critical radical and socialist feminists have given some left cover to this, allied with websites and blogs that have been attacking the so-called "transgender lobby" for years.[425]

When the GRA was drafted in 2004 it was certainly progressive. However, much had changed by 2015. The number of trans people referring to gender identity clinics had increased dramatically, although the number applying for a gender recognition certificate had not risen proportionately. By the second decade of the 21st century many people, not just trans people, had recognised that there were a number of outdated and unnecessarily restrictive provisions in the Act. For example, it assumes that everyone falls within the gender binary, and that all trans people want to transition between these two gender poles. The Act makes no explicit recognition of non-binary people.

As well as suggested changes to legislation the government proposed to make current practices, staff training and guidance circulating in various public bodies such as the NHS more trans supportive. This was in response to trans people's concerns about inadequate and often transphobic NHS staff and facilities.

The report of the Women and Equalities Parliamentary Committee stated:

> High levels of transphobia are experienced by individuals on a daily basis (including in the provision of public services) — with serious results. About half of

young trans people and a third of trans adults attempt suicide. The recent deaths in custody of two trans women, and the case of a trans woman who was placed in a men's prison, are particularly stark illustrations of the issues... The Gender Recognition Act 2004 was pioneering but is now dated. Its medicalised approach pathologises trans identities and runs contrary to the dignity and personal autonomy of applicants. The Government must update the Act, in line with the principle of gender self-declaration.

It continued:

Protection for trans people under the Equality Act 2010 was a huge step forward. However, the terms "gender reassignment" and "transsexual" in the Act are outdated and misleading; and may not cover wider members of the trans community. The protected characteristic should be amended to that of "gender identity". The NHS is letting down trans people: it is failing in its legal duty under the Equality Act. Trans people encounter significant problems in using general NHS services, due to the attitude of some clinicians and other staff who lack knowledge and understanding— and in some cases are prejudiced. The NHS is failing to ensure zero tolerance of transphobic behaviour. GPs too often lack understanding and in some cases this leads to appropriate care not being provided. A root-and-branch review must be conducted, completed and published by the NHS.

And it concluded:

Across the board, government departments are struggling to support trans people effectively, with the 2011 Advancing Transgender Equality action plan remaining largely unimplemented.[426]

No doubt one explanation for failing to implement the

Advancing Transgender Equality action plan has been institutional transphobia. Another must be almost ten years of neoliberal austerity and cuts to welfare and support services since the financial crash of 2008.

The committee's report could also have mentioned the often severe impact of social class and poverty on trans people's experiences of accessing NHS health care, support for transition, and applications for the GRC. But predictably it did not. Other reports and writers have done so, however. Trans activist Pat Clinton wrote:

> As with all medical treatment there is a two tier system. One tier is exclusively for those who can afford it, where waiting times are virtually non-existent and discrimination is based on cash rather than any other social factor. And there is a lower tier with devastating cuts, brutally long lists and treatment decisions based on how much those providing it think you deserve it rather than whether you need it.[427]

This view is backed by other evidence. In 2016 the TUC's advice for trade union reps on transgender people at work included this in the introduction:

> Trans people face massive discrimination in the workplace. In March 2016 a study by a recruitment company showed that 60 percent of trans workers have experienced some form of discrimination in the workplace and 53 percent have felt the need to hide their trans status from their colleagues. A 2011 Government survey showed similar levels of discrimination and added that "88 percent of respondents said that ignorance of transgender issues was the biggest challenge they faced in employment".[428]

Some of the parliamentary committee's recommendations such as better NHS staff training, better data protection procedures and so on, were uncontroversial. Lowering the age of consent under the GRA, the possibility of introducing a new gender category for official documentation and replacing the term "gender reassignment" with "gender identity" in the Equality Act caused rather more debate. But it was the proposed introduction of self-declaration to obtain a GRC that proved to be particularly controversial.

Self-declaration takes the responsibility for deciding a person's gender identity away from medical professionals and legal panels and gives it to the trans person. It is an important step away from the current medicalised or pathologised approach to transgender people.

As Stonewall and Mermaids spokespeople (and many others) have pointed out, the current situation, especially for young trans people, can be deeply damaging if left unaddressed. A high proportion of trans and non-binary people suffer bullying, discrimination and self-harm.

Refusal to implement even currently available support and advice for trans people needs to be seen against this backdrop. To do nothing but hang on to the status quo would mean effectively to ignore or downplay the high levels of transphobia that trans people face.

There have been debates on transgender rights and the proposed amendments in some trade union conferences, most notably a motion tabled at the Easter 2017 National Union of Teachers conference. Self-declaration was overwhelmingly endorsed by NUT delegates.[429] Since then other unions, such as the Communication Workers Union (CWU), and the University and College Union (UCU) have followed suit.

But the following from an article by Kiri Tunks, President of the National Union of Teachers/National Education Union (NUT/NEU) from 2018, gives a flavour of the views held by some labour movement critics of the proposals:

> The ability to define one's own "gender" will undermine the legal characteristic of "sex" and could lead to serious implications for women and their ability to fight sex discrimination and oppression...

> The demand for self-identity has huge implications for all of us and how we are defined. And, because women

are an oppressed group (whose fight for equality has never been won or sustained) it is women who are the most affected by the proposals...

Terms that are used to describe people of and from specific groups must be determined by all the people in those groups.[430]

Not all feminists have taken such trans-critical viewpoints. A 2016 article by Lori Watson, a radical feminist cisgender woman who identifies as a woman but is often read as trans or as a man, spelt out her sympathetic position towards trans people. She made it clear that she believed trans women are women and she rejected any feminism that excludes trans women.

Her article is interesting in that it discusses what it is like to deal, practically and emotionally, with being challenged for "being a man" in women's spaces such as public toilets. Her experiences of being socially interpreted as male but identifying as female enabled her to empathise with the reality of what trans people and especially trans women face daily. She criticised trans-critical feminists for their underlying essentialist notions of sex. Watson writes:

The criticism of trans women failing to act in ways that are consistent with an ideal of liberation from sex and gender is a little like criticising any of us for making a decent living under capitalism, or investing our retirement funds in the stock market, if the aim of liberation is the destruction of capitalism as a social, political, and economic system. Even Karl Marx had to eat in the here and now.[431]

Grasping the nettle of self-identification

The proposed change to self-identification in the GRC application would, almost at a stroke, remove some of its more onerous and intrusive aspects. It would not, however, mean that a person could simply declare their intention to identity as the "other" gender one fine day and thus get a GRC over the counter, as some trans critics and transphobes have suggested, trivialising the proposed process.[432]

Self-identification would still involve a formal process of registration, a legally sworn and witnessed declaration, and a paper trail but, as in Ireland and in several other jurisdictions, the applicant would need to complete perhaps a two page document rather than the dozens of pages plus letters from doctors and psychiatrists, personal medical history and so on currently required in Britain.

Admittedly it is still fairly early days in Ireland, where the new GRA with self-ID was passed in 2015, but there have been no reports of misuse of the process in the way some critics are suggesting could happen if the change is made in Britain. Besides, self-declaration already exists without any apparent problems not just in Ireland but in Malta, Denmark, Norway, Argentina, Mexico City, California and Belgium (since 2017) and Pakistan and Portugal (since 2018). India, Pakistan, Nepal and New Zealand have also allowed third gender declarations on passports and other documents.

There have been a number of specific arguments that have been deployed against the self-identification proposal. These relate to safeguarding children, access to single sex spaces, the introduction of a third or non-binary gender category, and the claim that trans women and trans men are not really women and men, particularly that trans women are still actually men and thus, following patriarchy theory, they also remain inherent threats to all women. I will address each of these in turn.

Safeguarding

In an article in October 2017 Andrew Gilligan, a journalist with *The Times*, sensationalised the issues around transgender children.[433] His article criticised the trans children's charity Mermaids for its alleged involvement in a 2016 case when a mother was accused of forcing her male child to dress and live as a girl. Gilligan has continued to publish articles attacking Mermaids and trans rights in the *Times* and on other plat-forms. His article in December 2018 referring to Mermaids as an "aggressive" group, as well as hostile campaigning by TV writer Graham Linehan and the Mumsnet online community, led to the Big Lottery Fund reviewing its £500,000 grant to the charity, putting at serious risk its support for trans and gender-variant children.

Subsequently the charity was widely attacked in the press and on social media. Mermaids issued a statement in response to negative coverage in the press.[434] Thankfully, after a two-month review the Lottery Fund confirmed that it would award the grant to Mermaids and published a report calling the allegations made against Mermaids by Gilligan, Linehan and others "baseless".[435]

Nevertheless, similar hostile and poorly informed press articles have picked up on the increased numbers of children and young people being referred to the only children's Gender Identity Clinic (GIC), the Tavistock in London, implying that there is a social epidemic of "transness" or that there must be a shadowy "trans lobby" encouraging a trans or gender variant mindset among young people.

The number of referrals to GICs in Britain has certainly been growing. The Tavistock Clinic has seen referrals increase steadily since 2010-11. In 2015/16 there was an unprecedented doubling of referrals, up from 697 to 1,419. The following year 2016/17 there were 2,016 referrals, up 42 percent, and in 2017/18 there were 2,519, a 25 percent rise.[436]

The increase in referrals to the current fourteen GICs has put enormous strain on their limited funding. Patients have been forced to wait months or years for first appointments and in the meantime they receive no formal help or advice.

However, it would be a serious mistake to assume that these increases are the result of a fad or fashion, as some anti-trans activists have suggested. Each referral is of a person seeking advice and support and they should have the right to be listened to. It is the greater visibility of trans people that has almost certainly encouraged others to come forward, just as the ending of punishments and stigma for being left-handed led to an apparent increase in the proportion of left-handed people, from 3 percent a hundred years ago to 11 percent today.[437]

Some practitioners feel that the rate of referrals will not go on increasing: the most recent figures may reflect a process of catching up and numbers may be starting to stabilise. Only time will tell.

In their evidence submitted to the 2015 parliamentary trans rights enquiry GIRES noted that in terms of NHS services for trans youth in Britain:

> Medical intervention for children and adolescents has lagged behind overseas expertise in the long-term and well-researched practices in Amsterdam and elsewhere. Intervention with hormone-blockers in early puberty, to suspend the development of unwanted secondary sex characteristics, was not introduced here [in the UK] until 2011... Initially, blocking treatment was only available from 12, rather than the early stage of pubertal development, incurring unnecessary delay and psychological trauma. Hormone-blockers are now given around the onset of puberty, if assessments have already been completed.[438]

GIRES and others have warned of the dangers associated with long delays before treatment. The risks of suicidal emotional states, self-harm and deteriorating mental health are increased. Moreover, this is a class issue — not only does this affect rights in the workplace but working class trans individuals and families who have no access to private resources will generally be waiting the longest and have least access to systems of support.

> Young trans people, especially those assigned female at birth, may adopt starvation as a way of stopping menses and breast development. This may be wrongly interpreted as "classic anorexia", and the cause of the not-eating is not addressed...

> Those who have sought treatment elsewhere or who, in desperation, have self-medicated are, under present protocols, excluded from the current UK service provision. This would appear to be unethical.[439]

And they pointed out that:

...it takes 4 ½ months to access the clinic; assessments take 6 months; hormones are only prescribed after 12 months of hormone-blocking, and never before 16. Even when eligible for hormones, the young person has a further 6 months of assessment by the endocrinology service. That amounts to a 28 ½ month wait for treatment. By contrast, the Harvard Medical School can, when appropriate, get a young person onto hormones within a week.[440]

The focus on children and trans children's rights is reminiscent of some of the attacks on gay rights 50 years ago.

In the past opponents of homosexual decriminalisation often used homophobic slurs which claimed that homosexuality was linked to paedophilia. This vicious and fallacious trope raised its head again when the issue of gay adoption was being debated a couple of decades ago.

Today "child abuse and child protection" has been the false flag under which trans people and trans organisations have been accused of malignly pushing young people into irreversible decisions and expensive life-altering medical intervention. Contrary to the evidence, some have claimed this constitutes a crucial safeguarding issue in education and social care. In fact, these claims amount to reactionary transphobic scaremongering.

It seems that the starting point for the trans critics' political position is not the distress and anguish of the children and young people themselves or their families, or concern about the bullying and transphobia that they may be facing. Instead, parents have been repeatedly attacked for allegedly indulging their children's "whims" or "fads".

Access to single-sex spaces

Trans critics and transphobes argue that women's safety could be put at risk by self-declaration.

Safe spaces for women, such as domestic violence refuges, were fought for by the women's movement and trade unionists decades ago, in the face of establishment indifference and hostility. They remain necessary because of women's widespread and continued oppression in capitalist society. Today there are struggles to keep such refuges open and refuges are having to turn away increasing numbers of women as a result of huge cuts through austerity.

Currently such single-sex spaces can be subject to exemptions on a case-by-case basis from the equal access normally guaranteed in law by the 2010 Equality Act.

A transphobic trope often retailed in this context is that women's safety in toilets and other single-sex spaces is put at risk if trans women have access to them because trans women, because they are really men, still possess inherent inclinations to harass or attack cisgender women.

It is vanishingly rare for those making these claims to mention the violence that trans people, especially trans women, and especially black and Hispanic trans women, already face on a daily basis whether from inappropriate placement in male facilities based on their birth-assigned sex and lack of a GRC, or from the simple act of needing to visit a toilet.

Attempts to exclude trans people also erase the reality of the assaults, domestic violence, self-harm and mental ill-health that they may be subject to. Nor is the question answered about where abused trans people *should* go for refuge, or to use the toilet, other than to suggest that there "ought to be" specifically designated trans facilities. This is an abstract and unrealistic suggestion that ignores people's immediate needs. The alternative would seem to be that trans and non-binary people should simply be turned away.

The way that this issue has often been posed, in particular the implication that trans women are potentially violent men in drag scheming to get into women's spaces in order to assault or ogle them, carries a basic implicit transphobic assumption — that trans women remain men after transition and vice-versa for trans men.

It also ignores several key facts. First, trans women are actually the group most at risk of violence in seeking to use such facilities. What do the transphobes think should happen to non-binary identified people? Should they only enter gender neutral facilities?

Second, refuges and other bodies assess the people who

approach them and they operate security measures to protect clients against, for example, violent former partners who may be male or female. Why would such an organisation need to operate a different policy towards a trans person when such assessments are made on a case-by-case basis?

Third, it is not the case that all men are violent and women are not. Most men are not violent, and some women can be violent. Domestic violence within lesbian relationships has become more commonly recognised in recent times. The potential for violence against women certainly comes mainly from men (most commonly the men that women live with, rather than strangers) but it can also come from other women — in prisons, domestic situations and so on.

The #MeToo campaign highlighted the extent of day-to-day harassment, objectification and commodification of women that goes on at work, in public and in institutions like parliament, some mainstream political parties, and by a range of well-known figures in film and the media.

It would be false to claim that there has *never* been *any* example of someone claiming to be a trans woman harassing or attacking women in single-sex spaces, despite institutions like prisons and refuges carrying out individual risk assessments. The case of trans prisoner Karen White was mentioned previously. There have been some rare cases of harassment or assaults in other situations by people who, as well as identifying as trans, also sometimes appear to have had some mental health issues. But reports of trans women harassing or attacking cisgender women in *toilets* are rare to non-existent.

Compared to the preponderance of incidents of harassment, inappropriate behaviour, verbal attacks, sexual assaults and murders, domestically and in public, by men-identifying-as-men, the few examples of violence by trans women against other women cannot reasonably be used to justify the transphobes' unacceptable alternative for trans people — that of policing and blocking trans access to single-sex spaces, thus leaving the trans person even more vulnerable and fearful.

Those promoting these views rarely seem to think through what their insistence on excluding trans women from "women's spaces" would mean in practice. Should trans women instead use the very limited unisex toilets available, or use men's toilets in accordance with their birth sex exposing them to obvious very serious safety risks? It also begs the question of how such "banning" would be policed. What sort of inspections are being proposed?

Would there be scrutiny of identity documents, including birth certificates? That would surely be harassment. Being in possession of a "gender appropriate" birth certificate also tells the person doing the inspecting nothing, since someone with a GRC can change their original birth certificate. To take the situation to its absurd extreme, even inspecting genitalia would not only be gross physical assault but would also settle nothing since genital reconstruction these days is generally cosmetically convincing.

Trans critics and transphobes ignore the fact that if a predatory man wants to cross-dress in order to try and gain access to women's facilities he can already do so. The specific proposals to make it easier to gain a Gender Recognition Certificate are irrelevant to this "danger" in practice.

The exclusion of trans people from single-sex spaces would only result in making life even more difficult and dangerous for them — at a time when they are facing an increasingly hostile world — and would do nothing to improve safety and quality of life for cisgender women.

It is legitimate to question the inconsistency in the attitude of trans critics on the left, in that they are hostile towards aspects of trans rights yet supportive of greater rights for workers and other oppressed minorities. The answer seems to lie in their acceptance of aspects of patriarchy theory and bourgeois feminist ideology. The prevalence of the belief that trans women pose a threat reflects a common strand in some feminist ideology — the essentialist myth of the inherent nurturing, non-violent nature of women, and the inherent violence of men.

Trans critics seem to have de facto collapsed into an acceptance of an essentialism that they are comfortable applying to transgender people even though they may deride essentialism when discussing *women's* oppression.

When it comes to trans people (especially trans women), the "trans critics" of Woman's Place UK, Fair Play for Women or the Women's Human Rights Campaign (co-founded by Sheila Jeffreys[441]) and their supporters, through a network of social media sites and blogs which share a common hostility to trans rights and trans lives, consistently invoke arguments that rely on essentialist distinctions between biology and gender and the impact of gender-differentiated socialisation.[442]

All these transphobic groups in the UK have formed since the proposals to amend the GRA first emerged and have developed sets of demands, manifestos and declarations which, if implemented, would universally exclude trans women from already established women's rights or from struggles for the extension or defence of women's rights.

Thus the Women's Human Rights Campaign's *Declaration on Women's Sex-Based Rights* implicitly demands the removal of trans women's legal protections.

Another document, the *Woman's Place UK Manifesto 2019*[443], lists undeniably important and necessary demands and reforms to promote women's rights across a range of areas of social life, legislation, employment and so on. But each one of these areas has embedded within it clauses which are clearly transphobic in intent. Again, if implemented they would exclude trans women from any participation in *and benefit from* campaigns for equal pay, pension rights, equal access to the labour market, campaigns against violence, harassment and abuse against women and girls, equal access to health care and so on.

The Manifesto also calls for the "robust defence of the human right to freedom of speech in academia". This is an outright bourgeois demand, not a working class demand, in practice one that is currently being promoted by right wingers to undermine the left and advance a right wing agenda especially in academia. It is a transparent agenda that, among other threats, masks the crucial distinction that socialists make between "free speech" and "hate speech".

Another section of the Manifesto states an aspiration to:

> properly resource the Equality and Human Rights Commission (EHRC) to ensure effective oversight and enforcement of the Equality Act by including clear

guidance on the existing legal protections for single-sex services and a commitment to strengthening them where necessary.

This in fact would severely undermine trans rights and the spirit of the 2010 Equality Act that afforded some protection under the "gender reassignment" protected characteristic by expanding, and encouraging, the legal right of exception whereby service providers have the right to exclude trans people from single-sex services.

There are also attacks on the rights of trans prisoners ("end the practice by the criminal justice system of allowing offenders to self-identity their sex..."); and in sport (support for sex-segregated sports, promoting a level playing field for competitors and encouraging and recognising the excellence of female competition).

Such measures, if ever implemented, would sweep away trans women's rights in particular and would in effect erase them as well as intersex people and those identifying as non-binary.

The point is that this pernicious political discrimination becomes possible once one (falsely) perceives that the roots of trans oppression are fundamentally *different* to the roots of women's oppression, and once one believes that trans women are just "woman-identified men". Such an othering process is the kiss of death for the any notion of unity of the oppressed, would escalate the dangers trans people face, lets the austerity-mongers off the hook, and is a gift to the bigots and far right.

Introducing a non-binary legal category

Concerns have also been expressed by some about the reality or otherwise of non-binary gender identities and how these should or should not be recognised legally or in terms of data collection and official documentation.

Some feminists and trans critics have suggested that the proposals would amount to the eradication of "woman" as a sex category and would have a detrimental impact on the potential to promote data exposing the continuing oppression of women. This data is clearly important when it comes to looking at possible gender-differentiated access to health and employment, the gender pay gap or the impact of austerity on women. It is claimed that proposed changes would distort and degrade the accuracy of data about the sex distribution of the British population. It would bring into existence a new category or categories of gender, not just the current (in reality *inaccurate*) two, and break the immutable link they perceive between biological sex and gender.

Woman's Place UK's first general campaign, for example, was a petition to oppose a tentative proposal that the Office for National Statistics might decide to include such a third, non-binary option on the 2021 National Census item asking people's sex.

Others have argued, on the contrary, that the objections to such proposals are misplaced both conceptually and in terms of the current or likely absolute numbers that might be reflected in such changes, which are very small. The proportion of trans and non-binary people remains small despite greater visibility today. Estimates suggest perhaps one or at most two percent of the population. The number who transition is even smaller. Many do not apply for a GRC. Only around 4,800 GRCs have been issued over 12 years in a population approaching 70 million. The distorting impact of such numbers ticking a third gender option in the Census and other data-gathering exercises on the statistics about equal pay, hate crime and so on would certainly be negligible.

Those in favour of the changes, which they regard as long overdue and which have begun to be introduced in other contexts and jurisdictions, suggest that the claim of distortion has been considerably exaggerated and that, predictably, those objecting make no mention of the *positive* potential for trans or non-binary monitoring that such a question might yield.

At some point, short of the British state continuing to insist that everyone must fall under one or the other pole of a binary gender classification, non-binary identification will almost certainly be introduced. Opposition to this on the basis that it may undermine the struggle for women's rights (claims that this will dilute the statistical category of "woman") looks very much like the deployment of a deeply bourgeois argument to undermine a long overdue reality check.

It is true that the change would impact official statistics and data gathering, to a very small extent, but surely the basic right to designate one's gender (comparable to designating one's sexuality) is more important than this, should be defended by socialists, and indeed will better reflect social reality?

At the same time as decrying the potential of a third option on the sex item trans critical feminists say that they do *not* accept trans women as women or trans men as men. Yet like other trans women, when it comes to answering the current Census question, I have to tick the "female" box in accordance with my gender identity and my official documentation, and thus I would be counted as officially female — despite my personal preference which would be to tick an "other" or "trans" option if one was available.

So there is a contradiction: trans men and trans women are currently effectively treated as their acquired gender, or presumed gender identity, in the Census, while those who deny the reality of transgender identity argue that trans people should continue to be subsumed within the statistical sex binary, that is, trans women ticking the "female" option.

Of course, it is certainly not a simple matter to think of a precise wording for an appropriate Census question which would satisfy all or most transgender or non-binary people. However, the preferred alternative for those opposing such a move seems to be to stick with the current invisibility or erasure of trans and non-binary people in the Census.

It ought to be possible to devise biographical survey items which could include other gender categories and/or ask people whether they are "living in the gender to which they were assigned at birth". This is roughly the form of words some trade unions (including my own, UCU) and other organisations are already using as a formulation which allows them to go beyond the binary box-ticking of most biographical data collection items.

This whole "problem", of course, disappears once people can accept that trans women are women, trans men are men, and some people are non-binary, and all should be treated with respect and acceptance in documentation and statistics.

The socialisation argument

There is a common objection to recognising trans women as women — that they are not "real" women because they have not been socialised as women from birth. Jenni Murray, presenter of Radio 4's *Woman's Hour*, got into some hot water in 2017 for making exactly this claim.

The suggestion that trans women cannot be "real" women because they have not shared the same experiences as natal women in terms of puberty and early life is an attractive one for some feminists but it completely misses the point.

First, the argument stems from a flawed identity theory approach — people are here being defined in essence by their individual social experiences and their assumed biology rather than how they experience themselves in interaction with collective social mores and expectations and their objective position in a class structured society.

Second, trans-critics and transphobes do not seem keen to accept that trans women who have transitioned post-puberty or later in life are what might be termed "late-onset women", although many are keen to claim that trans people who come out as children or young adults are evidence of "Sudden Onset Gender Dysphoria" (or SOGD), an entirely mythical condition propagated to de-legitimise many people's lived experience.

Third, what ought to be an obvious response to this denial is that after their transition transgender women are subject to oppression as women — so why would any decent feminist or socialist want to deny them support, solidarity and equal rights?

In addition, something which transphobes and many trans critics ignore is that in their earlier lives trans and non-binary people will have very likely been subject to a form of oppression which cisgender women have not — transphobia. They will also have likely spent their entire childhood internalising the shame, guilt and trauma of having to hide who you are.

The objection to transgender women being regarded as women on the grounds of differential socialisation also ignores the fact that not all women have the same experience. Women's socialisation is neither a class-neutral nor homogenous phenomenon. Ivanka Trump's socialisation will have been very different to that of a working class immigrant woman in Los

Angeles, or a working class or poor woman anywhere.

There are also undercurrents in this line of argument reminiscent of the historical marginalisation of some women's concerns, needs and experiences within the women's movement itself. These have been women who, like many trans women, will also have been socialised very differently. Sometimes, for instance, this has involved the systematic exclusion of such women, like black women or lesbians, by dominant sections of the middle class white women's liberation movement of the 1970s.

Change the individual or change society?

Trans-critical feminists have also accused trans people of copping out by opting to change themselves and their bodies in order to better fit into gender binary societies as they exist, rather than seeking to change society to accept them as they are.

Presumably they expect trans people to put on hold their efforts to feel more comfortable and authentic in their bodies and lives until capitalist society magically evolves, or is overthrown, or is forced to become more ideologically and politically accommodating to transgender people.

Such a view reflects an abstract, idealist position. While some trans people will certainly want nothing more than to fit seamlessly into their acquired gender role after transition, others will want to change both themselves and the society which oppresses them. Either view is legitimate and should be supported. There is no contradiction in this.

A final thought on self-identification: no other oppressed group or protected characteristic is denied the right to the self-identification that some people critical towards trans rights want to deny when it comes to trans people. Self-identification is a basic democratic and human right. No-one has the right to tell trans people what they can or cannot be. Choosing to live in a gender different from that assigned at birth, or no gender at all, should be respected and not denied by others or by the state.

The socialist response — a way forward

Women and trans people are two groups hit hardest by austerity and anti-worker globalisation. Trans women are one of the highest risk groups for HIV infection — around 19 percent were HIV positive according to a worldwide meta-analysis published in *The Lancet* in 2013.[444]

Likewise the clock has been turned back decades for women facing domestic abuse, particularly working class women with minimal resources. Restricted access to legal aid, cuts to benefit entitlements, hundreds of thousands of benefits sanctions, changes to housing benefit rules that deem women in refuges ineligible, all threaten the financial viability of women's refuges and make life even more financially precarious for women. An *Independent* article in 2017 reported funding for women's refuges and support workers had been slashed by almost a quarter between 2010 and 2017.[445] Three quarters of councils have cut funding for women's refuges and many are now forced to turn away desperate women and children.

In this context it is tragic if the kind of transphobic and trans-critical views outlined above result in people seeing trans rights and women's rights as being in competition with one another. This needs to be strongly resisted, both through presenting clear arguments as to why such views are mistaken, but also by proposing ways to undermine such tendencies to division among oppressed groups and promote unity in the face of the attacks we all face. Equal rights is not a finite cake where different oppressed groups have to fight each other for bigger slices. Austerity and racism affect all of us: there is a common class enemy. Socialists start from the notion that an injury to one is an injury to all.

What is needed today are practical political demands to address both women's and trans people's oppression and work towards the achievement of active solidarity between their struggles.

This means refusing to be pessimistic about the potential of such struggles to win, offering solidarity to each other and agreeing appropriate concrete demands and proposals for joint organisation to achieve these. Activists should support demands for practical improvements to maximise safety and minimise risk for *all* women, trans or cisgender.

Some examples could be fighting to restore lost funding for refuges, support and advice groups, social services and so on.

We should demand that women's services have sufficient staff and staff training, that facilities are adequately supervised and monitored. How about fighting to get funding for attendants in toilets, secure individual bedrooms in shelters and cells in prisons, good lighting in streets and premises, emergency help buttons in homes, toilets and other facilities?

This necessity for joint struggle is recognised not just by many trans people but also by many women's rights organisations as well. In the next chapter, we will explore what sort of politics we need to build a movement for trans rights and trans liberation that can also challenge oppression in capitalism in general.

Chapter 10
What politics do we need?

Identity theory and the retreat from class

Many activists today who want to fight racism, women's oppression, homophobia or transphobia probably share a political worldview that draws on some form of identity theory.

Identity politics arises from what may appear to be a common sense view that only those who experience a particular form of oppression can define it or resist it, that everyone else has relative privilege and benefits from that oppression, and that by not sharing a particular characteristic (being a woman, or black, or Muslim, or LGBT+ for example) other people in society to a greater or lesser extent have an interest in maintaining that oppression. This is the basis of identity politics and for those holding this rather pessimistic view, what is required, as Sharon Smith has put it, is that:

> ...each oppressed group should have its own distinct and separate movement. Such movements therefore tend to be organised on the basis of "autonomy" or independence — from each other and from the socialist movement. They tend also to be organised independent of any class basis.[446]

Identity theory is currently under ideological attack by the right and the far-right. This hostility emanates from a variety of often well-funded sources. It includes the American fascist Richard Spencer, who first popularised the term "alt-right", far-right popularisers like Steve Bannon (formerly Donald Trump's adviser) associated with the online media outlet Breitbart, and the gay self-publicist Milo Yiannopoulus.

These attacks from the far-right are very different to the criticisms of identity politics made by Marxists. The far-right seek to deny that there are any genuinely oppressed categories of people, and to promote the false notion that oppression is exaggerated and driven by "political correctness gone mad." They claim that there are fundamental values (family values, "our way of life", "race realism", and so on) that must be defended against those who would undermine them. These include Muslims, socialists, LGBT+ people, women's movement campaigners and non-white migrants.

The propaganda of far-right groups like Generation Identity, whose aims include "defending Europe" and promoting "ethnopluralism" (segregating people along ethnic lines) give a flavour of the deeply racist, white European outlook being promoted.

This motley crew of the religious right, the alt-right, white supremacists, racist and fascist organisations and identitarians aim to subvert and replace identities based on class or oppression, which are also identities of *resistance*, with identities based on the cultural superiority of particular nations or ethnicities. But such identities actually *promote* the oppression of marginalised and disadvantaged groups and so stand for the defence of reactionary values and the preservation of capitalism.

While all those fighting oppression need to stand together against the right, we cannot ignore the fact that different understandings of particular oppressions and their causes will give rise to different understandings about how best to fight back. These differences should not fracture our attempts to build united fronts of resistance but they do need to be discussed in comradely ways in our campaigns, unions and activities.

Disagreements over whether and how trans people should be included within the parameters of particular identity categories have been played out especially within feminism and LGBT+ politics. Trans people have, in the process, often come in for quite a battering.

Because identity theories don't address the class roots of

oppression in capitalism, they offer no substantive basis for fundamentally challenging the system. Indeed, because they focus on ever finer categories of difference rather than on solidarity and unity in action, they can sometimes lead away from effective challenges.

The greatest trap they fall into is to base their political aims and objectives on *appearance* and the *particular* in capitalism rather than on the *reality*, the *essence* and the *universal*.

Falling into such an ideological trap has been made more likely since the early 1970s because of the absence in most of the industrialised world of large scale industrial action from which workers could generalise positive lessons about class struggle. No theory of power in society emerges independently of its social context. Identity theory, which at best sees class, or "classism", as merely one among a range of power differentials structured by particular identity categories, emerged out of a period of defeat and retrenchment for the left and for movements against oppression in the 1970s and 1980s.

Class versus individual differences

Even though different forms of identity theory may recognise class, they don't conceptualise it in the same way as Marxists do. They only see class as a category of *difference*. The working class is not recognised as embodying the potential to transform society through revolution.

Nor is the working class recognised as encompassing the vast majority of the oppressed within its ranks: rather, oppressed groups are viewed as effectively devoid of class character. This was illustrated in practice as identity theories gained traction in the 1970s through their marginalisation and exclusion of many of the radical and revolutionary gay activists from the gay movement and even from Prides by the mid-1970s. Instead, they focused on explicitly reformist strategies — including separatist strategies — aimed at maximising equal rights *within* the system.

Any emphasis on exploitation and profit accumulation as the purpose of capitalism and as the source of oppression was rejected by identity theorists as being evidence of Marxist "economic reductionism." Class struggle — over pay, conditions, pensions and so on — tended to be perceived as economistic and inherently failing to recognise oppression. This has sometimes been caricatured as Marxists ignoring struggles over oppression such as abortion rights, racism, or sexual and transphobic harassment, within and beyond the workplace.

Not only is this historically false but in fact any such Marxist perspective on industrial and workplace struggles would be fundamentally mistaken. Abortion rights in Britain, along with Equal Pay legislation, gender discrimination, LGBT+ rights and anti-racist campaigns are just a few examples of where socialist activism, including by Marxist individuals and organisations in the trade unions and more broadly in the working class, have been central to building the pressure needed to win significant reforms.

It was socialist and socialist feminist women who took the demands for abortion rights into the trade unions and won support from male workers. It was often socialist lesbians and gay activists who in the 1970s and 1980s took demands for LGBT+ rights, opposition to Section 28, and the fight against HIV/Aids to their straight workmates and won their support.[447]

The idea that a person's oppressed identity supersedes class divisions and should be tackled independently of class solidarity has invariably had a corrosive impact on the potential for working class resistance to oppression. Class divisions are rejected in favour of assumed essential gender differences and rigid distinctions between sex and gender — the liberal mirror to bourgeois notions of sex, sexuality and gender.

The eclipse of any mass adherence to socialist or Marxist explanations of LGBT+ oppression in favour of identity theories in the last quarter of the 20th century took a heavy toll on LGBT+ thinking and activism and helped to marginalise the legitimate demand for gay and trans liberation.

Postmodernism's influences

The theoretical soil from which identity politics grew was postmodernism. Postmodernist theory's originators — Derrida, Leotard and others[448] — held that the big theories of the past, such as Marxism which sought to analyse modern society, the development of capitalism and class struggles through a historical materialist approach, no longer fitted "postmodern", post-industrial societies in which power is dispersed, reality is relative and essentially ahistorical, and there are potentially equally valid alternative discourses available.

Choonara and Prasad have put it this way:

> The theoretical backbone of identity politics was the rise of post-Marxist and postmodernist theories in academia. This break with Marxism held that the era of "grand narratives"—attempting to understand society as a whole—was over. The stress was now on uncertainty, indeterminacy, and the multiple and fragmented character of reality. Postmodernism reflected the politics of a generation of activists and academics demoralised by the defeat of the mass movements of 1968 as well as the general pessimism of an era in which Francis Fukuyama could famously announce that the triumph of liberal capitalism signalled the "end of history".[449]

Approaches derived from postmodernist roots therefore start from a very different understanding of the origins and distribution of power in society to that of Marxism.

Power is envisaged as localised and multifarious and "struggle" frequently boils down to individualised resistance or acts of "subversion" rather than collective mass action. Challenging oneself and one's privileges becomes the site of political activity.

Marxists, on the other hand, start from the centrality of exploitative class relations in capitalism and look to strengthen our side, our class, by standing as the "tribunes of all the oppressed", as Lenin put it, recognising that the capitalist class is the common enemy of all working class people in whatever oppressed group they might be.

That means socialists need to focus on promoting working class unity in action and not endorse ways of thinking and political strategies and tactics that, in practice, further entrench differences between working class people.

Building such unity means developing organisation which

can not only bring together activists to address particular forms or issues of oppression but who also understand that the roots of oppression lie deep in the class nature of the capitalist system. When social movements against sexism, racism, LGBT+phobia emerge socialists need to be actively involved in these, but social movements are volatile and can rise and fall quickly. We also need to develop ongoing socialist organisation which can learn from being part of these social movements and can help to shape them and make victories more likely. I examined the emergence and subsequent limitations of the Gay Liberation Front in an earlier chapter but similar political reversals also happened to the Black Power and Women's Liberation movements.

Tragically, some of the LGBT+ radicals of the 1960s and 1970s did not survive the Aids epidemic from the 1980s. Some others had never been all that radical to start with and treated the real radicals like Sylvia Rivera, the GLF and socialist LGBT+ people with suspicion. They were very ready to embrace homonormativity and a set of limited reformist aspirations.

Many other former radicals and activists aspired to join the middle class and followed well-worn political paths into mainstream reformist politics (the Democratic Party in the US, the Labour Party in Britain), becoming local and in some cases national politicians.

Others have been busy carving out careers in academia for decades, often becoming increasingly remote from the grassroots where some of them had cut their political teeth.

Queer theory — the great postmodernist hope?

The emergence of queer theory was an apparently radical rejection of liberal identity theory and its adherence to essentialist notions of sex and gender. However, it stands as an example of the contradictory nature of postmodern responses to the retreat from class and class struggle.

Queer theory and queer politics were developed from the writings of the French philosopher Michel Foucault[450], the founder of deconstruction, Jacques Derrida, and later the work of Judith Butler.[451]

Some years before his death in 1984 Foucault had rejected

Marxism following the failure of the 1968 events in France. This was articulated in his *History of Sexuality*, which owed more to the existentialist Nietzsche than to Marx. His ideas, later developed by Judith Butler, emerged from a broad postmodernist and poststructuralist ideological framework, partially in opposition to liberal identity theory's approach to women's and LGBT+ oppression.

Queer theory gained popularity, especially in academia, from the late 1980s. It is, however, a contradictory phenomenon. While it rejects the rise of the comfortable individualism and homonormativity of a minority of relatively affluent gays, and likewise the predominance of the Pink Pound and the notion of the "safe gay", it also continues to express the retreat from class politics and Marxism that had its theoretical origins in the decline of class struggle throughout the West after the early 1970s.

Queer theorists are rightly critical of the bulk of the lesbian and gay politics which became prominent during the 1980s and the way these became subsumed within an individualistic, consumer-oriented, apolitical niche-market ethos of "gay rights".

It is true that in some respects Marxists and queer theorists share a common starting point. Both reject the de-politicisation and commercialisation of the gay movement and demand a return to the activism and radicalism of the early gay rights movement. Beyond that starting point, however, the remedies proposed are radically different.

Queer theory, as Noel Halifax has put it, is quite good at recognising the fluidity and social construction of sexuality and gender identity, quite good at describing the "how" of being gay or, in Judith Butler's work, of "performing" man or woman, but it doesn't say anything about the "why".[452] Queer theory fails when its proponents try to expand its insights to become a theory of everything.

Queer theory argues that the process of "queering" mainstream approaches to any field of study, not just gender studies and sexuality, contributes a subversive quality which can challenge or "trouble" prevailing power relations and help to empower the disadvantaged.

But in practice such politics lead to inward-looking identity politics rather than an engagement with efforts to collectively change the world and create the conditions for sexual and gender liberation.

Surya Munro, who herself writes from a poststructuralist position, describes queer theory in this way:

> One of the hallmarks of queer theory is the destabilisation and subversion of existing categories. Queer theory deconstructs gender and sexual identities, primarily via interpretations of cultural texts... For instance, Butler... interprets drag and cross-dressing as queer and as challenging heteropatriarchal norms because they expose the ways in which gender is constructed. Thus gender identities are enacted with the aim of destabilising the normalisation of certain types of gender and sexuality, so that we are made aware of how *all* genders and sexualities are fictitious. Queer theory also creates space for imagining alternatives to the rigid gender binary system.[453]

However, trans activist Viviane Namaste is highly critical of queer theory for its neglect of the everyday lives of transgender people. "Critics in queer theory", she says, "write page after page on the inherent liberation of transgressing normative sex/gender codes, but they have nothing to say about the precarious position of the transsexual woman who is battered and who is unable to access a woman's shelter because she was not born a biological woman".[454]

She accuses Butler of distorting transgender realities in order to privilege explanatory schema based exclusively on race and class. By downplaying the significance of transgender in the lived realities of trans people Namaste suggests that Butler is contributing to the same denial and erasure of trans reality which is found in sociological and medical approaches to trans people's lived experiences, and in the treatment of gender variance by some gay writers and theorists where trans is subsumed within a treatment of sexual orientation.

Queer theorists are critical of the notion that there is a

"gay movement" or a "gay community" at all. This may be a fair point: it may make more sense to talk about LGBT+ *communities*. LGBT+ history does reveal the existence of a variety of gay, lesbian, transgender, bisexual, non-binary, intersex, etc, groups with a variety of origins and aspirations who have sometimes been mutually antagonistic or dismissive of one another.

Judith Butler, to her credit, is not numbered among those feminists who promote trans exclusionary or trans-critical politics. Queer theorists in general seem supportive of trans identities, seeing them as inherently subversive of the gender binary.

In an interview with a trans blogger in 2014 Butler was invited to comment on the views of Sheila Jeffreys and Janice Raymond, two prominent critics of transgender/transsexuality. She responded:

> I have never agreed with Sheila Jeffreys or Janice Raymond, and for many years have been on quite the contrasting side of feminist debates. She appoints herself to the position of judge, and she offers a kind of feminist policing of trans lives and trans choices. I oppose this sort of prescriptivism, which seems to me to aspire to a kind of feminist tyranny.[455]

We can see such radical feminist "tyranny" in action in the attitudes of some radical feminists to trans people in general, and trans women in particular. Monro sums this up well:

> The radical feminist stance on trans has had a profound and damaging impact on the relations between trans people and the feminist movement. Since the feminist debates of the 1970s, typified by Raymond's position on transsexuality, transsexual women have experienced a very considerable amount of exclusion from the lesbian and feminist communities. This has included, for instance, female transsexual employees in women's organisations being forced to resign, transsexual women who have been raped being refused support by Rape Crisis Centres, and Women's Centres refusing them access.[456]

Nevertheless, queer theory is open to criticism from a Marxist perspective.

While queer theorists are fundamentally critical of sexual and gender relations in capitalism and look for radical change they do not see the working class as the agent of that change. This rejection, in practice, is fatal to any idea that queer theory can constitute a viable theory of collective liberation for LGBT+ people.

Privilege theory

Privilege theory emerged in the late 1980s and proposes that a range of power advantages are inherent in the fact of someone being white (in a racist society), or heterosexual (in a homophobic society), or cisgender (in a transphobic society), or middle class.[457]

For many people who see that sexist, racist, homophobic and transphobic ideas are deeply rooted in the socialisation we all experience and the institutions we are part of, the idea that we should all "check our privileges" can seem to make sense.

Thus those who have one or more privilege(s) ought to become self-aware ("check their privilege"), or indeed may need to have their privilege pointed out to them so that they can become more self-aware and use this awareness to address the inequality in power relations between individuals who belong to oppressed categories.

Choonara and Prasad have summarised privilege theory in this way:

> At the heart of privilege theory is the idea that oppression works through a series of unearned advantages enjoyed by those who do not suffer a particular oppression. So all men, white people or straight people, for example, will gain privileges that come from not facing sexism, racism or homophobia. The beneficiary of these privileges may be completely unaware of them — in fact much emphasis among privilege theorists is on what they would describe as "making privilege visible" — alerting people to the unearned advantages they may take for granted. Similarly individuals do not choose

whether or not to have these "privileges" — they are automatically bestowed by virtue of someone's race, gender, sexuality and so on. Through this framework, class becomes just one of a myriad of oppressive divisions in society.[458]

This obviously poses a problem in terms of how to collectively fight back against oppression. Resistance based on a Marxist understanding of oppression starts from asserting the need to tackle the structural transphobia (or racism or sexism) around us rather than focusing on changing the individual.

Marxists argue that individuals are most likely to change their views when directly engaged in struggles and campaigns. The experience of the Stonewall Rebellion radically affected many participants' political consciousness through exposing them to the state's class nature on the one hand and the potential for change through mass struggle on the other.

In the process people engaged in such struggles can learn that any concessions to racism, sexism, homophobia and transphobia undermine the potential of the very collective struggle they are part of. Choonara and Prasad write:

> Because privilege theory's primary focus is on the inequality between individuals it cannot arm us for a fight that is ultimately against the system as a whole. But the damage is not just in the way it limits the horizons of struggle; it also risks hampering the battles against prejudice and discrimination that are taking place in the here and now.[459]

It is neither helpful nor progressive for privilege theorists to insist that the best that white anti-racists can do — or straight anti-homophobes, or male feminists, or cisgender trans advocates for that matter — is act as supporters of black people, women, gays or trans people. The notion that fighting racism, or sexism or transphobia is very much in the direct interests of *all* working class people regardless of their particular oppression is unfortunately alien to privilege theory.

Marxists support the notion that oppressed groups

have a right to self-organise and a right to insist that others cannot achieve liberation on their behalf. The voices of all the oppressed have a right to be heard — not least because the working class is composed of oppressed people who share the experience of exploitation by the capitalist class.

It is not the role of self-appointed advocates and spokespersons to assume the right to speak for oppressed groups. And it is unfortunately true that there have been plenty of instances where some left activists have either been blind to the multiple oppressions experienced by many oppressed people or have assumed the right to speak on behalf of them.

Nevertheless, self-organisation raises a crucial issue. At heart here is the matter of whether oppressed groups can achieve their liberation *on their own.* This has certainly been argued by many black nationalists, lesbian separatists, radical feminists, and some gay rights groups. One reason this is mistaken is because oppressed groups are almost always minorities. In the case of trans people, a very small minority of society, in fact.

From a socialist perspective it is one thing to insist on the right to self-organisation of oppressed groups, to develop group cohesion and confidence in safe environments and so on, but quite another to operate as if no-one outside the oppressed group can genuinely work alongside and share the demands of the group because they do not identify as being of that group.

The central problem with privilege theory derives from its identity theory roots that focus on differences and divisions between those whose real interests would be best served (indeed ultimately *can* only be best served) by class solidarity and unity in action.

Privilege theory does not address a supposed gap that some writers on women's oppression claim to have identified in Marx's thinking about oppression.[460] It tends instead, by starting at the level of the individual and her experience of oppression relative to other individuals, to ignore the reality, central to Marxist theory, that we cannot understand the social relations in any society (including the existence of systemic oppression) without recognising the central role played by the actual productive forces of that society — how production is organised to use the tools, technology and so on to produce things and distribute them.

The key relationship between who owns or is excluded from the control of these means of production, and people's ways of thinking about the world and their place in it — their ideas or consciousness — is not a passive or static one. Each acts upon the other in a reciprocal or dialectical way. When Marx wrote that:

> Men make their own history, but they do not make it just as they please; they do not make it under circumstances chosen by themselves, but under given circumstances directly encountered and inherited from the past. The tradition of all the generations of the dead weighs like a nightmare on the brain of the living.[461]

he was arguing against any static, economic reductionist, or idealist understanding of how peoples come to hold certain ideas. The material circumstances give rise to the ideas rather than the other way round, but not in a crudely mechanical way.

Marx's historical materialist approach is, Marxists argue, a *sufficient* explanation of how the economic and social relations in society give rise to class conflict over who owns the means of production, and how oppressions such as transphobia or sexism arise. While the particular conditions in any given society will be different and require careful analysis, the general explanation shows no evidence of a "gap" in theory that requires a "bolt on" theory of oppression such as privilege theory. Rather the Marxist method can be applied to new and changing circumstances.

Privilege theory is in fact an impediment to the development of a comprehensive theory of oppression. Because it neither recognises that the roots of oppressions such as transphobia lie in the social relations of class society nor recognises the potential that collective struggle, especially class struggle, has for encouraging the agency of the working class itself to end oppression by challenging the class rule of the capitalist minority, it represents an ahistorical political path away from the historical materialist, class struggle approach that is necessary for trans liberation. It thus needs to be sensitively but robustly opposed by socialists.

At the level of praxis its corrosive impact can often be appreciated from witnessing discussions on social media and within campaigns. Many of us will have witnessed discussion forums that have degenerated into destructive accusations of unacknowledged racism, sexism or homophobia to the extent that potential activists and those offering solidarity are driven into silence and withdrawal.

While it can certainly be the case that even well-meaning people can exhibit internalised oppressive assumptions and behaviours, and should be challenged if these become apparent, when such people get dismissively told to step back, check their privilege, review their behaviour and beliefs, or that they are "bullying" by arguing and discussing tactics or expressing disagreement, this can undermine any notion of collective, inclusive unity in action among those otherwise keen to be part of challenges to institutional and societal oppression.

Who benefits?

It is not a privilege for a cisgender person not to get beaten up for not being trans. Rather, it should be a right, just like for anyone else, for trans people *not* to be subject to such hate crime. Seeing things in terms of rights and not "who benefits" can help shift the debate from divisive and exclusionary tactics towards the development of collective, inclusive ones.

Marxists deny that all men benefit from women's oppression or that all whites benefit from racism. We might ask, for example, how men benefit when women's average earnings in Britain remain around 18 percent below those of men's for equal work. Do male workers pocket the difference? To ask the question is to answer it: the difference in fact is pocketed by the employer, not the male workers. Do men living in families with women workers benefit from their lower earnings? In reality the whole family, including any men and boys, suffers materially through a lower standard of living.

Black people — mostly black men — in Britain continue to be subject to high levels of stop and search by police and deaths in custody, and proportionately are much more likely to end up in prison than white men. This is also true in the United States where the extent of police killings of black people is a 21st century scandal.

Stephen Lawrence's murder in 1993 and the catalogue of police corruption, incompetence and endemic state racism that followed exposed the racism at the heart of the British state, as did the recent Windrush scandal and the Grenfell Tower fire, which killed 72 people in the summer of 2017. None of these examples of racism benefit white people, and certainly not white working class people.

When police who kill, harass or mistreat black people are protected by senior officers, prosecutors and the courts it makes them more confident to mistreat white working class people and other oppressed groups like trans people.

Our activism should not consist merely in demanding that those who possess more power by virtue of their wealth and position should, or might, give it up merely by having it pointed out to them, as in effect privilege theory does. The realities of inequality and oppression under capitalism need to be collectively challenged and those who really do benefit should be stripped of their class power and potential to do so.

Intersectionality

Many LGBT+ activists, feminists and others, particularly younger ones and those moving into political activism for the first time, have embraced the notion of intersectionality. For them it represents inclusivity and solidarity with other oppressed people rather than separatism. Intersectionality or intersectional thinking is seen as a fresh new idea and one which addresses the divisive shortcomings of identity theory.

On these grounds many strongly opposed the behaviour of the small group of lesbian separatists who hijacked the front of the 2018 Pride in London parade, putting them on the same side as socialists and the trans activists who were the main target of the transphobic group.[462] Many of them were among the thousands who signed the letters of protest that quickly drew a public apology from the Pride in London organisers.[463]

Yet, intersectionality is not a new concept, having first emerged in multiracial feminist theory in the 1970s. It was popularised by Kimberlé Williams Crenshaw who used the term in several articles from the late 1980s onwards.[464]

Crenshaw articulated a rejection of the notion that within second-wave feminism, from the late 1960s on, white women's experiences of women's oppression could simply be extended to those of black women, ie that black women's experiences could be, or could remain, subsumed within white women's experiences as the experiences of *all* women.[465]

At the same time, partly as a result of their experiences in social movements and some left organisations, and the partial incorporation/partial defeat of autonomous political movements through the final decades of the 20th century (anti-war, Black Power, women's liberation, gay liberation), some black women activists and also many lesbian activists wanted to develop a theoretical response to their perceived erasure or invisibility. This was certainly a justified critique, especially in the US where the women's movement was much more middle class and the involvement of trade unions and the left was much weaker than in Britain. It articulated a partially progressive politics within feminism compared to the prevailing bourgeois feminism.

Intersectionality theory, however, has failed to really explain the origins of oppression and what is at the root of the multiple oppressions we experience in class societies. Its basic claim is that oppressed people often have multiple intersecting vectors of oppression — such as gender, ethnicity, class and sexuality (the black, lesbian, disabled person for example) — and that the lived experience of marginalised people is based on such multiple identities which contribute to their systematic social inequality. Individuals can and do experience oppression differently. Black women can experience sexism differently to white women; lesbians can experience oppression differently to straight women; trans women can experience oppression — sexism and transphobia — differently to cisgender women.

A person's "intersectionality experience" will be greater than the sum of the parts — the specific forms of oppression they experience. As a description, this is a step forward from the invisibility experienced by some multiply oppressed groups.

However, on the crucial question of how to explain these

oppressions, how to resist them and fight for liberation, there is little on offer in intersectionality theory other than the notion that we should seek greater self-awareness to "increase self-value" and achieve "a stable self-definition".[466]

Intersectionality theory had contradictory elements even in the context of the women's movement at the time it emerged. It was partly a progressive critique in arguing that gender could not be discussed without reference to class, race, sexuality, disability and so on. It rightly critiqued bourgeois white feminism's effective erasure of the ways in which women's oppression impacted the lives of black women in the USA. But from an historical materialist perspective it was at the same time regressive in its rejection of the primacy of class and class struggle. Like privilege theory, its weaknesses become most evident when its theorists have tried to develop its insights into a theory of everything.

Theorists like Patricia Hill Collins promoted a more explicit rejection of an historical materialist analysis of capitalism. They explicitly rejected Marxist insights and theories and further retreated from challenging the capitalist system.

In response, others have sought to reassert Marxist analysis. Marxist-feminist Martha Gimenez, for example, in discussing Black feminism in the US and responding to those who argued that Marxism is "economic reductionist", wrote:

> To argue, then, that class is fundamental is not to "reduce" gender or racial oppression to class, but to acknowledge that the underlying basic and "nameless" power at the root of what happens in social interactions grounded in "intersectionality" is class power.[467]

Eve Mitchell, in her widely shared blog article "I am a woman and a human: a Marxist feminist critique of intersectionality theory" presents an interesting and highly critical account of intersectionality's rise to its current hegemonic position. Part of Mitchell's conclusion is that:

> Since identity politics, and therefore intersectionality theory, are a bourgeois politics, the possibilities for

struggle are also bourgeois. Identity politics repro-duces the appearance of an alienated individual under capitalism and so struggle takes the form of equality among groups at best, or individualized forms of struggle at worst.[468]

There are debates among those who use the notion of intersectionality about the nature of particular social catego-ries and the relationships between them, as well as interest in theorising the experiences of people who cross the bounda-ries of societally constructed categories, such as transgender people.

While those influenced by intersectionality, like those who define as feminists, should be regarded by Marxists as co-fighters against oppression, it is not a theory that can be approached uncritically. Marxists argue that intersectionality can *describe* situations of multiple oppression but does not *explain* them.

Some on the left have argued that intersectionality can provide a bridge to Marxism in developing an effective theory and practice for resisting oppression.[469] Marxists certainly need to engage in joint struggles with those influenced by intersec-tionality theory but they also assert that exploitation of our labour power is more fundamental than the various forms of oppression: oppression is how the ruling class tries to keep us divided and subjugated in order that they can more effectively maintain their rule and exploit our labour power.

We therefore need to recognise the centrality of class struggle as the crucial way to radically change the balance of class forces in capitalism and empower workers' confidence, self-esteem, and self-value. Fundamentally that struggle is engaged in the workplace. While recognising the importance of social movements and struggles against oppression there is a danger that seeking to accommodate Marxist theory and strategy to intersectionality would seriously detract from a recognition of the importance of struggles that can bring workers together at the site of their exploitation — in the workplaces. Without this recognition, intersectionality can in practice act as a bridge that leads *away* from Marxism rather than one that leads towards Marxist historical materialism.

Reasserting materialism

The experience in recent decades of capitalism's growing instability, endless wars, accelerating environmental degradation, gross and increasing inequalities, and particularly the severe financial and economic crisis of 2008, has prompted some writers and activists to seriously question approaches like queer theory and to begin to re-examine materialist explanations and analysis.[470]

James Penney, for example, offers a cogent critique of queer theory's shortcomings and suggests the need for a materialist approach rooted in Marx on the one hand and Freudian and Lacanian psychoanalysis on the other.[471] This, however, seems in danger of offering an unnecessarily obscure alternative which would in any case prove unable to break free from postmodernist and post-structuralist premises.

A Marxist, historical materialist analysis is crucial to offering the working class and its organisations the ideological and political tools to understand oppression in general and transphobia in particular.

When we march and attend vigils and protests in solidarity with people threatened with deportation, or protest at trans people's treatment in prisons, or pass trans-supportive resolutions in our trade unions, or turn up to support workers' picket lines, it would be the height of sectarian numbskullery to refuse to link arms with or seriously engage with some of the people there, or, worse, deny their right to be present, because they have a different way of understanding this or that particular oppression, or because they do not see the centrality of class and organised labour. Socialists have a responsibility to work with others to help build the biggest and most effective campaigns and movements against oppression.

But in the inevitable discussions about how best to fight back, Marxists will argue, as Choonara and Prasad have aptly put it, that:

> By locating the sources of oppression in class society,
> we can see the structural capabilities and potential

power that workers have within capitalism. While intersectionality rightly points out that there are many interrelated divisions in society, like privilege theory it relegates the question of class to just one of a series of oppressions. This misses out what is unique about class in capitalism. It is a source not just of oppression—but of power—and is the potential basis on which people of many backgrounds and intersecting oppressions can unite. Marx called the working class the *universal class* not because everyone in the working class is the same, but because all working class people share a common relationship to capitalism and together form the unique force that has the power to abolish class society altogether.[472]

The task of Marxists is to dig deeper than the surface appearance of many oppressions, to understand the underlying material bases of those oppressions. This helps us to uncover the fact that simply fighting for equality within capitalism will never be enough to rid us of oppression altogether.

Chapter 11
Eyes on the prize

The level of trans visibility today would have been unthinkable to transgender people a mere half century ago.

Most trans people report a sense of relief and at least partial fulfilment in coming out, perhaps transitioning, and living a more authentic life. But being trans can carry severe stress and very real risks despite also having the potential to be life-enhancing. Trans people by their very existence negate the constricting and damaging parameters of a heterosexist and gender binary orthodoxy. Transgender, genderqueer, agender, genderfuck, gender rebels, non-binary people, and so on, can fight back alongside straight and cisgender supporters and be at the forefront of consigning the old system to history's dustbin.

Trans people are increasingly to be seen on vigils, protests, prides and in the media. More trans people are out at work, in unions and in communities. Some are now involved electorally. But visibility does not amount to liberation. So the question arises: is trans liberation achievable within the confines of the current system?

Many people may agree that to alleviate suffering, end wars, reverse climate change and create a safer world we need socialism. They want radical change, but everything in capitalist society is geared towards making them feel powerless to bring about that change themselves. Some would tell us that these changes can only be achieved by electing a majority of socialist MPs in parliament and then legislating for equal rights, effective environmental controls, workers' rights, the nationalisation of corporations and utilities and so on. Others might add that extra-parliamentary activity is also required — perhaps some demonstrations and petitions.

But these proposals alone fail to adequately explain or offer a solution to the source of the problem for oppressed and exploited people — the capitalist system itself.

Nonetheless, workplaces and trade unions, as well as communities, official politics and the media, are arenas within which today's fights for trans rights are being waged. It is encouraging, therefore, that the Labour Party and almost every trade union in Britain currently have national policies that support trans rights and the proposed amendments to the GRA.

Likewise, ensuring workplaces have good policies on trans issues and that unions hopefully have in place some appropriate training for reps is important. Trans supportive policies should not just be a set of fine words but should encourage staff and union reps to treat trans rights as an industrial issue intimately linked to pay, contracts, job security, pensions and working conditions for trans staff.

And often the most effective response by workers and students to equality deficits, bullying, harassment and victimisation in workplaces and on campuses is immediate solidarity action, including strikes and walkouts, and not limiting resistance to the pursuit of individual grievances and a casework approach. Quick, sharp mass responses like this can often concentrate employers' and managers' minds because it threatens their bottom line or their public reputation.[473]

Today there is no shortage of issues and demands that should be raised by LGBT+ activists and fought for by workers' political and trade union organisations. We can:

⬜protest, march and hold vigils against examples of hate crime, ensuring that the victims of such attacks are also offered meaningful practical support and solidarity;
⬜campaign for our organisations — student unions, trade unions, campaign groups — to adopt explicit policies supporting trans rights, especially the proposed amendments to the GRA and the introduction of nonbinary status to censuses, surveys and data bases.

This will be crucial to mounting opposition should the government ultimately renege on support for these.

■ argue to turn Prides into protests, not corporate fun days[474];

■ work with others to support or initiate Trans Prides, and win trade union and community backing for these;

■ encourage trans organisations to work with women's groups to demand the reversal of cuts to LGBT+ and women's support organisations;

■ encourage support for the international Transgender Day of Remembrance (20th November), International Day Against Homophobia, Transphobia and Biphobia (IDAHOT Day),[475] and Trans Visibility Day (March 31st) in our localities and workplaces;

■ organise trans history and awareness events as part of LGBT History Month every February;

■ ensure our organisations support anti-racist, anti-Islamophobic initiatives and campaigns, and support refugees and migrants, especially those who are LGBT+.

Recovering our memories

There is much to be learnt from working class history and how struggles for LGBT+ rights are impacted by and integral to many other past struggles. Trans people have a long history of resistance to transphobia despite this often having been hidden or partially erased. Today, compared to even 50 years ago at the time of Stonewall, trans people are better organised and more visible in many parts of the world and in a much better position to fight collectively for their liberation.

A crucial conclusion that can be drawn from examining the history of working class struggle in general and the fight against oppression is that the highest points of struggle and achievement for LGBT+ rights have been when there have been the greatest working class challenges to capitalist rule, and vice versa.

Several recent books have demonstrated the crucial role that trade unions and socialist activists within the labour movement have played for decades in the fight against LGBT+ oppression and the struggle to win our legal, social and human rights.[476] Trans people's history also includes important contributions that have been made in seeking to clarify concepts of gender, sex and sexuality.

But the relatively small number and limited social weight of LGBT+ people is also relevant to how the fight can be waged. Trans people especially are a small proportion of society and while self-organisation can certainly achieve important advances, such organisation on its own ultimately lacks the power to fundamentally change society. Consequently self-organisation is self-limiting if it does not look to link up with the potential power of the working class organised in workplaces.

No oppressed minority, no collection of individuals defined by having particular identity characteristics such as being women, or trans, or BAME, can retreat into its own bunker, fight its own corner and still hope to win liberation.

Workers have no option but to sell our labour power. Workers now constitute the largest social class in the world. Our common exploitation is the critical shared characteristic that makes the working class a *collective* and not just a *collection* of oppressed individuals.

Whatever our particular forms of oppression in other ways. We are all exploited, we do not receive in our wages and salaries the full value of our labour power because the capitalist employer appropriates a portion of it as profit. This means that we all have a crucial common interest not just in maximising wages and improving working conditions in day to day struggles but also the more fundamental shared interest of ending the economic system that exploits our labour power in the first place.

When oppressed people actively oppose their oppression the chances of winning are hugely improved by linking such struggles to the collective power of workers in the workplace. Thus it was crucial that the labour movement fought for equal pay for women, against sex discrimination, for LGBT+ rights, for abortion rights and for the criminalisation of racial discrimination.

This works both ways: to fight successfully in day-to-day struggles in workplaces workers have to confront the diverse and sometimes contradictory or prejudiced ideas about others that their workmates may hold. Given the prevalence of reactionary and regressive ideas in capitalist society in general, it is no surprise that some of these ideas may be racist, sexist, transphobic and so on.

Workers' best option for victory is to maximise their unity against the employer while arguing with the sexist, racist or homophobic fellow worker at the same time. Racists then have to decide whether they are going to strike and picket alongside BAME and Muslim workmates, sexists have to decide whether to accept the leadership of women strike leaders, people with transphobic views have to decide whether to link arms with trans workers and so on. In other words, will they put their class interests ahead of identity, group or national interests. There have been workplace disputes which give glimpses of this kind of inspiring solidarity.[477]

Today's critical times demand that creative and inclusive ways need to be found to achieve the greatest possible unity of oppressed and exploited people to work together to defend gains, win reforms, and ultimately overthrow the corrupt and inhumane capitalist system. In the UK the numbers of strike days have been at historic lows, but taking part in strikes and mass movements has the potential to radically change people's consciousness.[478] Often strikes which begin as defensive industrial action over apparently straightforward economic issues such as pay and working conditions will quickly progress to offensive political strikes about repression, workers' rights, particular laws and so on. Similarly, struggles against oppression can feed into the fight over economic power.

This is what happened in country after country during the Arab Spring of 2011, and what began to happen in struggles such as the Sudanese revolution of 2019. Protests and strikes can begin over bread or democratic rights, but can grow to threaten the dictator's rule, the political establishment and the economic system itself.

In the course of such struggles people themselves begin to change. Women were at the forefront of the Sudanese struggle, leading the protests and organising in unions and communities. Stereotypes about the "meekness" of Muslim women were challenged, and long-hidden histories of women warriors were once again told.

Trans people, like the courageous fighters Sylvia Rivera and Marsha P Johnson, have often been foremost among those calling most loudly for solidarity and unity of *all* the oppressed and not just those identifying as trans or even LGBT+.

Today trans people can offer solidarity to those who are also under increasing attack — Muslims, women, disabled people, black people, workers — not least because many trans people *are also* those oppressed and exploited people. Many, perhaps most, oppressed people are multiply oppressed, many, perhaps most, are also workers. Offering active solidarity invites reciprocal solidarity and so helps to generate the unity that can block and defeat the bigots and the far-right, resist employers' offensives, and help us all move forward to win the prize of human liberation.

Organisation

The question of organisation is a crucial one. In a 2019 article assessing the situation for LGBT+ people on the 50th anniversary of Stonewall, Yuval Noah Harari put it this way:

> Nothing has been determined yet, and however gloomy the future may seem to some of us, in 1969 the future looked ever gloomier. In the end, most of the dystopian scenarios that frightened people in 1969 did not materialise, because many people struggled to prevent them. If you wish to prevent the dystopian scenarios of the 21st century, there are many things you can do. But the most important thing is to join an organisation. Cooperation is what makes humans powerful. Cooperation is what the Stonewall riots were all about.[479]

Winning changes demands effective organisation to fight for those changes. Winning revolutionary change demands revolutionary socialist organisation. Human individuals are very small when faced with powerful social and political forces, but together we can achieve great, even profound, things.

Nicola Field has pointed to the role that socialists and Marxism can play in developing the organised resistance to threats faced by LGBT+ people and promoting the fight for liberation:

> Marxism is about turning small, everyday struggles into the big historical revolt. Small battles, conflicts and skirmishes can lead to a genuine mass class confrontation on the scale seen in Russia in 1917 and which almost occurred in several European countries at that time. The key to that transformation is organisation.[480]

The need for fundamental change

Prominent throughout this book has been the notion that the struggle for trans liberation needs to be informed by a historical materialist approach if we are to properly understand and act on the roots of trans oppression. A Marxist approach is the only one, I have argued, that can offer a sound understanding of the relationship between the exploitation of workers and the systemic oppression that women, trans people and a range of other oppressed groups are subject to under capitalism.

The fundamental changes that human society needs in order to create properly democratic and equal societies — socialist societies — can only be achieved through working class resistance and rebellion. This will necessarily involve creating social movements that mobilise masses of people on the streets plus, crucially, generalised workplace industrial action to maximise pressure on profit generation and to seize democratic, collective control of the production process. Both elements need to be energised and united by a socialist vision and a Marxist strategy for revolutionary change.

The costs of the failure to fundamentally transform our societies would be catastrophic for humanity. Rosa Luxemburg's famous phrase about the choice facing humanity being socialism or barbarism rings as true today as when she said it in 1915.[481]

Without socialism the crisis-ridden capitalist system will continue squeezing maximum short-term profits and chasing after the own goal of continuous economic growth while careering towards environmental and climatic dystopias and generating murderous inequality, violence and instability along the way. The capitalist system is irretrievably built on the profit imperative — as Karl Marx put it in Volume 1 of *Capital*, "Accumulate, accumulate! That is Moses and the prophets!"[482]

Capitalism is a system that celebrates and magnifies the wealth of the minority and disregards the lives and wellbeing of its workers beyond their ability to turn up for work and generate profits. In the 21st century, amid wildfires, floods and melting icecaps, as bombs supplied by Britain and the US rain down on men, women and children in Yemen, Afghanistan, Syria and elsewhere, as migrants fleeing war, poverty and climate change drown in their thousands in the Mediterranean, freeze or suffocate to death in containers or languish in teeming refugee camps, Vasily Grossman's words in his epic novel Stalingrad seem apt:

> There is a power that can raise huge cities from the dust, but no power in the world can lift the almost weightless eyelashes that have closed over the eyes of a dead child.[483]

In this terrifying context, oppressed people are increasingly vulnerable. To win liberation for trans people and others and enable the free expression of human sexuality and gender variance we need to break from capitalism.

Apologists for capitalism constantly tell us that there is no alternative to it and things have to be this way, but this is propaganda not reality. There is an alternative vision to capitalist Armageddon — that of genuinely democratic human societies, creative, liberated and producing for human need not profit — that could take root once the ideological, social and economic prison walls of capitalism have been decisively breached.

Such societies would protect the right of everyone to live authentically, to challenge gender binary prescriptions and proscriptions and to express their gender and sexuality in whatever way they wish as long as it caused no harm to others.

In 1995 an International Bill of Gender Rights (IBGR) was adopted in Houston, Texas.[484] One of its clauses, The Right to Define Gender Identity, argued that:

All human beings carry within themselves an ever-unfolding idea of who they are and what they are capable of achieving. The individual's sense of self is not determined by chromosomal sex, genitalia, assigned birth sex, or initial gender role. Thus, the individual's identity and capabilities cannot be circumscribed by what society deems to be masculine or feminine behaviour. It is fundamental that individuals have their right to define, and to redefine as their lives unfold, their own gender identities... Therefore, all human beings have the right to define their own gender identity regardless of chromosomal sex, genitalia, assigned birth sex, or initial gender role; and further, no individual shall be denied Human or Civil Rights by virtue of a self-defined gender identity which is not in accord with chromosomal sex, genitalia, assigned birth sex, or initial gender role.[485]

From the right to define should follow the right to free expression of that gender identity and a host of other human and civil rights. Of course, the IBGR has no legal standing and is in essence a wish list, but it has the merit of clearly laying out a set of human rights for trans people even though it says nothing about how these can be achieved.

The reality is that even this quite liberal wish list effectively pits trans people against the capitalist system where social relations derive from the exploitation of workers' coerced labour power and the system of social reproduction rooted in the nuclear family. It is by no means automatic, but trans people who find themselves individually and collectively driven up against societal and institutional transphobia and gender binary expectations simply in order to live their lives can come to recognise that capitalism is fundamentally transphobic and the enemy of all trans and oppressed people.

The prize

Capitalism is set to go on driving the world towards environmental and climatic catastrophe and intensifying the oppression of vulnerable minorities along the way. 2019 saw large portions of the forests of the Amazon, Madagascar and Indonesia being deliberately burned for profit, record high temperatures in Europe, rapid melting of ice sheets in Greenland and Antarctica, and hurricane Dorian, perhaps the most severe hurricane on record, energised by rising sea temperatures, that destroyed large areas of the Bahamas and killed hundreds of people.

None of this can be successfully addressed piecemeal and time is now extremely short to force the necessary system change. The inspiring international strikes and protests by climate change campaigners in 2019, which involved millions of people in over 150 countries, marked for the first time direct solidarity and action on a tremendous scale between school student activists and workers in trade unions. A new environmental movement driven mainly by young people has been born, young people of all genders and none, who will be inheriting the devastation wreaked by capitalism.

Environmental authors Bellamy Foster, Clark and York have aptly summed up the situation:

> Today we face the challenge of forging a new organic revolution in which the struggles for human equality and for the earth are becoming one. There is only one future: that of sustainable human development.[486]

The conclusion from history seems clear: to achieve a socialist society requires a particular sort of system change, a revolutionary break from the exploitative and oppressive system that is wrecking the planet and constrains us all in a heteronormative, binary gendered oppressive set of social values and expectations.

In hir seminal book *Transgender Warriors* Leslie Feinberg concluded that:

> None of us will be free until we have forged an economic system that meets the needs of every working person. As trans people, we will not be free until we fight for and win a society in which no class stands to benefit from fomenting hatred and prejudice, where laws restricting

sex and gender and human love will be unthinkable.[487]

In a socialist world, where production will be organised for need and not for profit and where the nuclear family and all its pervasive ideological underpinnings will no longer be the sole incubator and primary socialiser of the current and next generation of labour, many different gender expressions, sexualities and creative humane arrangements for living together will be possible. For trans and non-binary people, as for all the oppressed and exploited, such a socialist society is the prize worth fighting for.

Appendix 1
Glossary of terms: Trans terminology

LGB and transgender terminology is both varied and evolving. The choice of whether to use "trans" or "transgender", however, is not something I have agonised over, preferring to regard the terms as synonymous. The choice of one over the other, for me, is essentially a stylistic matter. Sometimes it simply feels better to use one rather than the other.

Some people prefer to use trans* to denote inclusivity towards those who describe themselves as non-binary, intersex and queer, and other terms as well. There is no problem with this but I have preferred to stick to the term trans partly because I think it is already fully inclusive, and because it is the one most used by organisations in this field and especially in the trade union movement.

Bisexual — a person capable of desiring or potentially desiring people of more than one gender.

Cisgender — a person whose gender identity is congruent with their sex appearance.

Coming out — informing others of your sexual preferences or gender variant status. This should always be a matter of personal choice.

Cross-dresser — someone who occasionally, regularly or permanently adopts the clothing, make-up, etc of the "other gender" than their ascribed sex. Cross-dressers generally do not desire gender transition.

Doxing (or **doxxing**) — revealing personal and private details about someone. With respect to trans and non-binary people, revealing a person's previous gender status before transition by investigating their personally identifiable information, eg home address, former name, workplace information and so on. Doxing is frequently an element of online bullying and harassment. The word is derived from "docs", short for "documents".

Drag queen — generally a gay cross-dresser (DRAG — Dressed As A Girl)

Drag king — generally a lesbian cross-dresser (drag used here to mean cross-dressed).

FTM — female-to-male transsexual or transgender person.

MTF — male-to-female transsexual or transgender person. These terms have become less used in recent years.

Gender Diverse — Trans and Gender Diverse (TGD) — An umbrella term sometimes used to describe all those whose gender identity is at odds with their biological sex.

Gender dysphoria — medical term since the Diagnostic and Statistical Manual of Mental Disorders - version V (DSM V) was published in 2013, referring to the persistent personal discomfort felt by transgender people arising from pressure to conform to society's gender expectations. Replaced "gender identity disorder". There is a general presumption that people will conform to society's rules about what is appropriate behaviour for a boy/man or girl/woman. Where this is not the case it may give rise to discomfort and anxiety in those who witness it and on the part of the **gender non-conforming** or **gender variant** individual.

Gender fuck — conflicting gender/sex signals, usually intentional.

Gender identity — the psychological identification of oneself as boy/man or girl/woman, or, outside the **gender binary model** (where gender is presumed to be either man or woman), as pan-gender, poly-gender, third-gender, genderqueer, neutrois, agender, gender neutral and other terms. Sometimes **trans*** is used to denote inclusion of all these terms.

Gender Identity Disorder (GID) — prior to DSM V in 2013, where GID became "gender dysphoria", GID was a diagnosis of a mental disorder suffered by transgender people. A diagnosis of GID was required to obtain a gender recognition certificate that is now superseded by a requirement for a diagnosis of gender dysphoria.

Gender queer — Alternative term to 'non-binary' preferred by some people. Indicates a rejection of conventional gender descriptions and the gender binary, and an identification with neither or both conventional genders, or a combination

Gender Recognition Certificate — can be obtained under the Gender Recognition Act 2004 and allows a trans person to change their birth certificate plus makes disclosure of the person's previous gender status an offence.

Gender role — is inherently social: the interaction with others that both gives expression to the inner gender identity and reinforces it. Interaction with society by people of a specific gender by following arbitrary rules defining appropriate clothing, behaviour, mannerisms, relationships, etc deemed appropriate for each sex.

Hir (and **Zie**) — gender neutral terms preferred by some trans and non-binary people to replace the gender specific pronouns her and she, or his and he. The American transgender activist Leslie Feinberg, among others, preferred to use these terms. Some non-binary people also prefer to use **they**. Some may also use **Mx** as a title in preference to the traditional Mr, Mrs, Miss, or the less traditional Ms.

Intersex — refers to a range of biological conditions at birth or later in development which are not typically or exclusively male or female and which may give doubt about the person's sex. An intersex person's assigned sex at birth may not accord with their **gender identity** and may require intervention later. Intervention too early, before the person can give informed consent, is generally now considered unethical following sustained campaigning by intersex advocacy organisations.

LGBT+phobia — relatively recent collective term to describe hostility towards lesbians and/or gays and/or bisexuals and/or trans.

Misgendering — referring to a trans person by the wrong pronoun, eg he instead of she. This may be a mistake (in which case a quick apology may resolve matters) or deliberate. Deliberate and persistent misgendering is transphobic and amounts to a refusal to acknowledge the trans person's gender presentation.

Passing — the ability to be accepted by most people as the preferred gender. The inability to do this is known as **being read**.

Passing privilege — a disdainful and elitist attitude adopted by some trans people who pass well in society directed at those who may not.

Queen — usually a gay man in drag, may be for entertainment purposes. Queens are generally not gender variant. Originally the term also encompassed transgender people as well as gay men in drag until trans/transgender became more differentiated from gay in the later 20th century.

Sex — refers to male/female physical development — generally relates to biological differences between male, female and intersex people.

Sexual orientation — who a person is sexually attracted to. A trans person may be gay (homosexual), straight (heterosexual), bisexual, or asexual. Sexual orientation is conceptually independent of gender identity.

Transgender or **trans** — inclusive term describing all those whose gender expression falls outside typical gender norms. Implies a situation where a person's gender identity does not accord with their sex appearance. Transgender should not be used as a noun, ie to refer to people as "transgenders".

Transsexual — originally a term describing a person who wished to transition their gender. Now an outdated term as it implies "crossing" from one (binary) sex or gender to "the other". More recently it has generally been replaced with transgender or trans.

Transvestite — outmoded term applied to occasional, regular or full-time cross-dressers, usually male, who did not want gender transition, to distinguish them from transsexuals who generally desired gender transition.

Trans men — those born with female appearance or ascribed female at birth (AFAB) who subsequently identify as men.

Trans women — those born with male appearance or ascribed male at birth (AMAB) who subsequently identify as women.

Transition — the process of permanently adapting the gender role in all spheres of the person's life over a period of time. Transition is not a change of gender identity. It is an adaptation of living to embody a person's gender identity. This may or may not involve **gender confirmation** (or **affirmation**) **treatment** such as hormonal therapy and/or genital surgery, and/or cosmetic surgery to help the person in their gender presentation. This is no longer referred to as "a sex change" or sex change surgery, or even gender reassignment.

[Includes material published by GIRES, the Gender Identity Research and Education Society, and Surya Monro, *Gender Politics* (London, 2005)]

Appendix 2
Useful trans organisations, Britain

Action for Trans Health — http://actionfortranshealth.org.uk/
Offers limited help with funding and seeks to engage the trans* community about health issues.
All About Trans — http://www.allabouttrans.org.uk/
Seeks to change how the media understands and portrays trans people.
All Out — https://allout.org
A global movement "working to build a world where no one will have to sacrifice their freedom because of who they are or who they love".
Beaumont Society — https://www.beaumontsociety.org.uk
Original British support organisation for cross-dressers/transgender people and their partners and families.
Gendered Intelligence — http://genderedintelligence.co.uk/
Gendered Intelligence is a not-for-profit Community Interest Company, established in 2008 working with the trans community and those who impact on trans lives. The organisation specialises in supporting trans people under 21.
Gender Trust — www.gendertrust.org.uk
A blog site for "all those affected by gender identity issues".
GIRES, The Gender Identity Research and Education Society — https://www.gires.org.uk/
Aims to improve the lives of trans and gender non-conforming people of all ages, including those who are non-binary and non-gender.
IMAAN — www.imaan.org.uk/index.htm

Describes itself as the UK's leading LGBTQ Muslim Charity

Intersex UK — https://www.facebook.com/intersexuk
British NGO-Human Rights Defenders, educating and consulting on a child's right to bodily autonomy and a family's right to support.

LGBT History Month — https://lgbthistorymonth.org.uk
Offers resources to schools and other organisations to celebrate LGBT history, especially during LGBT History Month in February.

LGBT+ Against Islamophobia
https://lgbtagainstislamop.wixsite.com/lgbtai
Lesbian, Gay, Bisexual, Transgender people, people from across the LGBTQIA+ community, in solidarity with Muslim communities under attack

Mermaids — https://www.mermaidsuk.org.uk
Offers support and advice for children and young people and their families about transgender and gender diverse issues.

Press for Change — www.pfc.org.uk/
Describe themselves as 'The UK's Leading Experts in Transgender Law'. Played a key role in lobbying for the 2004 Gender Recognition Act

Polish Rainbow in the UK — www.facebook.com/polishrainbowinuk/
First Polish LGBTQ Group in the UK

Samaritans — www.samaritans.org/Samaritans/
Supporting anyone who needs help. Can be called free any time from any phone on 116 123.

School's Out — http://www.schools-out.org.uk/
Aiming to make schools safe and inclusive for everyone.

Scottish Trans Alliance — https://www.scottishtrans.org/
Works to improve gender identity and gender reassignment equality, rights and inclusion in Scotland.

Stand Up to LGBT+ Hate Crime
www.facebook.com/standuptolgbtqhatecrime/
A political coalition of LGBT+ Groups and their Allies fighting rising levels of anti-LGBT+ hate incidents in the UK, and forging international solidarity against bigotry

Stonewall — www.stonewall.org.uk/
Stonewall campaigns for the equality of lesbian, gay, bisexual

and (since 2014) trans people across Britain.

Trades Union Congress — https://www.tuc.org.uk/
Umbrella organisation for most (around 50) British trade unions representing 5.6 million members.

TransActual — www.lgbtconsortium.org.uk/directory/trans-actual-uk
Aims to highlight issues affecting the trans community in Britain and beyond, to dispel myths and promote trans rights by sharing facts, research, examples of international policy and best practice, as well as amplifying the voices of Trans people.

Trans*formation — https://www.transformationuk.com
To undertake activities to end discrimination and promote the welfare of Trans* and non-binary people in the UK. Primarily aimed at people in the work environment.

Trans Info UK — https://twitter.com/UKTransInfo
A national organisation focused on improving the lives of trans & non-binary people in the UK.

Trans Media Watch — www.transmediawatch.org
A charity dedicated to improving media coverage of trans and intersex issues.

Trans Pride Brighton — https://transpridebrighton.org/
Trans Pride Leeds — https://www.facebook.com/TransPrideLeeds/
Trans Pride South West — http://www.outbristol.co.uk/transpridesouthwest
Trans Unite — https://www.transunite.co.uk
A UK directory of support groups for gender-variant people.
UK Intersex Association — www.ukia.co.uk/
An education, advocacy, campaigning and support organisation which works on behalf of Intersex people.
Wipe Out Transphobia — http://www.wipeouttransphobia.com
An international volunteer-led project aiming to reduce and wipe out if possible the transphobia in society that regularly affects anyone who strays away from the traditional binary idea of gender as assigned at birth.

Notes

Introduction

1 Terminology in general use around trans issues can be quite complex. New terms to describe people's identity, particularly various non-binary identities, have emerged in recent years and continue to evolve. The use of the collective acronym LGBT+ has become much more widespread, especially in the trade union movement. In general in this book I have used terminology appropriate to particular time periods (for example, 'homosexual', 'gay and lesbian', 'transsexual', 'LGBT', 'LGBT+') but on occasions, where I have intended to refer to all those who fall under what we would today consider the range of sexual orientations or gender variance, I have tended to use 'LGBT+' as a shorthand inclusive term even if this was not in use at that time. Why I have used this at particular points should be clear from the context. See Appendix 1 for a glossary of terms.

2 ILGA Europe, Rainbow Europe 2018, https://www.ilga-europe.org/rainboweurope/2018.

3 For example see Sue Caldwell, 'Marxism, Feminism and Transgender Politics' *International Socialism* 157, Spring 2018; Laura Miles, 'Transgender Oppression and Resistance', *International Socialism* 141, Winter 2014; and Laura Miles, *Pride, Politics and Protest: A Revolutionary Guide to LGBT Liberation* (Socialist Workers Party, 2014).

4 Nick Clark, The downfall of Golden Dawn in Greek elections is a crucial lesson for the left, *Socialist Worker*, 8 July 2019, http://bit.ly/33YtAed.

Chapter 1: Trans visibility and backlash

5 Jacqueline Rose, 'Who Do You Think You Are?', *London Review of Books*, 5 May 2016.

6 It is difficult to find any reliable figures for the proportion of trans people in the British population due to lack of monitoring. State surveys like the national census do not yet include a relevant question. The Gender Identity Research and Education Society (GIRES) carried out a prevalence study but this was published in 2009 and would probably be considered an underestimate in 2018. The monitoring (or lack thereof) problem is discussed in a later chapter.

7 We should note that Tambor suggested in late 2017 that he would not be returning to *Transparent* after two women co-workers made allegations of sexual misconduct against him and investigations were opened.

8 See for example Cathy Brennan's negative review 'It's winning awards but *Girl* is no victory for trans representation', *BFI*, 30 October 2018, https://www.bfi.org.uk/news-opinion/news-bfi/features/girl-lukas-dhont-trans-representation.

9 http://www.mermaidsuk.org.uk/.

10 Andrew Gilligan, 'Mermaids UK charity ban as boy forced to live as girl', *The Times*, 8 October 2017, https://www.thetimes.co.uk/article/mermaids-uk-charity-ban-as-boy-forced-to-live-as-girl-dvx3j99cn.

11 CJ Atkinson, *Can I Tell You About Gender Diversity: A Guide for Friends, Family and Professionals*, (London, 2017): Sally Weale, 'Book explaining gender diversity to primary school children sparks furore', *The Guardian*, 2nd January 2017.

12 'Record number of children calling Childline over gender issues', *STV*, 13 December 2016, https://stv.tv/news/scotland/1375527-record-number-of-children-calling-childline-over-gender-issues/.

13 Natasha Devon, 'I received rape and death threats after I suggested schools use gender-neutral language', *TES*, 23 November 2017, https://www.tes.com/news/school-news/breaking-views/i-received-rape-and-death-threats-after-i-suggested-schools-use.

14   Ewan Palmer, 'Lucy Meadows: Coroner Slams Daily Mail over Transgender Teacher's Suicide', *International Business Times*, 1 July 2014, http://www.ibtimes.co.uk/lucy-meadows-transgender-teacher-suicide-daily-mail-472282.

15   Ruth Smith, 'Lucy Meadows was a transgender teacher who took her own life. Her story must be remembered', *The Independent*, 19 November 2017, http://www.independent.co.uk/news/long_reads/lucy-meadows-transgender-teacher-ruth-smith-media-press-daily-mail-lgbt-rights-a8063946.html.

16   Letter to the BACP concerning Transgender Trend, http://bit.ly/343s0rF.

17   UN Human Rights Council Report, *Discrimination and Violence against Individuals Based on their Sexual Orientation and Gender Identity*, 1 June 2015, http://www.ohchr.org/Documents/Issues/Discrimination/LGBT/A_HRC_29_23_One_pager_en.pdf

18   Kristina Mastropasqua, 'Global discrimination against LGBT persons: 2015 United Nations report', *Journalist's Resource*, 8 June 2015, http://journalistsresource.org/studies/international/human-rights/global-discrimination-against-lgbt-persons-2015-united-nations-report

19   Trans Respect, 'Trans Day of Remembrance (TDoR) 2018', Press Release, 12 November 2018, https://transrespect.org/en/tmm-update-trans-day-of-remembrance-2018/

20   TDoR and National Coalition of Anti-Violence Program, *Annual Hate Violence Report*, 2015.

21   For example see: Kae Greenberg, 'Still Hidden in the Closet; Trans Women and Domestc Violence', *Berkeley Journal of Gender, Law and Justice*, 2012, ps198-251, and: *Stonewall and NFPSynergy Report, Supporting trans women in domestic and sexual violence services*, 2018, https://www.stonewall.org.uk/system/files/stonewall_and_nfpsynergy_report.pdf.

22   Suicide Prevention Australia, *Suicide and Self-harm Among Gay, Lesbian, Bisexual and Transgender Communities*, 2009, https://www.suicidepreventionaust.org/content/suicide-and-self-harm-among-gay-lesbian-bisexual-and-transgender-communities.

23   NatCen, *British Social Attitudes 34*, 2017, http://www.bsa.natcen.ac.uk/latest-report/british-social-attitudes-34/key-findings/context.aspx.

24   See for example A T Norton and G M Herek, 'Heterosexuals' Attitudes Toward Transgender People: Findings from a Probability Sample of US Adults', *Sex Roles 68*, no. 11-12, June 2013. See also the Scottish Social Attitudes Survey 2015: *Attitudes to Discrimination and Positive Action*, 30 September 2016, https://www.gov.scot/publications/scottish-social-attitudes-2015-attitudes-discrimination-positive-action/.

25   GLAAD, *Accelerating Acceptance Report 2019*, 24 June 2019, https://www.glaad.org/publications/accelerating-acceptance-2019.

26   NatCen, *British Social Attitudes 34: Moral Issues, Sex, Gender Identity, Euthanasia*, 2017, pp11-16, http://www.bsa.natcen.ac.uk/media/39147/bsa34_moral_issues_final.pdf.

Chapter 2: Has oppression always existed?

27   In other words that sex is founded on certain immutable binary biological characteristics, and gender follows suit.

28   For example see Leslie Feinberg, *Transgender Warriors*, (Boston, 1996)

29   Chris Harman, *A People's History of the World*, (London, 1999), p8.

30   hir and zie are gender-neutral pronouns preferred by some non-binary people.

31   Feinberg, 1996, p43.

32   David Greenburg, *The Construction of Homosexuality*, (Chicago, 1988), p64.

33   Merlin Stone, *When God Was a Woman*, (New York, 1976)

34   See Feinberg, 1996, p41.

35   See for example Pat Califia, *Sex Changes: The politics of Transgenderism*, (New Jersey, 1997), ps145-147.

36   Pat Califia, 1997, Chapter 4.

37   See Feinberg, 1996, Chapter 3 for a

discussion of these terms.

38 Will Roscoe, *Changing Ones: Third and Fourth Genders in Native North America*, (New York, 2000),

39 See for example the Online Archive of California, *Will Roscoe papers and Gay American Indians records*, (San Francisco, 2014), http://www.oac.cdlib.org/findaid/ark:/13030/c85d8sd4/entire_text/.

40 Martin Cannon, 'The Regulation of First Nations Sexuality' in Maureen FitzGerald and Scott Rayter, *Queerly Canadian: An Introductory Reader in Sexuality Studies* (Toronto, 2012), p52.

41 For example, see the *Will Roscoe archive*, 2014: See also S Jacobs, W Thomas, and S Lang, *Two-Spirit People: Native American Gender Identity, Sexuality, and Spirituality*, (Chicago, 1997); and W Williams, *The Spirit and the Flesh: Sexual Diversity in American Indian Culture*, (Boston, 2006).

42 See Pat Califia, 1997, Chapter 4.

43 Johnathan Ned Katz, *Gay American History: Lesbians and Gay Men in the USA*, (New York, 1976)

44 Susan Stryker, *Transgender History*, (Seattle, 2008).

45 Feinberg, 1996, ps 51-53.

46 Friedrich Engels, *The Origin of the Family, Private Property and the State*, (Peking, 1978 (1884)).

47 Lewis Morgan, *Ancient Society: Or, Researches in the Line of Human Progress from Savagery, through Barbarism to Civilization,* (New York, 1877).

48 Some writers on women's oppression have been dismissive or highly critical of the *Origins*. Heather Brown and some other Marxist or socialist feminist writers have sought to distinguish between Engels' supposed economic determinism and Marx's dialectical approach to the relationship between humanity and nature in relation to production and reproduction. While the anthropological limitations of Engels' sources in 1884 should be recognised, his method and conclusions, I would argue, have been vindicated by much subsequent evidence and analysis. See Heather Brown, *Marx on Gender and the Family: A Critical Study* (Boston, 2012). See also Eleanor Burke Leacock, *Myths of Male Dominance: Collected Articles on Women Cross-Culturally*, (New York, 1981), as a keynote work. And Sally Campbell, 'Engels Revisited', *Socialist Review* 378, March 2013; and Chris Harman's defence of Engels: 'Engels and the Origins of Human Society', *International Socialism* 2:65, Winter 1994.

49 Engels, 1978 (1884), p195.

50 Mario Mieli, *Towards a Gay Communism: Elements of a Homosexual Critique*, (London, 2018), p61.

51 Feinberg, 1996, Chapters 5 and 6; Also see Harman, 1999, especially Chapters 2-4.

52 Feinberg, 1996, p53.

53 Feinberg, 1996, Chapters 9-11; Harman, 1999, Parts 3 and 4.

54 Feinberg, 1996, p 25.

55 Feinberg, 1996, p29.

56 Feinberg,1996, p23.

57 Feinberg, 1996, Chapter 9.

58 For example see Jeffrey Weeks, *Sex Politics and Society*, 4th Ed, (Abingdon, 1981): Jeffrey Weeks, *Making Sexual History*, (Cambridge, 2000)

59 John D'Emilio, 'Capitalism and Gay Identity', in *Making Trouble: Essays on Gay History, Politics, and the University* (New York, 1992).

60 Friedrich Engels, *The Condition of the Working Class in England*, (Oxford, 2009 (1845)).

61 See for example Karl Marx, *Capital Volume 1*, (London, 1974 (1867)), Chapter 10.

62 D'Emilio, 1992, p13.

63 Weeks, 1981, p36.

64 See Judith Orr, *Abortion Wars: The Fight for Reproductive Rights*, (Bristol, 2017)

Chapter 3: Biology, gender and gender identity

65 Cordelia Fine, *Testosterone Rex: Unmaking the Myths of our Gendered Minds*, (London, 2017), p181.

66 Myra J. Hird, *Sex, Gender and Science*, (Basingstoke, 2005), p8.

67 'Trump is 'declaring war' on the LGBT community by appointing this man to defend trans rights, groups say',

Pink News, 24 March 2017, https://
www.pinknews.co.uk/2017/03/24/
trump-is-declaring-war-on-the-lgbt-
community-by-appointing-this-man-
to-defend-trans-rights-groups-say/.

68 NOM is funded by wealthy right wing
anti-LGBT+ donors, reportedly with
links to the Mormon Church. See Fred
Karger, 'Is the Mormon Church
Hiding Its Funding of the National
Organization for Marriage?',
Huffington Post, 25 May 2011,
https://www.huffingtonpost.com/
fred-karger/is-the-mormon-church-
hidi_b_220587.html.

69 Dominic Holden, 'This bus is on a road
trip to convince you that transgender
people aren't real', *BuzzFeed News*, 22
March 2017.

70 Simon LeVay, 'A difference in
hypothalamic structure between
homosexual and heterosexual men',
Science 253, 1991, p1034–1037.

71 John Gray, *Men are from Mars, Women
are from Venus*, (New York, 1992)

72 Deborah Cameron, *The Myth of Mars
and Venus: Do Men and Women Really
Speak Different Languages?* (Oxford,
2008), p3-4.

73 Although Sheila McGregor has pointed
out that the experience of pregnancy
and childbirth became physically
different in different societies. She
writes: "It isn't possible to know
exactly what the experiences were
in our prehistory. However, we do
know that men and women have
lived in egalitarian societies in which
production and reproduction were
closely linked and where pregnancy
and childbirth were quite different."
Sheila McGregor, 'Social Reproduction
Theory: Back to (which) Marx?',
International Socialism 160, Autumn
2018, p88.

74 Fine, 2017, p190.

75 Intersex Society of North American,
'How Common is Intersex?', nd,
http://www.isna.org/faq/frequency.

76 Dsdfamilies http://www.dsdfamilies.
org/.

77 UNFE Intersex Factsheet, https://
unfe.org/system/unfe-65-Intersex_
Factsheet_ENGLISH.pdf.

78 Hird, 2005, p48.

79 UK Intersex Association, http://

www.ukia.co.uk.

80 For some reactions from the scientific
community to the the IAAF ruling
and the Court of Arbitration for
Sport appeal ruling see Science
Media Centre, May 1 2019, https://
www.sciencemediacentre.org/
expert-reaction-to-ruling-on-caster-
semenya-appeal-regarding-athletes-
with-differences-of-sex-development-
and-testosterone-levels/.

81 Both men and women generate
testosterone (a natural androgen)
and while men usually have higher
androgen levels than women there
is a wide variation within both
men and women and in the same
man or woman at different times
depending on age, lifestyle, drug use
and so on. It is not common but some
women may have higher average T
levels than some men. There is also
an assumption that testosterone
level is the key factor in physical
performance, which is debateable.
The fact that testosterone levels in
men are not considered by the athletic
authorities as something to be tested
despite likely considerable variation
might suggest that such testing and
potential consequences including
banning affected women athletes is
more about lack of knowledge and
gender and race discrimination than
about creating a level sporting field.
See Marthe de Ferrer, 'Like Caster
Semenya I have hyperandrogenism.
The IAAF's ruling will hurt millions
of women like us', *The Independent*, 1
May 2019, for an interesting take on
this. https://www.independent.co.uk/
voices/caster-semenya-iaaf-ruling-
sports-heightened-testosterone-
pcos-a8895226.html.

82 For example see E. Luders, F. J.
Sánchez, C. Gaser, A. W. Toga, K. L.
Narr, L. S. Hamilton, et al., 'Regional
Gray Matter Variation in Male-to-
Female Transsexualism', *NeuroImage*,
Vol. 46, No. 4, 2009, pp904-907.

83 J.-N Zhou, M.A Hofman, L.J Gooren,
D.F Swaab, 'A Sex Difference in the
Human Brain and its Relation to
Transsexuality', *International Journal
of Transgenderism* 1:1, 1997.

84 See for example H Berglund, P

Lindstrom, C Dhejne-Helmy, & I Savic, 'Male-to-female transsexuals show sex-atypical hypothalamus activation when smelling odorous steroids', *Cerebral Cortex*, 18 (2008), pp1900-1908.

85 European Society of Endocrinology, 'Transgender brains are more like their desired gender from an early age', 22 May 2018, https://www.ese-hormones.org/media/1506/transgender-brains-are-more-like-their-desired-gender-from-an-early-age.pdf.

86 Rebecca Jordan-Young, *Brainstorm: The Flaws in the Science of Sex Differences*, (Amherst, 2010).

87 For an excellent discussion of these issues see S Satel and S O Lilienfeld, *Brainwashed: The Seductive Appeal of Mindless Neuroscience*, (New York, 2013).

88 B McEwen and T Milner, 'Understanding the broad influence of sex hormones and sex differences in the brain', *Journal of Neuroscience Research*, Jan 2017 2:95, pp24-39.

89 Karl Marx and Friedrich Engels, *The German Ideology, 2nd Edition*, (London, 1974 (1846)), p52.

90 Marx and Engels, 1974, p51.

91 Marx and Engels, 1974, p50.

92 Romanian dictators who had misruled and bled dry Romania for decades who were overthrown in the Romanian revolution of 1989.

93 C A Nelson, E A Furtado, N A Fox, & C H Zeanah, 'The deprived human brain: Developmental deficits among institutionalized Romanian children — and later improvements — strengthen the case for individualized care', *American Scientist*, 97, 2009, p222–229, http://dx.doi.org/10.1511/2009.78.222.

94 Eleanor A. Maguire, Katherine Woollett and Hugo J. Spier, 'London Taxi Drivers and Bus Drivers: A Structural MRI and Neuropsychological Analysis', *Hippocampus* 16, 2009, p1091–1101.

95 Christine Jorgensen, *Christine Jorgensen: A Personal Biography,* (New York, 1967). See also April Ashley's autobiography, April Ashley with Douglas Thompson, *The First Lady*, (London, 2006); Gina Large, *Gina: The Woman Within*, (London, 2002); Helen Boyd, *She's Not the Man I Married: My Life with a Transgender Husband*, (Seattle, 2007).

96 Eugenics — a term coined by Francis Galton, the belief that a human population can and should be 'improved' by selective breeding. A popular theory even on the left in the early 20th century, it has been discredited since being most notoriously applied by the Nazis who used forced sterilisation, selective breeding and extermination of the 'inferior' stock in their efforts to breed an Aryan 'master race'.

97 American Psychiatric Association, *Diagnostic And Statistical Manual of Mental Disorders*, Fifth Edition, 2013.

98 Julia Serano, *Outspoken: A Decade of Transgender Activism and Trans Feminism*, (Oakland, 2016).

99 Juno Roche, *Queer Sex: A Trans and Non-Binary Guide to Intimacy, Pleasure and Relationships,* (London, 2018).

100 Juno Roche, 'I haven't failed to 'pass' as a woman, I want to look transgender', *iD magazine,* 28 April 2018, https://i-d.vice.com/en_uk/article/kzxjnw/i-havent-failed-to-pass-as-a-woman-i-want-to-look-transgender.

101 For example see: Shon Faye, 'I'm trans, and I don't care if we were 'born this way'. Neither should you', *The Guardian*, 30 May 2018.

102 Some may argue that the acronym should be LGBTQI (Q for queer or questioning, I for intersex) but I have used LGBT+ as being the most accessible acronym, the one which is most common in the labour movement and the one which arguably makes fewest concessions to separatist and identity politics.

103 "It is not the consciousness of men that determines their being, but, on the contrary, their social being that determines their consciousness." Karl Marx, *Preface to A Contribution to the Critique of Political Economy, (Moscow, 1977 (1859)),* https://www.marxists.org/archive/marx/works/1859/critique-pol-economy/preface-abs.htm.

104 Judith Orr, 2017, p107.

105 'Gender ideology' is detested by the alt right in that it is seen as claiming women's equality and equal rights for trans people and thus posing a demographic threat. See, for example, Cole Parke, 'The Right's "Gender Ideology" Menace Rolls to Africa', *Political Research Associates*, 4 May 2018, which refers to the proposed visit to Nairobi of the '#Free Speech Bus' mentioned at the beginning of this chapter.https://www.politicalresearch.org/2018/05/04/the-rights-gender-ideology-menace-rolls-to-africa/.

106 In May 2019 the Alabama state legislature voted to ban all abortions except 'where the mother's life is in danger'.

107 Surya Monro, *Gender politics: Citizenship, Activism and Sexual Diversity*, (London, 2005), pp12-14.

108 One piece of research carried out by practitioners at the main UK gender identity clinic, Charing Cross Gender Identity Clinic, Tavistock and Portman NHS Foundation Trust, concluded that: "Of the 3398 patients who had appointments during this period,[1 August 2016 to 1 August 2017] 16 (0.47 percent) expressed transition-related regret or detransitioned. Of these 16, one patient expressed regret but was not considering detransitioning, two had expressed regret and were considering detransitioning, three had detransitioned, and ten had detransitioned temporarily. The reasons stated by patients for their regret or detransition included: social factors, reporting physical complications, and changing their mind about their gender identity and identifying as their gender assigned at birth. The 16 patients consisted of 11 trans women, two trans men, two cis men, and one person assigned male at birth who said their gender identity was "trans". Study findings are consistent with previous research showing low rates of detransition. Detransition was most often prompted by social difficulties rather than changes in gender identity or physical complications and was most often temporary. Only three patients made a long-term detransition." Davies, S, McIntyre S, Rypma, C, *Detransition rates in a national UK Gender Identity Clinic*, paper delivered at the Third Biennial EPATH Conference Inside Matters. On Law, Ethics and Religion, 11-13 April 2019.

109 For example see the discussion of comments by Germaine Greer, Julie Bindel, Sheila Jeffreys, Janice Raymond and others in chapter 9.

110 Sheila Jeffreys, *Gender Hurts: A Feminist Analysis of the Politics of Transgenderism,* (Abingdon, 2014).

111 For a useful discussion of these issues see Ana Campoy, 'A conspiracy theory about sex and gender is being peddled around the world by the far right', *Quartz,* 4 November 2016, https://qz.com/807743/conservatives-have-created-a-fake-ideology-to-combat-the-global-movement-for-lgbti-rights/

112 Serano, 2016, p70.

113 Viviane K. Namaste, *Invisible Lives: The Erasure of Transsexual and Transgendered People*, (Chicago, 2000).

114 Namaste, 2000, pp135-136.

115 Namaste, 2000, p141.

116 Joseph Harry, 'Derivative Deviance: The Cases of Extortion, Fag-Bashing and the Shakedown of Gay Men', *Criminology* 19 (1982): pp546-563.

117 B Von Schultess, 'Violence in the Streets: Anti-lesbian Assault and Harassment in San Francisco' in G Herek and K Berril (eds), *Hate Crimes: Confronting Violence Against Lesbians and Gay Men*, (London, 1992), pp65-75.

118 Suzanne Kessler and Wendy McKenna, *Gender: An Ethnomethodological Approach,* (New York, 1978).

Chapter 4: A brief history of trans

119 Feinberg, 1996, p43.

120 Katie Barclay, 'Cross-dressing in historical perspective', *Women's History Network* blog, 2010, https://womenshistorynetwork.org/cross-dressing-in-historical-perspective/

121 For example see David Kynaston, *Family Britain 1951-1957,* (London,2009), p214.

122 Jean E Howard, 'Cross-dressing, The Theatre, and Gender Struggle in

Early Modern England', *Shakespeare Quarterly*, Vol 39, 4 (Winter 1988), p421.

123 Howard, 1988, p421.

124 Howard, 1988, p422.

125 See Rebecca Jennings, *A Lesbian History of Britain: Love and Sex Between Women Since 1500*, (Oxford, 2007) Chapter 2.

126 Jennings, 2007, p25.

127 Jennings, 2007, p30.

128 Jennings, 2007, p34.

129 Jennings, 2007, p37.

130 See David Jones, *Rebecca's Children: a study of rural society, crime and protest*, (Oxford, 1994).

131 See Rhian E Jones, 'Occupy the Tollgates: The Rebecca Riots as Myth, Meme and Movement', *Wales Arts Review*, 13 November 2015, http://www.walesartsreview.org/occupy-the-tollgates-the-rebecca-riots-as-myth-meme-and-movement/

132 Feinberg, 1996, p79.

133 See Feinberg, 1996, Chapter 11.

134 Rictor Norton, 'The Raid on Mother Clap's Molly House 1726', *The Gay Subculture in Georgian England*, 5 February 2005, http://rictornorton.co.uk/eighteen/mother.htm.

135 See Jeffrey Weeks, *Sex, Politics and Society: The Regulation of Sexuality Since 1800*, 2nd ed. (London, 1989). See also Sherry Wolf, *Sexuality and Socialism: History, Politics, and Theory of LGBT Liberation*, (Chicago,2009); Susan Stryker, *Transgender History*, (Berkeley, CA,2008).

136 *Stella*, a play by Neil Bartlett exploring the life of Stella Boulton, was performed at the Theatre Royal Brighton in June 2016 as part of the Brighton Festival and London International Festival of Theatre.

137 Holly Williams, 'The cross-dressing gents of Victorian England', *BBC*, 8 June 2016, http://www.bbc.com/culture/story/20160608-the-cross-dressing-gents-of-victorian-england

138 Wilde's socialism was strongly influenced by the anarchist ideas of the Russian Peter Kropotkin and celebrated the potential of socialism to foster real and liberated individualism.

139 Edward Carson was an Ulster loyalist and staunch opponent of Irish Home Rule. Seventeen years after the Wilde trial he organised an armed militia, the Ulster Volunteer Force, to oppose Irish Home Rule. Wilde's mother was a lifelong Irish nationalist, although Wilde himself does not appear to have had a public position on the issue. Wilde did seriously consider converting to Catholicism but did not go through with it.

140 The phrase was actually coined by Wilde's lover Bosie, the poet Lord Alfred Douglas, 'I am the Love that Dare not Speak its Name'.

141 In 1897 Havelock Ellis published one of the earliest studies on homosexuality, *Studies in the Psychology of Sex: Sexual Inversion* (Philadephia, 1901).

142 Magnus Hirschfeld, *Transvestites: The Erotic Urge to Cross-Dress*, (New York, 1991). It took another 50 years, however, before a recognisable transgender movement driven by trans people themselves would emerge in the United States, Britain and elsewhere.

143 For a discussion of why the German revolution failed see Chris Harman, *The Lost Revolution: Germany 1918 to 1923*, (London, 1982).

144 Laurie Marhoefer, *Sex and the Weimar Republic: German Homosexual Emancipation and the Rise of the Nazis*, (Toronto, 2015), p55.

145 Laurie Marhoefer, 2015, p59

146 See Joanne J Meyerowitz, *How Sex Changed: A history of Transexuality in the United States*, (Cambridge, Massachusetts; London, England, 2009) p19.

147 Laurie Marhoefer, 2015, p60

148 V I Lenin, *What is to be Done?* 1902 (Moscow, 1947)

149 VI Lenin, *The Right of Nations to Self-Determination*, 1914 (Moscow, 1947).

150 See Cathy Porter, *Alexandra Kollontai: A Biography*, (Pontypool, Wales, 2013) especially chapter 13 for a summary of Kollontai's work in the period immediately after the 1917 Revolution. See also Emma Davis, *A Rebel's Guide to Alexandra Kollontai*, (London 2019) for a useful summary of her life and political influence.

151 Dan Healey, *Homosexual Desire in Revolutionary Russia: The Regulation of Sexual and Gender Dissent*, (Chicago, 2001), p111.

152 Healey, 2001, pp12-13.

153 Healey, 2001, p115.

154 Healey, 2001, p116.

155 Healey, 2001, p122.

156 Healey, 2001, p125.

157 Stryker, 2008 Kindle edition, Loc 659

158 See Heinz Heger, *The Men With the Pink Triangle: The True Story of Homosexuals in the Nazi Death Camps*, (Boston, 1994), for a first-hand account of Nazi brutality.

159 See Hannah Dee, *The Red in the Rainbow: Sexuality, Socialism and LGBT Liberation*, (London 2010).. Also Sheila Rowbotham, *Edward Carpenter: A Life of Liberty and Love*, London 2009

Chapter 5: From post-war repression to Stonewall

160 Report of the first ever 'gay pride' march in the world, New York, 28 June 1970, billed as a march for Christopher Street Liberation Day a year after the Stonewall rebellion. This description is in Martin Duberman, *Stonewall*, (New York, 1993) p278.

161 Quoted in David Carter, *Stonewall: The Riots that Sparked the Gay Revolution*, (New York, 2004), p191.

162 For a selection of personal accounts of being gay in the 1950s see Geraldine Bedell *Coming out of the dark ages*, The Guardian 24 June 2007.

163 There are two films that cover Turing's life: One in 2014, *The Imitation Game*, starring Benedict Cumberbatch, and *Breaking the Code*, 1996, starring Derek Jacobi. Both detail his work at Bletchley Park and his persecution and ultimate suicide in 1954. *The Imitation Game* has been criticised for implying that Turing may have covered up a colleague's espionage. Jacobi's portrayal of Turing in *Breaking the Code* has been considered by some to be more accurate and sympathetic.

164 The Campaign for Homosexual Equality still exists: see http://www.c-h-e.org.uk/

165 Jeffrey Weeks, Making Sexual History,

(Cambridge, 2000) p138.

166 A biographical note and podcast about Harry Hay can be found here: https://makinggayhistory.com/podcast/harry-hay/

167 Michael Dillon, Self: A Study in Ethics and Endocrinology, (London, 1946) p53.

168 See April Ashley's autobiography, *The First Lady*, (London,2006).

169 Georgina Somerset, *A Girl Called Georgina* (Lewes, 1992).

170 Harry Benjamin, *The Transsexual Phenomenon; a Scientific Report on Transsexualism and Sex Conversion in the Human Male and Female* (New York, 1966), https://archive.is/20130105202900/http://www2.rz.hu-berlin.de/sexology/ECE6/html/benjamin/

171 Alfred Kinsey, Paul Gebhard, Wardell Pomery et al, *Sexual Behavior in the Human Male* (Philadephia,1948) and *Sexual Behavior in the Human Female* (Philadelphia, 1953)

172 This troubled relationship continues to generate a considerable literature. As a useful starting point see Paisley Currah and Susan Stryker (eds) 'Postposttransexual: Key concepts for Twenty-First-Century Transgender Studies, *Transgender Studies Quarterly*, Volume 1, Issue 1-2, 1 May 2014.

173 World Professional Association for Transgender Health, 'The Standards of Care for the Health of Transsexual, Transgender, and Gender Nonconforming People', Version 7, *International Journal of Transgenderism*, 13:4, pp165-232, http://www.wpath.org/publications/soc.

174 Standards of Care for the Health of Transsexual, Transgender, and Gender Nonconforming People, *World Professional Association for Transgender Health*, https://www.wpath.org/media/cms/Documents/SOC percent20v7/Standards percent20of percent20Care_V7 percent20Full percent20Book_English.pdf

175 For a useful summary of how services developed from this period see R Combs, L Turner L and S Whittle,

Gender Identity Services in England: The Mapping Project Report, (London, 2008).

176 DSM-III, The third edition of the Diagnostic and Statistical Manual of Mental Disorders from the American Psychiatric Association, (1980) https://www.ncbi.nlm.nih.gov/m/pubmed/3787052/.

177 The Intersex Society of North America produced a film in 1996 in which intersex people described their experiences. *Hermaphrodites Speak!* (Chase, 1997) Available from ISNA, Box 3070,Ann Arbor, MI, 48106.

178 Stryker, 2008, loc 2145

179 'A Change of Sex', *Inside Story*, BBC2, 1979, https://www.bbc.co.uk/programmes/p04frfp9

180 For a personal take on the problems by a service user see Abigail Robinson's blog, 17 June 2016, 'A Visit to Foucault's Clinic — The West London GIC at Charing Cross', https://abigailrobinsonblog.wordpress.com/2016/06/17/a-visit-to-foucaults-clinic-the-west-london-gic-at-charing-cross-hospital/.

181 In addition to Jorgensen's autobiography, *Christine Jorgensen, A Personal Biography*, (New York, 1967) see also Joanne Meyerowitz, *How Sex Changed: A History of Transsexuality in the United States*, (Cambridge, Mass, 2004), which follows Jorgensen's life story and discusses the medical and social context.

182 See Stryker, 2008, Chapter 2

183 Lily Elbe's story is told in her own words in Niels Hoyer (ed), translated by James Stebbing, *Man Into Woman: The First Sex Change. A Portrait of Lily Elbe*, (London, 2004)

184 The full judgement, including Justice Ormrod's 'test' was published by Press For Change can be read here: Corbett v Corbett (otherwise Ashley) The Judgement of Justice Ormrod, 1 February 1970, https://swarb.co.uk/corbett-v-corbett-otherwise-ashley-fd-1-feb-1970/

185 Jan Morris, *Conundrum*, (New York, 2006).

186 See Chris Harman, *The Fire Last Time: 1968 and After*, (London, 1988)

187 Harman, 1988, pvii.

188 Duberman, 1993, p193.

189 Duberman,1993, p194.

190 Duberman, 1993 p196.

191 See the November 2017 Netflix documentary about Marsha P Johnson and Sylvia Rivera which recognised the courageous roles they played. *The Death and Life of Marsha P Johnson*, Director David France, https://www.netflix.com/gb/title/80189623

192 Quoted in Duberman,1993, p198.

193 Quoted in Carter, p190-191.

194 Quoted in Carter, p191-192.

195 Carter,2004, p197.

196 Duberman,1993, p170-171.

197 Feinberg, 1996, p107.

198 Carter,2004, p198-199.

199 See: 'Gay Liberation in New York City', *OutHistory.org*, http://outhistory.org/exhibits/show/gay-liberation-in-new-york-cit/intro/timeline

200 The founding statement of the GLF can be found in Carter, 2004, p219.

201 As well as the Mattachine Society there were also groups such as The Daughters of Bilitis, originating in San Francisco, which offered help and support for lesbians and a social alternative to the lesbian bars which were subject to police raids and harassment. A number of the homophile organisations were part of ERCHO, the Eastern Regional Conference of Homophile Organisations, which was deeply suspicious of the GLF's radicalism (see Duberman 1993 pp226-233)

202 For a more detailed discussion of the internal arguments in the GLF and GAA at this time see Duberman 1993 pp215-244, and Carter, 2004, chapters 13 and 14.

203 Mario Mieli, *Towards a Gay Communism: Elements of a Homosexual Critique*, (London, 2018) p100. Mieli's work was originally published in English translation in 1980 by the London Gay Men's Press.

204 Quoted in Duberman, 1993, p238.

205 Sylvia Rivera, 'Y'all Better Quiet Down,' 1973, www.youtube.com/watch?v=Jb-JIOWUw1o

206 See Stryker, 2008, Chapter 3.

207 Susan Stryker and Victor Silverman, *Screaming Queens: The Riot at Compton's Cafeteria*, 2005.

www.youtube.com/watch?v=G-WASW9dRBU

208 Stryker and Silverman, 2005.

209 Mario Mieli, 2018, p 213

210 An early example of this was the exclusion in 1973 of Beth Elliott, a transsexual lesbian singer and activist from the San Francisco chapter of the Daughters of Bilitis. She was accused by a former friend and separatist feminist of being a "violator of women's space" through her transsexualism and was denounced and vilified. Music engineer Sandy Stone was another target in 1977. As the US political right stoked up its anti-homosexual campaigning at the time some radical feminists unfortunately turned on an even more marginalised group. See Zackary Drucker's interview with Sandy Stone, 'On Living Among Lesbian Separatists as a Trans Woman in the 70s', *Vice*, 19 Dec 2018 https://www.vice.com/en_us/article/zmd5k5/sandy-stone-biography-transgender-history

211 See for example Janice Raymond, *The Transsexual Empire: The Making of the She-Male* (Boston, 1979). Raymond attacked trans women's authenticity as women and their right to be part of the women's movement. Also see Sandy Stone's response, 'The 'Empire' Strikes Back: A Posttranssexual Manifesto', *Camera Obscura* (1992) 10 (2 (29)): pp150-176. available at https://sandystone.com/empire-strikes-back.pdf. Echoes of this transphobia persist among some radical feminists today.

212 Postmodernism was developed by thinkers like Michel Foucault, Jacques Derrida, Fredric Jameson and Jean-Francois Lyotard. See chapter 10.

213 The Terrence Higgins Trust, http://www.tht.org.uk/

214 See Riki Wilchins, *TRANS/gressive: How transgender activists took on Gay Rights, Feminism, the Media and Congress ... and Won!* (Riverdale, New York, 2017).

215 The UK Intersex Association www.ukia.co.uk

216 Organisation Intersex International in the United Kingdom http://oiiuk.org/

217 Stryker, 2008, loc 2081

218 See: Stonewall announces new Trans Advisory Group, 27th October 2015, https://www.stonewall.org.uk/news/stonewall-announces-new-trans-advisory-group

219 Stonewall response to inaccurate reports of splitting, 23rd October 2019, https://www.stonewall.org.uk/about-us/news/stonewall-response-inaccurate-reports-splitting

220 See Purton,2017, chapter 5 for a discussion of this process.

221 Stryker, 2008, loc 2113.

Chapter 6: Trans voices around the world

222 TransOralHistory.com records many stories of trans oppression and resistance.

223 Amrou Al-Kadhi, 'As a gay man born in Iraq, I know that western intervention is to blame for the murder of LGBT Iraqis', *The Independent*, 5 July 2017.

224 Trans Murder Monitoring, 2019, https://transrespect.org/en/map/trans-murder-monitoring/.

225 KAOSGL, 29 March 2010, Turkish minister's gay comments protested in Istanbul, https://www.kaosgl.org/en/single-news/turkish-ministerrsquos-gay-comments-protested-in-istanbul

226 Human Rights Violations of LGBT Individuals in Turkey, Republic of Turkey submission to the United Nations Universal Periodic Review, November 2014 https://ilga.org/wp-content/uploads/2016/02/Shadow-report-16.pdf.

227 LGBT activist Asli Zengin, quoted in ''She insulted my manhood'; murder underlines Turkey's LGBT backlash', *The Guardian*, 16 August 2018, https://www.theguardian.com/global-development/2018/aug/16/she-insulted-my-manhood-turkey-faces-fresh-scrutiny-lgbt-rights

228 Quoted in BBC News, 'Hande Kader: Outcry in Turkey over transgender woman's murder', 21 August 2016, https://www.bbc.co.uk/news/world-europe-37143879.

229 'Trans woman commits suicide in Turkey', *LGBTI News Turkey,* 22 August 2016, https://lgbtinewsturkey.com/2016/08/22/trans-woman-commits-suicide-in-turkey/

230 "I wanted and tried to kill myself': What it's like being transgender in Turkey, Europe's trans murder epicentre', *Pink News*, 21 July 2018, https://www.pinknews.co.uk/2018/07/21/transgender-turkey-europe-highest-murder-rate/.

231 'Lacking a supportive community, many LGBT people in Turkey live double lives', *PRI*, 4 June 2015, https://www.pri.org/stories/2015-06-04/lacking-supportive-community-many-lgbt-people-turkey-live-double-lives.

232 'Hundreds protest over murder of trans woman in Istanbul', *Al Jazeera*, 22 August 2016, https://www.aljazeera.com/news/2016/08/hundreds-protest-murder-trans-woman-istanbul-160821192103933.html

233 Quoted in 'Hande Kader: Outcry in Turkey over transgender woman's murder', *BBC News*, 21 August 2016, https://www.bbc.co.uk/news/world-europe-37143879.

234 In May 2013 mass protests erupted against plans to develop Taksim Gezi Park in Istanbul. The protests, involving sit-ins, marches and strikes were a lightning rod for discontent against the Turkish regime. Nearly 3,000 people were arrested, 11 people were killed by police and 8,000 injured by riot police using tear gas and water cannon as protests and demonstrations were sparked right across Turkey in defence of freedom of the press, free speech and secularism.

235 'Turkey LGBT: Scuffles at banned Istanbul transgender event', *BBC News*, 19 June 2016, https://www.bbc.co.uk/news/world-europe-36571303

236 'Turkish police fire teargas at crowds gathered for banned Istanbul Pride march', *The Independent*, 30 June 2019, https://www.independent.co.uk/news/world/middle-east/lgbt-pride-turkey-march-ban-tear-gas-istanbul-police-a8981751.html.

237 Trans Pride Press Statement, 19 June 2016, https://lgbtinewsturkey.com/2016/06/19/trans-pride-press-statement/.

238 Joseph Goh, 'Trans*cending tribulations: Malaysian Mak Nyahs', *New Mandala*, February 11, 2014, http://asiapacific.anu.edu.au/newmandala/2014/02/11/transcending-tribulations-malaysian-mak-nyahs/.

239 See Asia Pacific Transgender Network, *Legal Gender Recognition in Malaysia: A Legal and Policy Review in the Context of Human Rights*, 2017, https://www.undp.org/content/dam/rbap/docs/Research percent20& percent20Publications/hiv_aids/Malaysia-APTN_Publication_OnlineViewing.pdf p10.

240 Human Rights Watch, 'I'm Scared to be a Woman', 25 September 2014, http://features.hrw.org/features/HRW_reports_2014/Im_Scared_to_Be_a_Woman.

241 Human Rights Watch, 2014

242 Justice for Sisters, *Evidence of state-sponsorred violence and discrimination against LGBT persons in Malaysia*, https://justiceforsisters.wordpress.com/2019/04/19/458/ April 19 2019,

243 Transgender, Muslim and banned in Malaysia', *Unreported World*, 18 March 2016, https://www.youtube.com/watch?v=bMCloNkQ6Qg

244 Human Rights Watch, 2014

245 'Is there room for transgender rights in the 'New Malaysia'?', *The Diplomat*, April 4 2019, https://thediplomat.com/2019/04/is-there-room-for-transgender-rights-in-the-new-malaysia/.

246 World Bank Open Data, https://data.worldbank.org/country/russian-federation.

247 Jon Stone, 'Russian government bans transgender people from driving', *The Independent*. 9 January 2015, https://www.independent.co.uk/news/world/europe/russian-government-bans-transgender-people-from-driving-9967132.html.

248 'Channel 4's Hunted — the Russian gangs who hunt gays for sport', *Pink News*, 5 February 2014, https://www.pinknews.co.uk/2014/02/05/preview-channel-4s-hunted-the-russian-gangs-who-hunt-gays-for-sport/.

249 Human Rights Watch Report, 'No Support: Russia's 'Gay Propaganda' Law Imperils LGBT Youth', 11 December 2018, https://www.hrw.org/report/2018/12/11/no-support/

russias-gay-propaganda-law-imperils-lgbt-youth.

250 Shaun Walker, Christian Davies and Robert Tait, 'Anti-LGBT rhetoric stokes tensions in eastern Europe', The Guardian 25 October 2019, https://www.theguardian.com/world/2019/oct/25/anti-lgbt-rhetoric-stokes-tensions-in-eastern-europe.

251 ILGA-Europe, European section of the International Lesbian, Gay, Bisexual, Trans and Intersex Association, https://ilga-europe.org.

252 Oliver Carroll, 'Prominent LGBT+ activist murdered in St Petersburg', The Independent, 23 July 2019, https://www.independent.co.uk/news/world/europe/lgbt-murder-st-petersburg-russia-elena-grigorieva-death-a9017766.html.

253 www.newnownext.com/chechnya-rainbow-railroad/04/2017/.

254 For example see Homa Khaleeli, 'Hijra: India's third gender claims its place in law', The Guardian, 16 April 2014, https://www.theguardian.com/society/2014/apr/16/india-third-gender-claims-place-in-law.

255 Jessica Hinchy, 'The long history of criminalising hijras', Himal Southasian magazine, 2 July 2019, https://himalmag.com/long-history-criminalising-hijras-india-jessica-hinchy-2019/.

256 Sridevi Nambiar, 'A Brief History of Hijra, India's Third Gender', The Culture Trip, 1 January 2017, https://theculturetrip.com/asia/india/articles/a-brief-history-of-hijra-indias-third-gender/.

257 AVERT, HIV and AIDS in India, 1 October 2019, https://www.avert.org/professionals/hiv-around-world/asia-pacific/india.

258 Maria Thomas, 'Timeline: The struggle against section 377 began over two decades ago', Quartz India, 6 September 2018, https://qz.com/india/1379620/section-377-a-timeline-of-indias-battle-for-gay-rights/.

259 Shamani Joshi, 'Queer Indians tell us how much has changed since gay sex was decriminalised a year ago', Vice, 6 September 2019, https://www.vice.com/en_in/article/evjze7/queer-lgbtq-gay-indians-tell-us-how-much-has-changed-since-gay-sex-was-decriminalised-a-year-ago-section-377.

260 Shivam Vij, 'India's ruling Bharatya Janata Party has a rape problem', Quartz India, 25 September 2019, https://qz.com/india/1715615/kathua-unnao-up-cases-show-modis-bjp-has-a-rape-problem/.

261 Trans activist Bindiya Rana quoted in 'Pakistan passes landmark transgender rights law', Aljazeera, 9 May 2018,https://www.aljazeera.com/news/2018/05/pakistan-passes-landmark-transgender-rights-law-180509095207950.html.

262 Zulfikar Ali and Shashank Bengali, 'Pakistani trans activist who was shot, then taunted at hospital, dies of injuries', Los Angeles Times, 25 May 2016, https://www.latimes.com/world/asia/la-fg-pakistan-transgender-20160525-snap-story.htm.

263 'Pakistan's transgender community cautiously welcomes marriage fatwa', BBC News, 28 June 2016, https://www.bbc.co.uk/news/world-asia-36648141.

264 Bindiya Rana quoted in Homa Khaleeli, 'India Third Gender Claims Place in Law', The Guardian, 16 April 2014, www.theguardian.com/society/2014/apr/16/india-third-gender-claims-place-in-law.

265 Asad Hashim, 'Pakistan passes landmark transgender rights law', Al Jazeera, 9 May 2018, www.aljazeera.com/news/2018/05/pakistan-passes-landmark-transgender-rights-law-180509095207950.html.

266 'Pakistan's transgender community cautously welcomes marriage fatwa', BBC News, 28 June 2016, https://www.bbc.co.uk/news/world-asia-36648141.

267 Trans Action Pakistan: https://transaction.org.pk.

268 'Pakistan's transgender people live in fear,' BBC News, 23 June 2016, https://www.bbc.com/news/av/world-asia-36606560/pakistan-s-transgender-people-live-in-fear.

269 Ta*, 'One year after the murders of Xulhaz Mannan and Mahbub Rabbi Tonoy', Amnesty International, 25 April 2017, https://www.amnesty.org/en/latest/news/2017/04/one-year-after-the-murders-of-xulhaz-

mannan-and-mahbub-rabbi-tonoy/.

270 'Transgender councillor elected Bangladesh first', *The Jakarta Post*, 16 October 2019, https://www. thejakartapost.com/news/2019/10/16/ transgender-councillor-elected-in-bangladesh-first.html.

271 For a summary see Global Human Rights Defence, *LGBT Rights in Bangladesh*, 25 January 2019, https:// ghrd.org/lgbt-rights-in-bangladesh.

272 Human Rights Watch, *World Report*, 2016, www.hrw.org/world-report/2016/country-chapters/ bangladesh#e81181.

273 'Bangladeshis Hijras first trans pride parade', *Planet Transgender,* 15 November 2014, Video, https:// planettransgender.com/bangladeshis-hijras-first-trans-pride-parade-video/.

274 'One by One, Bangladesh's Activists Are Being Hacked to Death', *Foreign Policy*, 25 April 2016, https:// foreignpolicy.com/2016/04/25/ one-by-one-bangladeshs-activists-are-being-hacked-to-death/.

275 Ta*, 'One year after the murders of Xulhaz Mannan and Mahbub Rabbi Tonoy', *Amnesty International*, 25 April 2017, https://www.amnesty. org/en/latest/news/2017/04/ one-year-after-the-murders-of-xulhaz-mannan-and-mahbub-rabbi-tonoy/.

276 Gambian President Yahya Jammeh quoted in, Heather Saul, 'Gambian president says gay people are 'vermin' and should be tackled like malaria-causing mosquitos', *The Independent*, 19 February 2014 https://www. independent.co.uk/news/world/ africa/gambian-president-says-gay-people-are-vermin-and-should-be-tackled-like-malaria-causing-mosquitoes-9139119.html.

277 Amnesty International, *The State of the World's Human Rights*, 2017/18, www.amnesty.org.uk/files/2018-02/ annualreport2017.pdf.

278 Feinberg, 1996, p34.

279 Feinberg, 1996, p44.

280 For example see John Newsinger, *The Blood Never Dried: A People's History of the British Empire*, 2nd Ed, (London, 2013).

281 Ifeatu Nnaobi, 'One year on from rainbow flag arrests, Egypt continues LGBT crackdown', *AllOut*, 24 September 2018, http://news.trust. org/item/20180924165447-0gsae/,

282 Human Rights Watch, 'Harsh Law's Severe Impact on LGBT Community', 20 October 2016, https://www.hrw. org/news/2016/10/20/nigeria-harsh-laws-severe-impact-lgbt-community.

283 For an example of extreme homophobia in Nigeria see Richard Akuson, 'Nigeria is a cold-blooded country for gay men — I have the scars to prove it', *CNN*, April 17 2019, https://edition.cnn.com/2019/04/17/ opinions/nigeria-opinion-lgbt-attack/ index.html: For a personal testimony on being a young Nigerian trans person see: 'Young Trans Nigerians: people need to see that we exist, *Open Democracy*, 30 April 2018, https:// www.opendemocracy.net/en/5050/ young-nigerian-trans-rights/.

284 Gambian President Yahya Jammeh quoted in, Heather Saul, 'Gambian president says gay people are 'vermin' and should be tackled like malaria-causing mosquitos', *The Independent*,19 February 2014 https:// www.independent.co.uk/news/ world/africa/gambian-president-says-gay-people-are-vermin-and-should-be-tackled-like-malaria-causing-mosquitoes-9139119.html.

285 Amnesty International UK, 'Uganda's Anti-Homosexuality Bill becomes law', 12 January 2018 https://www.amnesty. org.uk/ugandas-anti-homosexuality-bill-becomes-law.

286 Quoted in David Smith, 'Why Africa is the Most Homophobic Continent', *The Guardian*, 23 February 2014, www. theguardian.com/world/2014/feb/23/ africa-homophobia-uganda-anti-gay-law.

287 Xan Rice, 'Ugandan'hang them'paper has no regrets after David Kato death', *The Guardian*, 27 January 2011, https:// www.theguardian.com/world/2011/ jan/27/uganda-paper-david-kato-death.

288 Princess Rihanna, 'The harsh reality of being transgender in Uganda', *The Washington Post*, 17 August 2016, https://www.washingtonpost.com/ news/in-sight/wp/2016/08/17/ the-harsh-reality-of-being-

transgender-in-uganda/.

289 Human Rights Watch, 'Angola decriminalises same sex conduct', 23 January 2019, https://www.hrw.org/news/2019/01/23/angola-decriminalizes-same-sex-conduct.

290 Human Rights Watch,'Kenya court upholds archaic anti-homosexuality laws', 24 May 2019, https://www.hrw.org/news/2019/05/24/kenya-court-upholds-archaic-anti-homosexuality-laws-0.

291 https://www.genderdynamix.org.za/

292 South African Hate Crimes Monitoring Project, http://hcwg.org.za/.

293 See for example Human Rights Watch, '"We'll show you you're a woman" Violence and Discrimination against Black Lesbians and Transgender Men in South Africa', 5 December 2011, www.hrw.org/report/2011/12/05/well-show-you-youre-woman/violence-and-discrimination-against-black-lesbians-and-.

294 For example, see: Cath Everett, 'South Africa Progressive on LGBT Rights but Gays Still Battle for Social Reform', *International Business Times*, 22 October 2014, www.ibtimes.co.uk/south-africa-progressive-lgbt-rights-gays-still-battle-social-reform-1471213.

295 See Sanet Oberholzer, 'Conversations: Transgender healthcare in crisis', *The Sowetan*, 5 April 2019, https://www.sowetanlive.co.za/s-mag/2019-04-05-conversations-transgender-healthcare-in-crisis/.

296 I am grateful to the South Korean organisation Workers Solidarity, a sister organisation of the UK's Socialist Workers Party, for much of the information in this section. They have been addressing issues of transphobia and trans-critical feminism from a revolutionary Marxist perspective, including publishing a book on the subject in early 2018.

297 Rainbow Action Against Sexual Minority Discrimination, *Human Rights Violations on the Basis of Sexual Orientation, Gender Identity, and HIV Status in the Republic of Korea*, March 2017, https://tbinternet.ohchr.org/Treaties/CAT/Shared percent20Documents/KOR/INT_CAT_

CSS_KOR_27029_E.pdf.

298 Quoted in AVERT, *Transgender people, HIV and AIDS*, 10 October 2019, https://www.avert.org/professionals/hiv-social-issues/key-affected-populations/transgender.

299 See Stonewall, *Global Legal Workplace Briefing: Colombia*, 2019, https://www.stonewall.org.uk/system/files/global_workplace_briefing_colombia_final.pdf.

300 See Anika Oettler, 'The Struggle for Gendered Peace and LGBT Rights in Colombia,' *Violence, Security, and Peace Working Papers* No 2, July 2019, http://www.lse.ac.uk/lacc/publications/PDFs/VSP2-Oettler-Gendered-Peace-LGBT-Rights-Colombia-web.pdf.

301 https://colombiadiversa.org/.

302 Stonewall, 'Trans Day of Remembrance: The alarming situation in Brazil', 20 November 2018 https://www.stonewall.org.uk/node/110736.

303 Andrea Martinelli and Leda Antunes, 'A Grisly Killing Shows the Rampant Transphobia in Brazil', *Huff Post Brazil*, 25 January 2019, http://bit.ly/2PjVewQ.

304 AVERT, *Transgender people, HIV and AIDS*, 10 October 2019.

305 For example see AVERT, *Transgender People, HIV and AIDS*, 10 October 2019, and World Health Organisation, *Transgender People and HIV: Policy Brief*, July 2015, https://www.who.int/hiv/pub/transgender/transgender-hiv-policy/en/.

306 UNAIDS, *The Gap Report*, 2014, www.unaids.org/en/resources/campaigns/2014/2014gapreport/gapreport; See also Winter, S et al, 'Transgender people: health at the margins of society', *Lancet* 16(10042) (London) June 2016.

307 See UNAIDS, *The Gap Report, 2014, Transgender People*, Geneva 2014, https://www.unaids.org/sites/default/files/media_asset/08_Transgenderpeople.pdf.

308 Transgender Europe, *Trans Rights and Europe Map and Index 2016*, 10 May 2016 : http://tgeu.org/trans-rights_europe_map_2016/.

309 Transgender Europe, *Trans Rights Europe and Central Asia Map and*

Index 2019, 17 May 2019, https://tgeu.org/trans-rights-europe-central-asia-map-index-2019/.

310 Transgender Europe, Celebrated & contested — breakthrough towards first French gender recognition law, 15 July 2016, tgeu.org/celebrated-contested-breakthrough-towards-first-french-gender-recognition-law/.

311 Irish Statute Book, Gender Recognition Act 2015, http://www.irishstatutebook.ie/eli/2015/act/25/enacted/en/html.

312 Transgender Europe, 'Norway approves Legal Gender Recognition based on Self Determination', 6 June 2016, https://tgeu.org/norway-lgr/.

313 Non-European countries which allow self-declaration are Colombia, Iceland and Argentina, plus the US state of California, and Mexico City, and Pakistan since 2018.

Chapter 7: Donald Trump, trans rights and the US bathroom wars

314 Carla Green, 'Transgender Honduran woman's death in US 'ice box' detention prompts outcry', *The Guardian,* 31 May 2018, https://www.theguardian.com/us-news/2018/may/31/roxana-hernandez-transgender-honduran-woman-dies-us-ice-box.

315 Clark Mindock, 'Donald Trump bans transgender people from serving in US military due to 'disruption' they would cause', *The Independent,* 26 July 2017, https://www.independent.co.uk news/world/americas/us-politics/donald-trump-bans-transgender-people-us-military-army-chelsea-manning-lgbt-rights-gay-president-a7861196.html.

316 'Protests erupt nationwide following Trump's transgender military ban announcement', *ABC News,* 27 July 2017, https://abcnews.go.com/US/protesters-rally-trumps-transgender-military-ban/story?id=48876355.

317 See The National Center for Transgender Equality, *The Discrimination Administration: Trump's Record of Action Against the Trans Community,* 2019, https://transequality.org/the-discrimination-administration.

318 'Transgender care cost military less than 1 percent of its health budget since 2016', *PBS Newshour,* 27 Feb 2019, https://www.pbs.org/newshour/nation/military-spent-about-8-million-on-transgender-care-since-2016.

319 Kimberley Amadeo, 'US Military Budget, Its Components, Challenges, and Growth', *The Balance,* April 22 2019, https://www.thebalance.com/u-s-military-budget-components-challenges-growth-3306320.

320 Janice Raymond, *Social And Ethical Aspects of Transsexual Surgery, Paper prepared for the National Center for Health Care Technology,* U.S. Department of Health and Human Services, 1980. See also Cristan Williams, 'Fact Checking Janice Raymond: The NCHCT Report', *Transadvocate,* 29 September 2018, http://transadvocate.com/.fact-checking-janice-raymond-the-nchct-report_n_14554.htm.

321 Janice Raymond, *The Transsexual Empire: The Making of the She-male,* (Boston, 1979).

322 Katy Steinmetz, 'The Transgender Tipping Point', *Time,* 19 May 2014, https://time.com/135480/transgender-tipping-point/.

323 Janet Mock, *Redefining Realness: My Path to Womanhood, Identity, Love and so much more* (New York, 2014).

324 Ann Haal, Phillip Rodgers, and Jody Herman, *Suicide Attempts among Transgender and Gender Non-Conforming Adults: Findings of the National Transgender Discrimination Survey,* (New York & Los Angeles, 2014) https://williamsinstitute.law.ucla.edu/wp-content/uploads/AFSP-Williams-Suicide-Report-Final.pdf.

325 Anthony Boyd and Sophie Evans, 'Orlando Pulse Club shooting: Recap after 50 killed in America's worst mass shooting when gunman stormed gay nightclub', *The Mirror,* 16 June 2016, http://www.mirror.co.uk/news/world-news/orlando-pulse-club-shooting-recap-8171546.

326 Stryker, 2009, loc 539.

327 John D'Emilio, *Making Trouble, Essays on Gay History, Politics, and the University* (New York, 1992).

328 Human Rights Campaign, *Violence Against the Transgender Community*, 12 May 2015, http://www.hrc.org/blog/alarming-number-of-transgender-people-killed-worldwide-in-the-last-seven-ye.

329 Human Rights Campaign, *Violence Against the Transgender Community 2018*, https://www.hrc.org/resources/violence-against-the-transgender-community-in-2018.

330 Joe Morgan, 'Shot, beheaded, and killed by family: 295 trans people murdered this year', *Gay Star News*, 16 November 2016, https://www.gaystarnews.com/article/shot-beheaded-murdered-family-295-trans-people-murdered-year/.

331 Alex Schmider, '2016 was the deadliest year on record for transgender people', *GLAAD*, 9 November 2016, https://www.glaad.org/blog/2016-was-deadliest-year-record-transgender-people.

332 'US gang member gets 49 years in prison for killing transgender teen', *The Guardian*, 16 May 2017, https://www.theguardian.com/us-news/2017/may/16/first-us-transgender-hate-crime-sentence-mercedes-williamson.

333 American Bar Association, 'The Gay/Trans Panic Defence: What It is, and How to End It', July 10 2019, https://www.americanbar.org/groups/crsj/publications/member-features/gay-trans-panic-defense/.

334 Ed Pilkington, 'Chelsea Manning jailed again as she refuses to testify before grand jury', *The Guardian*, 17 May 2019, https://www.theguardian.com/us-news/2019/may/16/chelsea-manning-jailed-again-as-she-refuses-to-testify-before-grand-jury.

335 Patrick Svitek. 'Lt. Gov. Dan Patrick fires back at criticism over "bathroom bill"', *Texas Tribune*, 11 January 2017, https://www.texastribune.org/2017/01/11/patrick-fires-back-critics-bathroom-bill/.

336 Christopher Harress, 'Alabama bathroom bill targets transgender rights', *AL.com*, 7 January 2017 http://www.al.com/news/index.ssf/2017/01/alabama_bathroom_bill_targets.html.

337 Britney McNamara, 'This Woman Was

Allegedly Harassed in a Restroom Because Someone Thought She Was Transgender', *Teen Vogue*, 17 May 2016, www.teenvogue.com/story/woman-mistaken-transgender-bathroom-attack.

338 https://www.youtube.com/watch?v=dYS-VsWJevY.

339 National Alliance to End Sexual Violence, 'Coalition of Leading 250+ Sexual Assault, Domestic Violence Groups Condemn Anti-Transgender Legislation', 21 April 2016 http://www.endsexualviolence.org/wp-content/uploads/2017/09/PRESS-RELEASE-APRIL-21-2016.pdf.

340 Joseph McCormick, 'Target faces boycott from lots of people who don't understand what transgender means', *Pink News*, 22 April 2016, www.pinknews.co.uk/2016/04/22/target-faces-boycott-from-lots-of-people-who-dont-understand-what-transgender-means/.

341 Daniel Kreps, 'Steven Van Zandt Talks Springsteen's Canceled North Carolina Concert', *Rolling Stone*, 9 April 2016, https://www.rollingstone.com/music/music-news/steven-van-zandt-talks-springsteens-canceled-north-carolina-concert-224724/.

342 ''Bathroom bill' to cost North Carolina $3.76 billion', CNBC, 27 March 2017 https://www.cnbc.com/2017/03/27/bathroom-bill-to-cost-north-carolina-376-billion.html.

343 CNN/ORC International, Transgender Rights Poll, 9 May 2016, http://i2.cdn.turner.com/cnn/2016/images/05/09/transgender.rights.pdf.

344 'Election 2016, North Carolina Results: Roy Cooper Wins', The New York Times,1 August 2017, https://www.nytimes.com/elections/2016/results/north-carolina-governor-mccrory-cooper.

345 Michael Lipka, 'Americans are divided over which public bathrooms transgender people should use', *Pew Research Center*, 3 October 2016, www.pewresearch.org/fact-tank/2016/10/03/americans-are-divided-over-which-public-bathrooms-transgender-people-should-use/?

346 Nick Duffy, 'Women don't actually

support laws to ban trans people from women's bathrooms', *Pink News*, 3 October 2016, http://www.pinknews.co.uk/2016/10/03/women-dont-actually-support-laws-to-ban-trans-people-from-womens-bathrooms/.

347 Centre for the Study of Hate and Extremism, *Report to the Nation: Factbook on Hate and Extremism in the USA and Internationally*, (California State University, 2019), https://csbs.csusb.edu/sites/csusb_csbs/files/CSHE percent202019 percent20Report percent20to percent20the percent20Nation percent20FINAL percent207.29.19 percent2011 percent20PM_0.pdf.

348 And in various other 'liberal' states, including in the UK where thousands of LGBT+ people have been subjected to such "cures" as well.

349 For example see the Ozanne Foundation, *Report of the Faith and Sexuality Survey 2018,* February 2019, https://ozanne.foundation/2019/02/20/2018-national-faith-sexuality-survey-results/.

350 Molly Woodstock, 'The Trump administration says it wants to define sex "on a biological basis". It gets the science wrong', *Washington Post*, 29 October 2018, https://www.washingtonpost.com/outlook/2018/10/29/trump-administration-says-it-wants-define-sex-biological-basis-it-gets-science-wrong/.

351 The Women's Liberation Front is a transphobic radical feminist group whose basic attitude towards trans is that 'Human beings can't change sex.' See their website https://womensliberationfront.org/.

352 Sam Levin, 'A critical point in history: How Trump's attack on LGBT rights is escalating'. *The Guardian*, 3 September 2019, https://www.theguardian.com/world/2019/sep/03/trump-attack-lgbt-rights-supreme-court.

353 Katelyn Burns, 'The rise of anti-trans"radical"feminists, explained', *Vox*, 5 September 2019 .

354 For example see Steven Rose, R C Lewontin and Leon J Kamin, *Not in Our Genes* (London, 1990) and Richard Lewontin, *It ain't necessarily so: The Dream of the Human Genome and Other Illusions* (London, 2000).

Chapter 8: Trans Rights and Transphobia in Britain

355 Benjamin Butterworth, 'Transgender woman Naomi Hersi murdered in London hotel room', *Pink News*, 26 March 2018.

356 See Rosenhan's study of admissions to psychiatric hospitals in America: D L Rosenhan, 'On Being Sane in Insane Places', *Science* 179, 1973, p250-258

357 Iain Ferguson, *Politics of the Mind: Marxism and Mental Illness* (London, 2017).

358 Pat Clinton, 'Harsh Realities of Trans Health', *Socialist Review* 421, February 2017.

359 A full index and links to the papers presented at the Gendys Conferences can be found at http://www.gender.org.uk/conf/index.htm.

360 Dave King & Richard Ekins, 'The First UK Transgender Conferences, 1974 and 1975', *Gendys Journal* 39, Autumn 2007, http://www.gender.org.uk/gendys/2007/39ekins.htm.

361 For example see https://blogs.lexisnexis.co.uk/futureoflaw/2017/02/lgbt-rights-in-review-transgender-identities-and-the-law/ for this and other legal anomalies; also Chris Baynes, 'UK government wrong to deny pension to transgender woman, rules European court', *The Independent*, 26 June 2018, https://www.independent.co.uk/news/uk/home-news/transgender-woman-pension-payments-uk-government-european-court-justice-ruling-a8417476.html.

362 Public Accountability and Inclusion Directorate, *CPS Transgender Equality Management Guidance*, February 2014, https://www.mermaidsuk.org.uk/assets/media/CPS percent20Transgender percent20Equality percent20Management percent20Guidance.pdf.

363 See Gendered Intelligence, *The 2010 Equality Act*, http://genderedintelligence.co.uk/projects/kip/equality/laws.

364 House of Commons Women and

Equalities Committee, *Transgender Equality First Report of Session 2015–16*, HC 390, London, 2016, https://publications.parliament.uk/pa/cm201516/cmselect/cmwomeq/390/390.pdf.

365 See Zoe O'Connell, 'Court of Appeal confirms: Stealth trans people having sex are criminals', *Complicity* blog, 27 June 2016, www.complicity.co.uk/blog/2013/06/court-of-appeal-confirms-stealth-trans-people-having-sex-are-criminals/.

366 Gendered Intelligence: genderedintelligence.co.uk.

367 For many years Stonewall only addressed issues of sexual orientation but in 2014 it decided to incorporate transgender issues as well.

368 Stephen Whittle, *The Transgender Debate: The Crisis Surrounding Gender Identity* (Reading, 2000), p44.

369 IMAAN LGBTQ Muslim Support: https://imaanlondon.wordpress.com.

370 There had been a spate of four deaths of trans prisoners in a short period of time: See 'Transgender prison deaths: Watchdog calls for action', *BBC*, 10 January 2017, www.bbc.co.uk/news/uk-38562714.

371 Peter Purton, *Champions of Equality: Trade Unions and LGBT Rights in Britain* (London, 2017), p169-70.

372 Lesbian and Gay foundation, now the LGBT Foundation, https://lgbt.foundation.

373 TUC, *Staying Alive: The Impact of 'Austerity Cuts on the LGBT Voluntary and Community Sector (VCS) in England and Wales*, 26 June 2014, https://www.tuc.org.uk/sites/default/files/StayingAlive.pdf.

374 Terry Reed, 'Written evidence submitted by GIRES to the Transgender Equality Inquiry', *GIRES*, 2015, fairplayforwomen.com/wp-content/uploads/2017/01/19292.pdf.

375 National Center for Transgender Equality, U.S. Transgender Survey Report,2015 https://vawnet.org/material/2015-us-transgender-survey-report.

376 Peter Purton, 'Young and LGB or T: at risk from austerity', *Stronger Unions*, 13 Mar 2014, stronger unions.

org/2014/03/13/young-and-lgb-or-t-at-risk-from-austerity.

377 Malen Davies, & Martin Mitchell, *Implications of Reductions to Public Spending on LGB & T people and services* (London, 2016), natcen.ac.uk/our-research/research/implications-of-reductions-to-public-spending-on-lgbt-people-and-services.

378 Transgender Europe (TGEU). See their *Trans Murder Monitoring (TMM) report for The International Day Against Homophobia, Transphobia and Biphobia* (IDAHOT), https://transrespect.org/en/research/trans-murder-monitoring.

379 Nick Antjoule, *The Hate Crime Report: Homophobia, biphobia and transphobia in the UK* (London, 2016), http://www.galop.org.uk/wp-content/uploads/2016/10/The-Hate-Crime-Report-2016.pdf.

380 Melanie Stray, *The Hate Crime Report 2019: Attitudes to LGBT+ people in the UK*, Galop (London) p2. http://www.galop.org.uk/wp-content/uploads/Hate-Crime-Report-2019.pdf.

381 The Galop Report 2019, p2.

382 Sally Weale, 'Almost half of trans pupils in UK have attempted suicide, survey finds', *The Guardian*, 27 June 2017, www.theguardian.com/education/2017/jun/27/half-of-trans-pupils-in-the-uk-tried-to-take-their-own-lives-survey-finds.

383 Homophobic hate crimes charges fall as reports soar, *BBC Radio 5 Live investigates*, 11 September 2019, https://www.bbc.com/news/uk-49509301.

384 www.schools-out.org.uk. An excellent source for advice and materials.

385 Equality Challenge Unit, *The experience of lesbian, gay, bisexual and trans staff and students in higher education,* Research report 2009, https://www.ecu.ac.uk/wp-content/uploads/2015/04/Experiences-of-LGBT-staff-and-students-in-he.pdf.

386 'Transgender hate crimes recorded by police go up 81 percent', *BBC News*, 27 June 2019, https://www.bbc.co.uk/news/uk-48756370.

387 Paris Lees, 'We're in the middle of an epidemic of violence against trans people', *The Guardian*, 22 January

2018, https://www.theguardian.com/commentisfree/2018/jan/22/epidemic-violence-transgender-people-experienced-stonewall.

388 Stonewall/Yougov Survey, *LGBT in Britain: Trans Report*, (London, 2018), https://www.stonewall.org.uk/lgbt-britain-trans-report.

389 Jay McNeil et al, *Trans Mental Health and Wellbeing Study*, (Edinburgh, 2012), https://www.gires.org.uk/wp-content/uploads/2014/08/trans_mh_study.pdf.

390 See Trades Union Congress, *The cost of being out at work: LGBT+ workers experiences of harassment and discrimination*, (TUC, 2017), https://www.tuc.org.uk/sites/default/files/LGBTReport17.pdf. Also, Trades Union Congress, *Transforming the Workplace: A TUC guide for trade union activists on supporting trans members*, (TUC, 2016), https://www.tuc.org.uk/research-analysis/reports/transforming-workplace-tuc-guide-trade-union-activists-supporting-trans.

391 For example see: Jill Miller, 'Workplaces must be more trans inclusive', *CIPD Community*, 6 November 2017, www.cipd.co.uk/Community/blogs/b/jill_miller/posts/workplaces-must-be-more-trans-inclusive.

392 This was widely covered in the media. For example see: John Harrington, 'Flop of the Month, NSPCC got it wrong over Munroe Bergdorf backlash', *PR Week*, 1 July 2019, https://www.prweek.com/article/1589584/flop-month-nspcc-wrong-munroe-bergdorf-backlash.

393 'Transgender Prison Deaths: Watchdog Calls for Action', *BBC news*, 10 January 2017, http://www.bbc.co.uk/news/uk-38562714.

394 House of Commons Library, *Transgender Prisoners,* 19 September 2018, https://researchbriefings.parliament.uk/ResearchBriefing/Summary/CBP-7420#fullreport.

395 See Jacqueline Beard, *Transgender Prisoners*, BRIEFING PAPER Number 07420, House of Commons Library, 19 September 2018 , https://researchbriefings.files.parliament.uk/documents/CBP-7420/CBP-7420.pdf.

396 'First UK transgender prison unit to open', *BBC News*, 3 March 2019 https://www.bbc.co.uk/news/uk-47434730.

397 Department for Education, *The national curriculum in England Framework document,* July 2013, p8, section 4.2, https:www.gov.uk/government/uploads/system/uploads/attachment_data/file/210969/NC_framework_document_-_FINAL.pdf.

398 Ofsted, *No Place for Bullying*, 2012, https://assets.publishing.service.gov.uk/government/uploads/system/uploads/attachment_data/file/413234/No_place_for_bullying.pdf.

399 Nick Duffy, 'Education magazine TES loses star columnist over transphobia row', *Pink News*, 11 May 2019, www.pinknews.co.uk/2019/05/11/education-magazine-tes-loses-star-columnist-transphobia-row.

400 Skills Funding Agency, *Sexual Orientation and Gender Identity Equality in Further Education*, 2011, https://assets.publishing.service.gov.uk/government/uploads/system/uploads/attachment_data/file/288670/Sexual_Orientation_and_Gender_Identity_Equality_in_Adult_Learning-_Published_August_2011.pdf.

401 Forum for Sexual Orientation and Gender Identity in FE, *Pride and Prejudice in Education*, 2016, https://sgforum.org.uk/wp-content/uploads/2016/02/Pride-and-Prejudice-in-Education-report.pdf.

402 *Trans Community Statement of Need*, 26 April 2019, https://www.gires.org.uk/trans-community-statement-of-need.

403 HM Government, *Advancing transgender equality: a plan for action*, December 2011, https://www.gov.uk/government/uploads/system/uploads/attachment_data/file/85498/transgender-action-plan.pdf.

404 *Trans Community Statement of Need*, 26 April 2019, https://www.gires.org.uk/trans-community-statement-of-need.

405 Purton, 2017.

Chapter 9: Contested rights in Britain today

406 Parent of a trans child alluding to the challenging, subversive and liberating potential of being transgender in an open letter to their child: 'A letter to... my non-binary child, who has officially laid my son to rest', *The Guardian*, 11 November 2017, https://www.theguardian.com/lifeandstyle/2017/nov/11/a-letter-to-my-non-binary-child-who-has-officially-laid-my-son-to-rest.

407 Claire Heuchan 'If feminist Linda Bellos is seen as a risk, progressive politics has lost its way', *The Guardian*, 6 October 2017, www.theguardian.com/commentisfree/2017/oct/06/feminist-linda-bellos-women-trans-male-violence.

408 The issues of safe spaces and no platform are discussed from a socialist perspective here: Sally Campbell, 'Safe Spaces?' *Socialist Review*, April 2015, http://socialistreview.org.uk/tags/no-platform.

409 For example see Freer Lives, *A Socialist Critique of Gender Ideology*, 1 January 2018, https://freerlives.wordpress.com/2018/03/01/left-resistance-to-trans-politics-developments-in-britain-2017.

410 'Lesbian activist Linda Bellos went to the Supreme Court to back Trump administration during landmark LGBT cases', *Pink News*, 9 October 2019, https://www.pinknews.co.uk/2019/10/09/lesbian-activist-linda-bellos-supreme-court-against-trans-rights.

411 ACLU, *RG and GR Harris Funeral Homes v EEOC and Aimee Stephens*, 10 September 2019 https://www.aclu.org/cases/rg-gr-harris-funeral-homes-v-eeoc-aimee-stephens.

412 'This is everything you need to know about Aimee Stephen's landmark Supreme Court case', *Pink News*, 8 October 2019, https://www.pinknews.co.uk/2019/10/08/supreme-court-aimee-stephens-landmark-transgender-discrimination-lgbt-rights.

413 Julie Burchill, 'Transsexuals Should Cut it Out', *Observer*, 13 January 2013.

414 Sheila Jeffreys, 'Transgender Activism: A Lesbian Feminist Perspective', *Lesbian Studies*, Vol 1 (3/4), 1997, pp59-60.

415 Calla Wahlquist, 'Germaine Greer tells Q&A her trans views were wrong, but then restates them', *The Guardian*, 11 April 2016, www.theguardian.com/books/2016/apr/12/germaine-greer-tells-qa-her-trans-views-were-wrong-but-then-restates-them.

416 Raymond, 1994.

417 I draw a distinction between transphobes, who are universally hostile to transgender people, do not support trans rights and accord little or no respect even at a personal level to trans people, and trans critics, who may support trans people's right to respect and to live their lives without discrimination, and even support trans rights in principle, but who believe or worry (wrongly, as I argue here) that trans rights undermine women's rights.

418 Linda Bellos, Lucy Masoud and others, 'Violence has no place in transgender debate', *Observer*, Letters, 24 September 2017, https://www.theguardian.com/world/2017/sep/24/violence-against-women-transgender-debate.

419 'Transgender activist Tara Wolf fined £150 for assaulting exclusionary radical feminist in Hyde Park', *Evening Standard*, 13 April 2018, https://www.standard.co.uk/news/crime/transgender-activist-tara-wolf-fined-150-for-assaulting-exclusionary-radical-feminist-in-hyde-park-a3813856.html.

420 'Improving the climate of debate around proposed changes to the Gender Recognition Act', *Morning Star*, Letters, 4 July 2018, https://morningstaronline.co.uk/article/improving-climate-debate-around-proposed-changes-gender-recognition-act.

421 'Labour: Row over inclusion of trans women in all-women shortlists', *BBC News*, 1 May 2018, https://www.bbc.co.uk/news/uk-politics-43962349.

422 The Murdoch papers have been prominent in this. For example see: Andrew Gilligan, , Parents' anger as child sex change charity Mermaids puts private emails online, *The Times*,

June 16 2019 https://www.thetimes.co.uk/article/parents-anger-as-child-sex-change-charity-puts-private-emails-online-3tntlwqln.

423 Government Response to the Women and Equalities Report on Transgender Equality, July 2016, https://assets.publishing.service.gov.uk/government/uploads/system/uploads/attachment_data/file/535764/Government_Response_to_the_Women_and_Equalities_Committee_Report_on_Transgender_Equality.pdf.

424 Consultation, *Reform of the Gender Recognition Act 2014*, 3 July 2018, https://www.gov.uk/government/consultations/reform-of-the-gender-recognition-act-2004.

425 For example see Canadian anti-trans blogger Meghan Murphy: www.feministcurrent.com .

426 House of Commons Women and Equalities Committee, Transgender Equality First Report of Session 2015–16, HC 390, London, 2016, https://publications.parliament.uk/pa/cm201516/cmselect/cmwomeq/390/390.pdf .

427 Pat Clinton, 'Harsh Realities of Trans Health', Socialist Review 421, February 2017, http://socialistreview.org.uk/421/harsh-realities-trans-health

428 TUC, *Transforming the Workplace A TUC guide for trade union activists on supporting trans members*, November 2016, www.tuc.org.uk/sites/default/files/Transformingtheworkplace.pdf

429 See Michael Dance, Socialist Review, Teachers' victory on trans rights, May 2017 (424), http://socialistreview.org.uk/424/teachers-victory-trans-rights.

430 Kiri Tunks, 'Sex Matters', The Morning Star, 8 August 2017.

431 Lori Watson, 'The Woman Question', Transgender Studies Quarterly, Vol 3, Numbers 1-2, May 2016, p249.

432 Some feminists associated with the Man Friday group, eagerly promoted by the website Mumsnet, have carried out stunts where they dressed as men on a given day and entered 'men's spaces' claiming this is equivalent to self-identification by trans women. See: http://www.huckmagazine.com/perspectives/opinion-perspectives/mumsnet-transphobia-online.

433 Andrew Gilligan, 'Mermaids UK Charity Ban as Boy Forced to Live as Girl', *The Times*, 8 October 2017.

434 Mermaids, 'A response to negative newspaper coverage on transgender rights', 16 October 2019, https://www.mermaidsuk.org.uk/when-its-hardest-to-speak.-speak.html.

435 See TNL Community Fund, Statement: Outcome of our review into Mermaids UK grant, 19 February 2019, https://www.tnlcommunityfund.org.uk/news/press-releases/2019-02-19/outcome-of-review-of-proposed-mermaids-grant; also; Third Sector, Lottery body finds no reason to withhold £500k grant from transgender charity, 19 February 2019; https://www.thirdsector.co.uk/lottery-body-finds-no-reason-withhold-500k-grant-transgender-charity/finance/article/1526168. Also; Nathalie McDermott, OnRoadM, 17 December 2018, In Support of our friends and colleagues at Mermaids, https://www.onroadmedia.org.uk/2018/12/17/in-support-of-our-friends-and-colleagues-at-mermaids.

436 See Tavistock and Portman NHS Trust, 'GIDS referrals increase slows in 2016/17', 27 April 2017, https://tavistockandportman.nhs.uk/about-us/news/stories/gids-referrals-increase-slows-201617/ and 'GIDS referrals increase in 2017/18', 17 May 2018 https://tavistockandportman.nhs.uk/about-us/news/stories/gids-referrals-increase-201718.

437 Chris McManus, Right Hand, Left Hand: The Origins of Asymmetry in Brains, Bodies, Atoms and Cultures, (London, 2002).

438 Gender Identity Research and Education Society (GIRES), *Written evidence submitted by GIRES to the Transgender Equality Inquiry*, 2015, https://fairplayforwomen.com/wp-content/uploads/2017/01/19292.pdf, p3.

439 GIRES, 2015, p4.

440 GIRES, 2015, p3.

441 Women's Human Rights Campaign, *Declaration on Women's Sex-Based Rights*, https://www.

womensdeclaration.com.

442 For example see the founding statement, *WPUK Manifesto* 2019 and other material: https://womansplaceuk.org.

443 *WPUK Manifesto* 2019, https://womansplaceuk.org/wpuk-manifesto-2019.

444 Dr Stefan Baral et al, 'Worldwide burden of HIV in transgender women: a systematic review and meta-analysis', *The Lancet*, 13:3, March 2013, p214-222, www.thelancet.com/journals/laninf/article/PIIS1473-3099(12)70315-8/abstract.

445 Lizzy Buchan, 'Women's refuge budgets slashed by nearly a quarter over past seven years', *The Independent*, 17 October 2017, https://www.independent.co.uk/news/uk/politics/women-refuge-budget-cut-quarter-domestic-violence-victims-children-support-a8003066.html.

446 Sharon Smith, 'Mistaken identity: Can identity politics liberate the oppressed?' *International Socialism* 62, Spring 1994, p3.

Chapter 10: Political strategies in the movement

447 See Purton, 2017, op cit, especially chapters 2 and 3.

448 See Alex Callinicos, *Against Postmodernism*, (Cambridge, 1989).

449 Esme Choonara and Yuri Prasad, 'Whats wrong with privilege theory?', *International Socialism* 142, Spring 2014, p87.

450 For example, Michel Foucault, *The History of Sexuality* (New York, 1976): Michael Foucault, *Madness and Civilization*, (New York, 1961).

451 Judith Butler, *Gender Trouble: Feminism and the Subversion of Identity*, (London, 1990).

452 Noel Halifax, 'History of Queer theory and Politics', *Marxism Festival*, 2016, https://www.youtube.com/watch?v=qtFutG4gbRU.

453 Surya Monro, *Gender Politics: Citizenship, Activism and Sexual Diversity* (London, 2005), pp31-32.

454 Viviane K Namaste, *Invisible Lives: The Erasure of Transsexual and Transgendered People* (London, 2000) pp11-12.

455 Judith Butler addresses TERFs and the work of Sheila Jeffreys and Janice Raymond, *The Terfs* website, 1 May 2014, theterfs.com/.../judith-butler-addresses-terfs-and-the-work-of-sheila-jeffreys-and-janice-raymond.

456 Monro, 2005, p 101.

457 For example see Peggy McIntosh, 'White Privilege and Male Privilege: A Personal Account of Coming to See Correspondences through Work in Women's Studies', 1988, reprinted in Michael S Kimmel and Abby Ferber (eds), *Privilege: A Reader* (Boulder, 2010).

458 Choonara and Prasad, 2014, p84.

459 Choonara and Prasad, 2014, p108.

460 For example, Heidi Hartmann, The Unhappy Marriage of Marxism and Feminism: Towards a More Progressive Union, in Linda Nicholson, ed, *The Second Wave: A Reader in Feminist Theory* (New York, 1997).

461 Karl Marx, *The Eighteenth Brumaire of Louis Bonaparte* (Peking,1978 (1852)) p9.

462 'Pride in London Organisers Face Backlash After Anti-Trans Activists, 'Lead Parade' Through Capital', *Huffington Post*, 7 July 2018, https://www.huffingtonpost.co.uk/entry/pride-london-organisers-anti-trans-activists-parade_uk_5b40cb76e4b07b827cc0e394

463 'Pride in London sorry after anti-trans protest', *BBC News*, 8 July 2018, https://www.bbc.co.uk/news/uk-england-london-44757403

464 Kimberlé Crenshaw, 'Mapping the Margins: Intersectionality, Identity Politics and Violence against Women of Color', *Stanford Law Review*, Vol. 43. No. 6 (Jul., 1991), pp. 1241-1299

465 See *The Combahee River Collective Statement of 1977*; http://circuitous.org/scraps/combahee.html

466 For example see P H Collins, *Black feminist thought: Knowledge, consciousness, and the politics of empowerment*, 2nd edition, (New York, 2000).

467 Martha Gimenez, 'Marxism and Class, Gender and Race: Rethinking the Trilogy', *Race, Gender & Class* (2001:Vol.8,No. 2), 22–33.

Available online at www.colorado.edu/ Sociology/gimenez/work/cgr.html.

468 Eve Mitchell, 'I am a woman and a human: a Marxist feminist critique of intersectionality theory,' *Libcom*, 12 September 2013, https://libcom.org/ library/i-am-woman-human-marxist-feminist-critique-intersectionality-theory-eve-mitchell.

469 For example see Sharon Smith, *Women and Socialism: Class, Race, and Capital* (Chicago, 2015); and Laura Miles, 'Can we combine intersectionality with Marxism?: A review of Sharon Smith's Women and Socialism: Class, Race and Capital', *International Socialism* 151, Summer 2016, pp2014-208.

470 See for example Holly Lewis, *The Politics of Everybody: Feminism, Queer Theory and Marxism at the Intersection* (Chicago, 2016) and Peter Drucker, Warped: *Gay Normality and Queer Anti-Capitalism,* Historical Materialism Book Series, Volume 92, 2015.

471 James Penney, *After Queer Theory: The Limits of Sexual Politics* (London, 2013).

472 Choonara and Prasad, 2014, p107.

Chapter 11: Eyes on the prize

473 One example in 2017 was a petition and student walkout at a London college demanding the right of a trans woman student to use the gender appropriate toilets. The action forced the college management to back down after they had initially acceded to transphobic objections. See: 'Students' solidarity flushed transphobia down the toilet', *Socialist Worker*, 28 February 2017, http://bit.ly/2sdU7XX.

474 In June 2019 New York City Pride was rivalled by a Queer Liberation march and rally attended by 45,000 people without corporate or police floats organised by activists who reject the corporatism of established Pride events. See https://reclaimpridenyc. org.

475 International Day Against Homophobia, Transphobia and Biphobia, May 17th. May 17th was chosen to mark the date in 1990 when the World Health Organisation declassified homosexuality as a mental disorder.

476 See for example Peter Purton, 2017; Nicola Field, *Over the Rainbow: Money, Class and Homophobia* (London, 2016); Christine Burns (ed), *Trans Britain: Our Journey from the Shadows,* (London, 2018).

477 In October 2019 hundreds of postal workers in the Communication Workers Union in Liverpool struck unofficially in protest at a manager's racist comment to a worker. 'Royal Mail staff storm out over claims of 'racist'comment to a Muslim worker', *Liverpool Echo,* 3 October 2019, https://www.liverpoolecho.co.uk/ news/liverpool-news/royal-mail-staff-storm-out-17019650.

478 Figures from the Office for National Statistics showed that in 2018 there were 273,000 working days lost due to labour disputes, the sixth-lowest annual total since records began in 1891: ONS, Labour disputes in the UK, 17 May 2019, http://bit.ly/2PyzH3D.

479 Yuval Noah Harari, '50 years after Stonewall: Yuval Noah Harari on the new threats to LGBT rights', *The Guardian,* 22 June 2019.

480 Field, 2016, p308.

481 The actual words were probably originally used by the German Marxist Karl Kautsky. Rosa Luxemburg, *The Junius pamphlet: The crisis of German social democracy* (Zurich, 1916), https://www.marxists.org/archive/ luxemburg/1915/junius.

482 Karl Marx, *Capital, Volume 1,* (Moscow) p558.

483 Vasily Grossman, *Stalingrad: A Novel, 1952* (London, 2018), Kindle version p527.

484 See Feinberg, 1996, p172.

485 *The International Bill of Gender Rights*, https://www.tolerance. org/classroom-resources/texts/ international-bill-of-gender-rights

486 John Bellamy Foster, Brett Clark, and Richard York, *The Ecological Rift: Capitalism's war on the Earth* (New York, 2010) p442.

487 Feinberg, 1996, p128.

Index